Pauperising Agriculture

Pauperising Agriculture

Studies in Agrarian Change and Demographic Structure

N Krishnaji

Published for
SAMEEKSHA TRUST
OXFORD UNIVERSITY PRESS
BOMBAY DELHI CALCUTTA MADRAS
1992

Oxford University Press, Walton Street, Oxford OX2 6DP
Oxford New York Toronto
Delhi Bombay Calcutta Madras Karachi
Kuala Lumpur Singapore Hong Kong Tokyo
Nairobi Dar es Salaam
Melbourne Auckland
and associates in
Berlin Ibadan

cak

First Published 1992

ISBN 0 19 563187 0

Typeset by Economic and Political Weekly, Bombay, and printed by Modern
Arts and Industries, 151, A-Z Industrial Estate, Lower Parel, Bombay-400 013
and published by S K Mookerjee, Oxford University Press, Oxford House,
Appollo Bunder, Bombay-400 039.

Preface

The Sameeksha Trust series of volumes, comprising selections of articles from *Economic and Political Weekly*, brings together contributions by different authors on a specific theme as well as the writings of a single author on an inter-related range of issues. The present volume, the sixth in the series, puts together N Krishnaji's contributions, published over a span of some two decades, dealing with changes in the Indian agrarian scene since the mid-sixties. The essays in the first part of the book focus on trends in agricultural production, wages and prices and the role of politics and the State in shaping them. The book's second part is concerned with the impact of demographic processes on agrarian structures. Like its predecessors, this volume will, we hope, attract a wide readership.

ASHOK MITRA
Editor of Publications
Sameeksha Trust

June 1, 1992

Acknowledgements

THESE essays, published originally in the *Economic and Political Weekly* over a period of two decades, were written during my affiliation to some leading centres of research in economics: The Indian Institute of Management, Calcutta, the Centre for Development Studies, Thiruvananthapuram, the Centre for Studies in Social Sciences, Calcutta, and the Centre for Economic and Social Studies, Hyderabad. At all these places I enjoyed practically unlimited freedom to pursue my studies, with light duties to meet other academic commitments. I was, moreover, in the company of several eminent colleagues in the profession. Their intellectual support contributed much to the shaping of my ideas. Among them are: Amiya K Bagchi, Sabyasachi Bhattacharya, Nirmal K Chandra, Paresh Chattopadhyay, I S Gulati, T N Krishnan, Ashok Mitra, P G K Panikar, R Radhakrishna, K N Raj, Ranjit K Sau, Asok Sen and A Vaidyanathan.

My younger colleagues—Nata Duvvury, T M Thomas Isaac, A V Jose, Chandan Mukherjee, C Rammanohar Reddy, P Satyasekhar and Mihir Shah—have helped me in ways hard to enumerate and describe.

The administrative staff and those in charge of the libraries, at the places I worked, had always supported my work on the friendliest of terms. My thanks in this respect are for Gouri Banerjee, Shika Chakraborty, C G Devarajan, Arun Ghosh, G Vijay Kumar, Susanta Ghosh, G Ravindran Nair and B Sankara Reddy.

Krishna Raj gave me more space than I deserved in the journal he edits. Ashok Mitra made sure of the compilation of this selection. To both of them I owe more than I can say.

Hyderabad
July 1991

N KRISHNAJI
Centre for Economic and
Social Studies

Contents

Introduction

DURING the late 1960s and early 70s, even as the neo-classical approach to the study of the Indian economy continued to be the dominant one, there began to develop an alternative approach, the method of Marxian political economy. There was significant earlier work in the Marxist tradition, but the method strengthened during this period. This was probably part of an international trend but here in India it had certainly something to do with the manner in which the so-called green revolution was developing and transforming the character of the agrarian economy.

Much of the effort of those early days—by a number of colleagues working in different parts of the country but always in close communication with each other, and publishing mostly in the *EPW*—tended to be theoretical and centred on the mode of production in Indian agriculture. Alongside, the discussion within the Marxist framework gradually extended to the economy as a whole and to the dynamic aspects of Indian agrarian structure in a historical perspective, bringing economists closer than ever before to scholars in other disciplines of social science.

There was in this exciting new way of looking at things scope for a statistician to do normal business without fitting production functions *a la mode*. Thus purely descriptive statistical accounts of the Indian economy could be placed within the more illuminating alternative framework. For example, while working out the econometrics of agricultural prices, it looked eminently sensible to ask oneself: what role does the state play? What, more generally, are the political, non-market factors that influence price movements? And so on. The studies reproduced in the first part of this volume refer to concrete questions such as what has been happening to production, wages or prices. They are statistical and descriptive in nature but influenced to some extent by those emerging trends in agrarian studies.

The two studies on agricultural prices in this volume—one referring to wheat prices during the early 70s, and one reviewing the evolution of price policy till recent times—lead to several issues in Indian political economy. Two further contributions included here refer to some of these questions. The paper 'Demand Constraint' examines the impact of foodgrain prices and that of the distribution of income on the structure of demand, in particular to see whether high and rising food prices have a dampening effect on the demand for manufactures. There is a huge amount of writing on the slow-down in industrial growth from about the mid-60s. Both an unwarranted inflation in foodgrain prices and a possibly worsening trend in inequalities have been cited as underlying factors. The paper examines some questions arising in that context. There is also a paper on the emerging trends in land relations and the left movement in Kerala, which deals with the nature of political support for 'remunerative prices' and its basis. Although the reference here is to the specific case of politics in Kerala, the issues discussed have wider relevance.

There were attempts during that early phase to look at the growing numbers of agricultural labourers, both absolutely and as a proportion of all workers in agriculture (including owner-cultivators and tenants, who do not work for wages), for not only making a quantitative assessment of the progress of capitalist relations in the sphere of agriculture, but also—through an analysis of the growing markets and of the changing attributes of the labouring classes—to identify the processes that convert independent producers into wage-dependent labourers. The 'debt mechanism' is one such; and much scholarly work in the Indian context attempts to show that markets tend to be 'inter-linked' and they work in ways that ultimately alienate the direct producer from land—the most important means of production—or leave the peasant with a tiny holding that cannot generate sufficient income from cultivation and hence force him into wage work. In sum, the processes of proletarianisation and pauperisation, linked in specific ways to the nature and growth of different markets constrained by pre-capitalist forms of production and exploitation.

This analysis applied to statistical data—as it has been actually done—proves to be defective in two respects. First, a count of numbers in the proletarianised/pauperised/de-peasantised classes must surely extend to the erstwhile independent producers in agriculture, and in other occupations in rural areas, who migrate to urban areas for wage work in 'industry' (including the activities in the so-called informal sector). However, the issues of growing proletarianisation/pauperisation were largely sought to be settled through statistics of agricultural labour (that pose formidable problems of comparability over space and time and divert the attention of capable scholars from important issues to trivial ones).

Rural-to-urban migration in the European historical experience is a vital part of the general model that is applied to the Indian case. And, Indian economists have debated much about the statistics of agricultural labour and whether the growth in numbers represents proletarianisation or pauperisation, but have paid very little attention to migration of labour. This was perhaps due to the fact that in formulating the analytical problems relating to the mode of production in Indian agriculture, the agrarian economy was treated in isolation, a mistake that is getting corrected in recent work that encompasses—as it should, in accordance with the general model—all economic activities. Not much has been written on this particular issue (i e, migration) and, therefore, the recognition of the defect in analysis as such must come from reflection and hindsight.

A more serious shortcoming in the analysis arises from the reluctance among Marxists to examine the impact of demographic variation on the changing structure of landholdings which has obvious implications for the pace of differentiation, although demographic change is only one among the several underlying factors. Indeed, at one extreme is the possibility that in particular families, demographic change alone—through increase in family size, sub-division of family holdings, etc—may lead to a change in the status of branch families from 'independent producers' to 'wage-dependent workers'. This is most likely to happen in the case of families unable to accumulate savings and augment their asset holdings or to improve the productivity of land to the required extent over two or three generations. All this is obvious and has clear-cut implications for the growth in the number of wage workers. The reluctance to examine the demographic question arises perhaps from the mechanical and religious—but invalid—identification (in this context) of demographic issues or even the word 'demography' with the Chayanovian model of the differentiation of peasantry. Those who look for Chayanov under every bed will no doubt find him lurking there but lose sight of an important component of the processes that induce wage-dependence.

From a statistical angle, it is however not easy to assess, given the nature of data at our command, the relative contributions of the exploitative and demographic factors to the growth of labour. A good first step to.take is, therefore, to use the available information on the interrelationships between demographic variables and those describing the agrarian structure. This will give us some idea about the structure of labour households (in terms of both demographic and economic specificities) and how it compares with that of middle peasant or big landowning families.

The papers in the second part of this book address demographic issues from one clearly specified angle: the variations in the size and structure of families ranging from poor rural households—mainly agricultural labour and poor peasant families—to those of rich peasants and large landowners. But the goal of sharply sketching these differences and understanding what lies behind them is not easily achieved because while statistics relating to household size are available in abundance those on fertility and mortality differences do not come in the right shape. However, with some speculation one arrives at the following inferences: household size tends to be small among the labour and poor peasant families, both because of higher mortalities and a higher propensity for them to be unitary or nuclear. In contrast, households with large landholdings are associated with a large household size, a high proportion of joint families and a distinctly possible lower mortality rate. Fertility differentials could be narrow, especially in the absence of control on fertility, but fertility levels in poor families are likely to be lower. (The remarkable observation of higher female-to-male ratios in poor families is analysed in a separate paper.)

The implications of these differences to the growth of labour are examined, in a somewhat speculative vein, in the third Daniel Thorner memorial lecture, 'Land and Labour in India: The Demographic Factor' (the text of which was published in *EPW*, May 5-12, 1990) reproduced in this volume. The question of rural-to-urban migration is treated in the context of processes of mutual adjustment between population parameters and land-use patterns (including labour-intensification) with the district as the regional unit of analysis, in the paper, 'Population and Agricultural Growth' (with P Satya Sekhar).

These papers were written separately over a long period of time when ideas were taking shape. There is, therefore some textual repetition, overlapping of statistical analysis, and the occasional inconsistency. They are left, nevertheless, as they originally appeared in the *EPW* and can be read independently of each other. The questions raised in these essays continue to be debated.

I
Agrarian Change

1

Wages of Agricultural Labour

THERE were two comprehensive enquiries into the living conditions of agricultural labourers, one in 1951 and the other in 1956. The data collected in these two studies, although not strictly comparable, indicate that real wages in 1956 were below their 1951 levels almost all over the country. Apart from these surveys, the government publishes on a regular basis wage data for a few villages in most districts of the country. The reason given for the collection and publication of these data is: "Agricultural wages constitute a major item in the cost of production of crops and it is essential to have an idea of agricultural costs."[1]

It is our purpose here to use this information[2] (data published by the Directorate of Economics and Statistics—DES for short) to study the trends in agricultural wages since 1956; we shall also attempt to compare the current wage levels with those of 1951. Since wages constitute the bulk of earnings for this class, we expect that such an analysis will throw some light on trends in earnings as well.

Throughout this paper we shall be concerned with the wage rate for adult male labourers. For most of the states for which data are published, wages of field labour—presumably an average for all agricultural operations (ploughing, harvesting, etc)—are available. For a few states, wages for the different kinds of operations are also given; in this case, we have taken the average overall agricultural operations. Thus we have developed data for the category of field labour uniformly for all the states. These data relate to the total cash equivalent of all payments made to labourers.

We may note at the outset that no information is available on how the villages are chosen within each district, except that villages are "so selected as to represent the wages and general agricultural conditions of the district".[3] Since there is considerable inter-village variation within the same district, it is difficult to assess the degree of accuracy in the resulting 'district averages'. Our final results are, therefore, subject to this important limitation.

A casual study of the wage data reveals that most villages do not exhibit any seasonal variation at all. This conflicts with the facts of real life and suggests that the data are of dubious value. We begin, therefore, by studying the pattern of variation over time (i e, months) and space, particularly to test the hypothesis that the published data do not reflect any seasonal variation. For this purpose we have selected the following four samples.

(A) 1956-57—16 districts in five states.[4]

(B) 1960-61—All (20) the districts of Andhra Pradesh. (In both (A) and (B) we have used averages of villages in each district as our basic data.)

(C) 1960-61—20 villages from five states (two districts from each state and two villages from each district).

(D) 1964-65—12 villages from three states (two districts from each state and two villages from each district).

In respect of two samples, (C) and (D), the village wage rate was the basic variable while in (A) and (B) the basic variable was the district average. Analysis of variance of these samples is given in the Appendix Tables (A), (B), (C) and (D), respectively. The analysis shows that most of the observed variation is accounted for by spatial variation; variation among months is insignificant in all but the 1956-57 sample. But in the 1956-57 sample, we have taken the district averages as the basic variable for the analysis of variance. On re-examination of the original data, we find that the number of villages available for estimating the district average is not the same over all months; moreover, in a few instances, even the villages (of a district) for which data are given are not the same in all months. Thus, what passes off as seasonal variation here includes a spatial component which cannot be separated. Also, the mean square among months (462) is very low compared to the mean square among districts (49405). All this goes to establish the fact that, if we ignore seasonal variation (i e, base our analysis on data for just one month), we shall not be losing much information (i e, our results will not be very different from those based on the data for all the 12 months).

A comparison of the 1956-57 DES data with the data from the Second Agricultural Labour Enquiry (1956) shows that the former are higher. While the two sets are not comparable, it seems reasonable to conclude that the DES data conform to peak-season wages. We have accordingly chosen one peak-season month for each state for estimating state averages: December for Andhra Pradesh, Assam, Bihar, Maharashtra, Gujarat, Mysore, Orissa, UP and West Bengal; April for Punjab and Himachal Pradesh; October for Kerala; November for Madhya Pradesh; and January for Tamil Nadu. We may add that, even if seasonal variation is present in the DES data (this can only happen if the samples we analysed were not representative—which is a very remote possibility), it will still be valid to compare wages prevailing in the peak-season month in one year with those in the same month in another year to estimate annual changes.

For each district, we have computed the average of all the villages (each year) for which data are available. Since considerable inter-village variation (within districts) is present this introduces a bias in the comparison of one year's average with another's if the villages are not the same. To estimate change over the years, therefore, it is essential to retain the same villages; but this will cut down the number of villages available for estimating the district average. We followed both procedures whenever sufficient data were available and found that the results are not very different except in one case. Details are given in the Appendix Table (E). Finally, we used the 1960-61 census figures of the number of male agricultural labourers in each district as a weight to compute the weighted state average wage rate for 1956-57, 1960-61, and 1964-65 (Table 1).

Table 1 also gives the labour bureau's index number of consumer prices for agricultural labourers. In the last two columns we give an index of real wages with 1956-57 = 100.

We can see that, in six out of the 14 states, viz, Assam, West Bengal, Maharashtra, Punjab, Himachal Pradesh and UP, real wages in 1964-65 were appreciably lower than their 1956-57 levels. In Bihar, Mysore, Gujarat and Madhya Pradesh they have remained more or less at the same level. It is only in Kerala, Orissa and Andhra Pradesh that we can say that real wages have risen during 1956-64.

We shall now attempt to compare the 1964-65 wage levels with those in 1951. Now, the wage data collected in the First (1951) and Second (1956) Agricultural Labour Enquiries (ALE) are not comparable because, in the first, payments in kind were converted into cash equivalents at retail prices, while in the second, this was done at wholesale prices.[5] Available price data[6] relate to those prevailing in towns; but if we assume that similar rela-

Table 1: Estimated Wage Rate of Male Agricultural Labourers

State	Wage Rate (Paise Per Day)			Consumer Price Index of Agri-cultural Labour			Index Number of Real Wages 1956-57=100	
	1956-57	1960-61	1964-65	1950-51=100 1956-57	1960-61	1960-61=100 1964-65	1960-61	1964-65
East zone								
Assam	236	230	225	117	107	131	107	81
West Bengal	164	163	206	108	110	137	97	83
Bihar	115	122	178	90	89	149	107	104
Orissa	100	125	189	101	109	143	114	120
South zone								
Kerala	148	169	246	104	114	133	104	114
Mysore	125	160	220	103	116	146	114	108
Andhra Pradesh	113	127	179	110	116	125	107	120
Madras	108	125	199	—	—	—	—	—
Central and west zones								
Maharashtra	141	138	186	—	—	151	—	89*
Gujarat	130	166	203	—	—	134	—	91*
Madhya Pradesh	101	127	146	106	106	139	126	105
North zone								
Punjab	294	273	354	101	103	139	90	84
Himachal Pradesh	269	258	302	101	103	139	94	79
Uttar Pradesh	98	157	174	—	—	160**	—	69*

Note: Price indices are computed from *Indian Labour Statistics*. The 1956-57 figures are averages of first six months of 1957, 1960-61 figures are averages of 12 months (July-June), 1964-65 figures are averages of 10 months, September-December 1964 and January-June 1965.
* 1960-61 = 100.
** Based on the first 6 months of 1965.

tions hold in rural areas it appears reasonable to assume that retail prices were higher than wholesale prices by 10-20 per cent in different areas. To this we must add the fact that only about 50 per cent of the wage payment was in kind (in 1956, according to the Second ALE). It then follows that, if we inflate 1956 wage rates by about 10 per cent they would then be comparable with the 1951 figures. In Table 2, we give these estimates along with an index of real wages in 1964-65 with 1950-51 = 100. This last column gives us a magnitude of change in relative wages over the period that roughly corresponds with the first three plans. We can see that only in Kerala and Orissa real wages have increased during 1950-64 to a significant extent; on the other hand, they have fallen appreciably in Assam and West Bengal and possibly in the Bombay region as well; in all the other states, real wages have remained more or less at their 1950-51 levels.

To conclude this section, we must now ask whether these falling trends have been reversed after 1964-65. For 1968-69, data on the wage rate are published for a few villages in the recent issues of *Agricultural Situation in India*. By comparing these with the wages for the same villages in 1964-65, we find that wages have risen between 25 and 50 per cent in different areas. Price increases in the same period were 33 per cent,[7] which show that living conditions of agricultural labourers probably continue to be the same today as ever before.

We hear the argument that the green revolution will lift agricultural labourers above the poverty line through increased pace of agricultural activity, greater demand for labour, and

Table 2: Estimated Change in Real Wages, 1950-64

State	Wages—Paise Per Day		Real Wages, 1950-51=100	
	1950-51	1956-57	1956-57	1964-65
Andhra Pradesh	97	95	89	107
Assam	190	169	76	62
Bihar	126	100	88	91
Bombay	101	95	—	—
Kerala	126	141	107	122
Madhya Pradesh	79	84	100	105
Madras	97	92	—	—
Mysore	90	92	99	107
Orissa	72	88	120	144
Punjab	184	218	117	98
Uttar Pradesh	118	101	—	—
West Bengal	166	157	87	72

Note: 1950-51 wages were taken from *Agricultural Labour in India: Report on the Second Enquiry*, p 110; 1956-57 wages were the result of adding 10 per cent to the 56-57 figures from the same source. Real wages were worked out using the price data given in Table 1.

APPENDIX: ANALYSIS OF VARIANCE
Table (A)
Sample (A), 1956-57:

    Assam—North Lakhimpur, Mangaldai, Barpeta and Karimganj.
    Bombay—Ahmednagar and Kolhapur.
    Madhya Pradesh—Sagar, Betul, Nimar, Chindwara and Raipur.
    Mysore—Chitaldurg, Kolar and Hassan.
    West Bengal—Midnapore and Hooghly.

Source of Variation	Degree of Freedom	Sum of Squares	Mean Square
Between states	4	646038	161509.50
Within states	11	95045	8640.45
Between districts	15	741083	49405.53
Between months	11	5079	461.73
Residual	165	36724	222.55
Total	191	782886	

Table (B)
Sample (B), 1960-61:

    The 20 districts of Andhra Pradesh for which data were available.

Source of Variation	Degree of Freedom	Sum of Squares	Mean Square
Between months	11	4184	380
Between districts	19	170408	8969
Residual	209	54112	259
Total	239	228704	

Table (C)
Sample (C), 1960-61:

    (1) Andhra Pradesh—Hyderabad (Arutla and Vennachadu); Karimnagar (Kodurpak and Cheppial).
    (2) Gujarat—Bhavnagar (Kundla and Umrala); Amreli (Khambha and Lathi).
    (3) Madhya Pradesh—Mandla (Shahpur and Bichhia); Betul (Samundra and Ranipur).
    (4) Orissa—Cuttack (Mahanga and Jagatsinghpur); Keonjhar (Champna and Anandpur).
    (5) Himachal Pradesh—Chamba (Sarol and Chowari); Mandi (Surajpur Bari and Kumi Behna).

In the following, a cell stands for the configuration of four villages of a state in a given month.

Source	df	ss	ms
Between months	11	5136	466.9
Between districts	9	1417070	157452.2
Districts × months	99	24456	247.0
Between cells	119	1446662	12156.2
Within cells (res)	120	187845	1565.3
Total	239	1634507	

Table (D)

Sample (D), 1964-65:

(1) Mysore—Chitradurg (Doddamagadi and Moradihally); Kolar (Mudurvadi and Doddasivara).
(2) Madhya Pradesh—Sagar (Sanodha and Basahari); Chindwara (Beradi and Chandangaon).
(3) Maharashtra—Ahmednagar (Rashin and Deolali); Kolhapur (Gargoti and Kadoli).

A cell here has the same meaning as in sample (C).

Source	df	ss	ms
Between months	11	40085	3644.0
Between districts	5	358052	71610.4
Districts × months	55	32091	583.4
Between cells	71	430228	6059.5
Within cells (res)	72	199145	2765.9
Total	143	629373	

Table (E): Estimated Change in Wages by Two Methods

(Per Cent)

State	Period	Method I	Method II
Andhra Pradesh	(1960-64)	42.0	40.0
Assam	(1956-60)	−2.6	−5.3
Bihar	(1956-60)	4.3	5.2
Maharashtra	(1956-60)	−17.6	−4.2
"	(1960-64)	31.4	31.1
Gujarat	(1956-60)	27.5	24.8
"	(1960-64)	49.1	52.6

Note: Method I refers to district averages based on whatever village data were available in each year. In Method II we retained the same villages at both points of time and is thus more reliable. The agreement is close except in the case of Maharashtra for the period 1956-60. Our final estimates for Maharashtra for 1956-57 are based on Method II together with the 1960-61 average wage rate.

higher wages. It is patently false because in those small pockets where the green revolution has penetrated to a significant extent (like Punjab) wages are kept low through the import of labour from neighbouring states. Also, the revolution is unlikely to spread wide enough to increase employment to a significant extent.

Table 1 also gives us an idea of the trends in inter-state disparities in the wage rate. These disparities appear to be shrinking; the coefficient of variation (a weighted index, with the number of male agricultural labourers as weights) has declined from 28.6 per cent in 1956-57 to 22.5 per cent in 1960-61 and to 19 per cent in 1964-65. This is, in a large measure, due to the fact that money wages increased at a faster rate in those regions where they were relatively low; in real terms, there were sharp falls in wages in Assam, Punjab, Himachal Pradesh and West Bengal where the wages are relatively high. If this process of inter-regional convergence continues, the wage rate will settle at a uniformly low rate all over the country.

We do not attempt to 'explain' the inter-state disparities here; however, a few comments are in order. The states of Punjab, Himachal Pradesh and Assam where the wages can be regarded to be relatively high contribute barely 2.5 per cent to the total agricultural labour population. In other states, like West Bengal, Maharashtra, Gujarat and Kerala where the wages are high compared to other states in the same regions, prices are also relatively high. If we take these two factors into account while reading Table 1, there is very little inter-state variation left to 'explain'. The conclusion is inescapable that stagnant agricultural wages characterise the whole country.

NOTES

1 *Agricultural Wages in India, 1964-65,* Directorate of Economics and Statistics, p 554.
2 *Agricultural Wages in India,* an annual publication.
3 *Agricultural Wages in India, 1964-65,* p 555.
4 Details are given in Appendix.
5 *Agricultural Labour in India: Report on the Second Enquiry,* Volume 1, All India, pp 110-11.
6 *Agricultural Prices in India,* 1956, Economic and Statistical Adviser, Ministry of Food and Agriculture.
7 *Indian Labour Statistics,* 1970. (The consumer price index rose from 139 in 1964-65 to 185 in 1968-69.)

September 25, 1971

2

Wheat Price Movements

I
INTRODUCTION

ANY review of price policy must begin with a clear understanding of the underlying objectives. A statement of these objectives is to be found in the terms of reference of the Agricultural Prices Commission (APC) formed in 1965. The APC is asked to advise the government on price policy through a relative price structure for various agricultural commodities which should be "in the perspective of overall needs of the economy and with due regard to the interests of the producer and the consumer".[1] The commission is exhorted to keep in view "the need to provide incentive to the producer..." and the "need to ensure rational utilisation of land..." as also the "likely effect of the policy on the rest of the economy...".[2] These considerations are reflected in some measure in the package of recommendations made year after year by the APC. But these are never accepted (Table 1 presents just one feature of this phenomenon) by the chief ministers who are the policy-makers. Could this be because the APC's recommendations are never in consonance with the real objectives of price policy as against the declared ones? The following analysis shows that the answer is in the affirmative.

II
THE POLICY INSTRUMENTS

In theory as well as practice the price structure is a three-tiered one comprising a minimum support price, the procurement price and the market price. One could add a fourth, viz, a statutory maximum price, to this scheme but it is of no significance because of the universally acknowledged existence of the black market. The conceptual framework of this price structure is easily understood: the minimum support price should cover costs plus

Table 1: *Procurement Prices of Wheat—Haryana, Punjab and UP*
(Marketing Season)

(Rs per quintal)

Year	State	Red		Common White		Superior		Mexican	
		APC*	Govt**	APC	Govt	APC	Govt	APC	Govt
1966-67	Haryana	53.00		57.00	59.50	61.00	63.50		
	Punjab	53.00		57.00	59.50	61.00	63.50		
	UP	53.00		57.00	94.45	61.00			
1967-68	Haryana	57.50		61.50	76.00	65.50	96.85		
	Punjab	57.50		61.50	85.00	65.50	81.00		
	UP	57.50	80.00	61.50	76.00	65.50			
1968-69	All states	66.00	72.00 to 74.00	70.00	76.00	74.00	81.00	66.00 to 70.00	76.00
1969-70	"	66.00	66.00 to 74.00	70.00	76.00	74.00		70.00	76.00
1970-71	"	66.00	71.00 to 74.00	72.00	76.00			72.00	76.00
1971-72	"	68.00	71.00 to 74.00	74.00	76.00			74.00	76.00
1972-73	"	66.00		72.00				72.00	

Notes: * Prices recommended by the APC.
** Prices fixed by the state governments.

Source: Reports of the Agricultural Prices Commission.

normal profits and hence should be a guarantee price to farmers at times when market price falls (or threatens to fall) appreciably in good years; the procurement price should be below the market price but above the support level and hence procurement should essentially be regarded as a tax. No one would dispute with this scheme if the overall objective is one of price reduction; but if it is not—and it is not—a reordering of the three tiers is needed. If, for example, the objective is to hike prices to the maximum possible extent there is no need for the procurement price to be below the market price and the support prices need play no role at all even in good years; the procurement and market prices can stay close to each other for ever. That the government had never any intention of accepting the distinction between support and procurement prices is clear from the preface to the APC's report on minimum prices for 1968-69 signed by a secretary to the government: "...it was decided not to announce the minimum support prices for wheat and gram for 1968-69 crop as government was already committed to purchase any quantity of foodgrains offered for sale at procurement prices. It was considered that as procurement prices were virtually fulfilling the role of the support prices, the announcement of minimum support prices might confuse the farmers and create apprehensions that the policy of offering incentive prices was being revised by the government... ."[3] And last year (1972) early December "saw the union minister of state for agriculture, A P Shinde, admitting in parliament that procurement of foodgrains in the kharif season was likely to fall considerably short of the target of 4.5 million tonnes...The reason for this failure to attain the target, he blandly explained, was that the government's procurement prices were currently much lower than the open market prices"![4] Procurement prices cannot stay behind (not far, anyway) market prices for long, as we have already remarked. Given this regime of prices it is easy to understand why the government is unable to procure grain in years of crop failure and it is equally legitimate to identify procurement as essentially a support operation in good crop years. No comment is needed on the relevance of this arrangement for a policy of price reduction. Procurement as an instrument of price policy cannot, however, be fully evaluated in isolation from the other instrument, viz, movement restrictions and it is to this that we now turn.

The subject of movement restriction by zoning has aroused

a great deal of controversy among economists as well as policy-makers but the essential point is that the case for movement restrictions rests on the single argument that the constitution of every state into a zone makes it easy for the government to pur-chase large quantities of grain in surplus states and also in surplus regions elsewhere.[5] A little reflection shows that the impact of a given combination of zoning and pricing policies on final prices would crucially depend on (a) the procurement price, (b) the amount procured and (c) where the procured grain is distributed and at what price. Now, these three elements can be so chosen as to increase the average all-India price in very much the same way as to decrease it. So much for the theory, but how did the combination actually work in practice? The year-to-year changes in the movement restrictions[6] might, at first sight, appear to be symptomatic of a St Vitus' dance, but closer examination reveals at least one simple empirical rule: relax restrictions in good years. We shall study in detail the impact of this policy on prices in a later section but it is clear that such a policy is advantageous to sellers because unfettered movement is an excellent cushion against a fall in prices in a bumper year while strict zoning might bring about a drastic price reduction.[7] This cushion is, of course, strengthened by the procurement price fulfilling the role of a support price.

III
PRODUCTION, IMPORTS, PROCUREMENT AND PRICES

Some all-India wheat statistics are given in Table 2. The rela-tionship between prices and production appears distinctly anomalous for the post-1968 period. That there was a decline in the overall deficit during this period, following a rapid rise in production, is reflected in the clearly declining trend in both imports and the quantum of public distribution of wheat. But one may argue that what is of relevance here is not just the demand-supply imbalance for wheat but the deficit of all foodgrains because the latter might also exert pressure on wheat prices. However, the declining trend is clearly visible in respect of the imports and public distribution of all foodgrains also (Table 3); on the other hand, the quantum of procurement has risen very rapidly. The APC has this to say on the question: "There is an obvious oddity in the situation in which prices

Table 2: *Wheat Statistics—All-India*

Year	Production (Million Tonnes)	Net Imports*	Procurement*	Public Distribution	Index Number of Wholesale Prices					
					Annual Average		April-June**		January-March**	
					61-62=100	52-53=100	61-62=100	52-53=100	61-62=100	52-53=100
1950-51	6.83	3.06	0.79	3.48				92.3		100.7
1951-52	6.18	2.55	0.78	2.98		96		94.7		92.0
1952-53	7.50	1.71	0.21	2.11		94		96.0		102.7
1953-54	8.02	0.20	—	0.98		100		92.3		90.7
1954-55	9.04	0.44	—	0.26		93		78.0		75.3
1955-56	8.76	1.10	—	1.15		75		60.7		85.0
1956-57	9.40	2.88	—	2.16		72		80.0		95.3
1957-58	8.00	2.71	—	2.95		88		90.7		84.6
1958-59	9.96	3.54	0.26	3.52		88		88.0		121.0
1959-60	10.32	4.38	0.40	3.52		105		95.0		96.0
1960-61	11.00	3.09	0.02	2.69		96		88.3		91.0
1961-62	12.08	3.25	—	3.34	100	90		87.3		97.3
1962-63	10.78	4.07	0.09	3.80	98	91	99.3	89.3	97.3	88.0
1963-64	9.85	5.62	0.38	6.85	106		96.7		121.3	
1964-65	12.26	6.57	0.22	5.94	138		116.7		157.3	
1965-66	10.39	6.57	0.80	5.94	149		144.0		152.0	
1966-67	11.39	7.83	2.37	8.14	178		152.0		215.7	
1967-68	16.54	6.40	2.42	7.37	214		205.7		212.3	
1968-69	18.65	4.77	3.18	5.75	204		194.0		211.3	
1969-70	20.09	3.09	5.08	5.20	205		199.3		233.1	
1970-71	23.25	3.42		5.34	209		206.0		210.0	
1971-72		1.81		4.44	208		201.0		218.0	

Notes: * Data refer to calendar years (the figure against 1951-52 refers to 1951, etc.)
      ** April-June prices refer to the average of the three-month-end indices and similarly January-March prices refer to the averages of the three corresponding months. Here the annual average 1952-53 and 1961-62 are taken as 100.

Sources: (1) Reports of the Agricultural Prices Commission.
        (2) *Bulletin on Food Statistics.*

Table 3: Government Operations Relating to All Foodgrains

(Million tonnes)

Year	Imports	Procurement	Public Distribution
1951	4.80	3.83	7.99
1952	3.93	3.48	6.80
1953	2.03	2.09	4.60
1954	0.84	1.43	2.15
1955	0.71	0.13	1.64
1956	1.44	0.04	2.08
1957	3.65	0.29	3.05
1958	3.22	0.53	3.98
1959	3.87	1.81	5.16
1960	5.14	1.27	4.94
1961	3.49	0.54	3.98
1962	3.64	0.48	4.37
1963	4.56	0.75	5.18
1964	6.27	1.43	8.66
1965	7.46	4.03	10.08
1966	10.36	4.01	14.08
1967	8.67	4.46	13.17
1968	5.69	6.81	10.14
1969	3.85	6.51	9.46
1970	3.59	6.74	8.86
1971	2.00	8.87	7.71

Source: Same as in Table 2.

undergo a spurt in the face of increasing production and mounting stocks of the cereal. That the producers have benefited from the wheat revolution is only as it should have been. But there must come a stage when the benefit starts percolating to the consumer too."[8] The post-1968 period also stands in marked contrast with 1953-54 to 1956-57 which was also characterised by production increases, minimal imports and low stress on the public distribution apparatus (Table 2); the earlier period (1953-57) was governed by a falling trend in prices (except for the last year of the period, i e, 1956-57, but note that this price was lower than the 1952-53 price by 12 per cent) in contrast to the queer trend of 1968-72. The difference, of course, was that in the earlier period there was practically no procurement and price support. We shall discuss the contribution of zoning policies to this difference in price behaviour in the two periods later on.

To explain price variation over the period 1951-72 we begin with the simple formulation that the price level, in the absence of governmental intervention. depends only on excess demand (i e, the excess of demand over supply). This gives rise to the question: how does one measure the demand-supply imbalance? We follow the usual econometric practice of looking for a 'proxy' for excess demand instead of trying to estimate the gap by using assumed consumption norms. The quantum of imports is the most obvious candidate for this purpose but we have considered the quantum of grain operated through the public distribution system as a competitor for the obvious reason that a part of the deficit is met through stocks to which locally procured grain also contributes. An extreme case may, perhaps, illustrate this more clearly. Suppose in a given year that there were no imports. Do we conclude that there was no deficit? No; because the deficit might have been met through depletion of stocks and both imports and procurement are used for stock-building. The grain released by the government might thus be a better indicator of shortage. Table 4 gives some simple correlations between all-India wheat prices and the 'proxies' discussed above. We have accordingly chosen to work with the quantum of public distribution of all foodgrains to serve as a 'proxy' for excess demand (of all foodgrains) to explain variation in wheat prices.

Our next step is to assume that movement restrictions simply shift the price curve (i e, price plotted against excess demand) parallel to itself (either upwards or downwards). However, broadly speaking, two kinds of zoning systems have been in force, viz, single state zones and larger zones. Under the latter, movement is relatively freer than under the former because of the presence

Table 4: Squares of Simple Correlation Coefficient

Price	Imports of		Public Distribution of	
	Wheat	All Foodgrains	Wheat	All Foodgrains
Annual average price	0.23	0.19	0.60	0.66
Harvest price*	0.19	0.13	0.52	0.61
Off-seasonal price**	0.26	0.22	0.63	0.68

* Average of three-month-end wholesale prices, April-June.
** Average of three-month-end wholesale prices, January-March.

of more than one state in a large zone and it is reasonable to expect a priori that the magnitude of the shift corresponding to the single state system would be higher than the shift due to the large zone system. This presents no difficulty in the analysis because the two systems are mutually exclusive and we merely introduce two 'shifter' (dummy) variables: L_t which takes the value 1 for those years when the large zoning system was in force and 0 for the rest of the years and similarly S_t which assumes the value 1 for the years corresponding to the single state system and 0 otherwise. (These values are given in Table 5.)

Our final step is to hypothesise that the procurement-cum-support operation also simply shifts the price curve parallel to itself; the fact that the procurement prices for common white and Mexican varieties of wheat have remained practically stable

Table 5: Values of the Dummy Variables

Year	S_t	L_t	D_t
1951-52	1	0	0
1952-53	1	0	0
1953-54	1	0	0
1954-55	1	0	0
1955-56	0	0	0
1956-57	0	0	0
1957-58	0	1	0
1958-59	0	1	0
1959-60	0	1	0
1960-61	0	1	0
1961-62	0	0	0
1962-63	0	0	0
1963-64	0	0	0
1964-65	0	1	0
1965-66	0	1	0
1966-67	0	1	0
1967-68	1	0	1
1968-69	0	1	1
1969-70	0	1	1
1970-71	0	0	1
1971-72	0	0	1

Note: The zoning system that prevailed in 1959 and 1960 was officially described as single state system but since freedom of movement of Punjabi wheat to Himachal Pradesh and Delhi was allowed we have re-designated the two years to correspond to the large-zone set up. The information on which this table is based is collected from the APC reports.

at Rs 76 per quintal (Table 1) since 1967 supports such a hypothesis. We have identified the period 1967-68 to 1971-72 as the period corresponding to support operations. It is explained earlier why the procurement price during 1968-72 should be regarded as a support price. The inclusion of 1967-68, a marketing year corresponding to a poor crop, in this period is dictated by the fact that high procurement prices were offered, particularly in UP (Table 1). We thus introduce a dummy variable D which takes the value 1 for the years corresponding to the support operation and 0 otherwise. (These values are given in Table 5.)

Based on the discussion of the preceding paragraphs we finally arrive at the following price equation:

$$p_t = a + b_1 I_t + b_2 D_t + b_3 L_t + b_4 S_t$$

where p_t is the annual average all-India price in the year t, I is the quantity of foodgrains (in million tonnes) operated through the public distribution system and D_t, L_t and S_t are dummy variables corresponding to support operations, large zoning and single zoning, respectively (Table 5).

We also assume that the same set of variables, viz, I, D, L and S determine the harvest prices (average of prices prevailing in April-June) and also the off-seasonal prices (average of prices during January-March). While the use of proxy I might be justified despite its crudity, for explaining variations in annual and year-end prices, its use for harvest prices might be objected to on the ground that excess demand gets determined only at the end of the year. But, if we assume that expectations on the level of the deficit determine harvest prices and that such expectations in the beginning of the year are well founded, the objection is at least partly met with. We have tried the alternative of using lagged production but the results are not satisfactory. The estimated price equations are given in Table 6.

For the purpose of this estimation we had converted the entire price series to the common base 1952-53 = 100 (this meant conversion of the series after 1961-62 to the old base) and hence all the following reckoning of the prices is in index terms with 1952-53 = 100. The results are interesting. The variables we have considered account for almost the entire variation in the harvest and annual average prices and only to a slightly smaller extent in off-seasonal prices. Shortages (as measured by I) have a greater impact on the off-seasonal price than on the harvest price, which is only to be expected. The impact of support operations (measured by the dummy D) on the harvest prices (67 points) is greater than the impact on off-seasonal prices (57 points). Thus, other things remaining unchanged, the support operation reduces the seasonal rise (defined as off-seasonal price minus harvest price) by 10 points and contributes significantly to intra-year price stability. Large zones make no significant impact on prices; single state zoning reduces the off-seasonal price by 23 points and the annual average by 12 points while it makes no significant contribution to harvest price variations (the annual average is not very different from the average of the two seasonal prices we have considered here). Hence the single state zoning system also has a tendency to reduce seasonal variation and bring about intra-year price stability. (Of course, this is in a way a restatement of the data for 1951-54, the period of single state zones, which exhibit very little seasonal variation—Table 2.) But this fact is of no moment for the period 1968-72 during which there were either no zones or only the larger zones which are now demonstrated to be ineffective.[9] The contrast between 1953-57 and 1968-72 with respect to price behaviour is now easily explained: in the first there was no significant support-cum-procurement drive and stiff zonal restrictions were present in 1953-54 and 1954-55 while the later period was characterised by both support and the virtual absence of movement restrictions; these facts explain the declining trend of 1953-57 and absence of such a trend during 1968-72.

And since the support policy enhances harvest price more than the off-seasonal price and, on the other hand, the absence of zones

Table 6: Estimated Price Equations—All-India, 1951-52 to 1971-72

Dependent Variable	Constant	Least Square Estimate of Coefficient of				R^2
		I	D	L	S	
Annual average price	68.87	6.03	64.54	1.84	−12.54	0.976
		(0.65)	(4.91)	(4.39)	(4.72)	
Harvest price	68.15	4.69	66.70	1.27	−5.01	0.973
		(0.59)	(4.81)	(4.30)	(4.63)	
Off-seasonal price	84.23	7.40	56.61	−0.01	−23.33	0.937
		(1.04)	(8.53)	(7.39)	(8.50)	

Note: Numbers in parentheses are standard errors of the coefficients.

implies a normal seasonal rise (which their presence might well neutralise) the two factors might combine to produce a measure of seasonal stability. Hence, the policy of relaxation of movement restrictions in good years must be interpreted as a deliberate measure to keep price at a high and fairly stable level throughout the year. We must also remember that the normal seasonal rise that can be attributed to market forces (i e, excess demand) gradually decreases with rising production. This, of course, eminently suits the large farmers because they need not wait for the seasonal rise till the end of the year but instead can dump practically all their surpluses in the harvest season thus saving on storage costs in the bargain. The expected result on the pace of market arrivals is to be found in the actual data (Table 7), with an increasing trend in the proportion of arrivals during the harvest season.

Turning back to the computed price equations we now wish to see if the seasonal pattern of market arrivals influences the seasonality in prices. For this purpose, strictly speaking, one must look at the seasonality in both these variables in all the four quarters but in this study we have concentrated on just the harvest and lean seasons. We simply used the proportion of arrivals in a season as an additional variable to see what difference it makes to the equations of Table 6. Market arrivals information is

Table 7: Seasonal Pattern of Market Arrivals of Wheat—All-India

Year	Number of Markets	Proportion of Arrivals (Per Cent) in			
		April-June	July-Sept	Oct-Dec	Jan-March
1958-59	31	56.1	19.1	13.4	11.3
1959-60	31	45.1	22.4	16.1	16.4
1960-61	60	48.3	14.6	15.6	21.5
1961-62	60	51.2	17.1	16.4	15.3
1962-63	60	54.8	14.8	11.2	19.2
1963-64	60	63.6	8.8	15.6	11.9
1964-65	60	52.2	18.7	14.4	14.7
1965-66	317	53.5	15.8	14.4	16.3
1966-67	317	56.6	15.9	16.2	11.3
1967-68	558	48.4	19.7	16.3	15.6
1968-69	558	67.2	17.9	7.8	7.1
1969-70	558	75.4	12.2	7.7	4.7
1970-71	558	67.8	19.8	7.5	4.9

Source: Same as in Table 2.

available only from 1958-59. After this year, excepting for 1967-68 when single state zoning was in force, there were either large zones or no zones at all. And, since large zones are ineffective we finally used I, D and the rate of arrivals (A) to explain variation in seasonal prices with the data for 1958-59 to 1970-71 except 1967-68.[10]

These are the estimated equations (omitting the suffix 't') based on the 12 observations:

(a) P_h = $76.63 - 0.21$ A_h + 5.24 I + 67.94 D
$\qquad\qquad\quad$ (0.43)$\qquad$ (0.71)$\quad$ (8.7)

$\quad$ R^2 = 0.977

(b) P_o = $133.72 - 3.52$ A_o + 7.92 I + 21.44 D
$\qquad\qquad\quad$ (0.83)$\qquad$ (0.85)$\quad$ (9.36)

$\quad$ R^2 = 0.978

where A_h and A_o denote the proportion of arrivals in the harvest season and off-season respectively and p_h and p_o denote the harvest and off-seasonal prices respectively.

It can be seen that the arrival rates do not influence the harvest prices but they have a significant impact on the prices in the lean season. Although these equations are estimated on the basis of fewer observations, the proportion of variation explained in (b) is very much higher than in the previous case (Table 6), lending credibility to the estimates. Except for the coefficient of D in (b) there is close agreement with the earlier estimates. Equation (b) implies a much smaller impact (21 points) of support policies on P_o than in the earlier estimates (57 points).

This is essentially because in the earlier estimate the price increase is mostly attributed to D while, as it is clear now, at least part of it should be attributed to the slackening of year-end arrivals. However we have already remarked that the arrival rate itself is determined by state policies. If this inter-dependence is taken into account in an appropriate manner much of this estimational difficulty will disappear. But it must be noted that the present set of equations, (a) and (b), only strengthen the conclusion arrived at earlier that support policies reduce the seasonal rise by raising the harvest price higher than they raise the off-seasonal price. However, they also imply a smaller impact (rise of 44 points) of support operations on the annual average price than estimated earlier (rise of 64 points).

IV
INTER-STATE VARIATIONS

So far we have been discussing the behaviour of the all-India average price. We now examine prices in the Punjab-Haryana region and Uttar Pradesh. Since price indices are not available we have estimated prices for these regions based on whatever little market information is available (Table 8). These estimates are not strictly comparable over time and we must bear this important limitation in mind in what follows. Data on pace of market arrivals in the two regions are given in Table 9. The change in the pattern of arrivals since 1968 can be seen to be more marked in the Punjab-Haryana region than in Uttar Pradesh.

Now, the bulk of the grain is procured in these two regions (Table 10) and we can reasonably expect the influence of support prices to be reflected in fair measure in the prices prevailing there. But UP's contribution appears to be marginal, except in 1968-69 and 1971-72. In any case, we have decided to work on the hypothesis that the period 1967-72 was governed by a regime of support prices for both the regions. Since Punjab-Haryana has always been a surplus region we have used the same set of variables, viz, I, L D and S, as in the case of all-India to explain price variations. The underlying assumption is that the all-India excess demand determines the Punjab price. Besides, we have also tried to see if the arrival pattern influences the seasonal prices (see Table 11).

The results are strikingly similar to the all-India ones. Since this analysis was done with wholesale prices in rupees per quintal, a comparison can be made with the coefficient in Table 6 (which are in index terms with 1952-53 = 100) by multiplying the coefficients of Table 11 by a factor 100 ÷ 34.5, this latter being the average Punjab price in 1952-53. It can be seen that support operations raise the annual average Punjab-Haryana prices by about 80 points while raising all-India prices by only 65 points (or 44 points if we were to go by an alternative estimate). Similar relations hold between Punjab and all-India in respect of seasonal prices. As in the case of all-India, large zones have no significant impact on prices; single state zoning has a far greater impact (a reduction by 33 points) on annual prices of the Punjab region than on all-India average prices (a reduction of 12 points).

All these conform to expectations but the implication of these facts to interregional inequalities cannot be over-emphasised: relaxation of zonal restrictions in good years is similar to the policy of support—both favour the farmers of Punjab-Haryana more than the others. We have already discussed the influence of these policies on seasonal stability in prices and the rate of market

Table 8: Wholesale Price of Wheat—Punjab-Haryana and Uttar Pradesh
(Rs per quintal)

Year	Punjab-Haryana			Uttar Pradesh		
	April-June	January-March	Annual Average	April-June	January-March	Annual Average
1952-53	33.9	34.8	34.5	45.5	55.1	50.9
1953-54	34.8	42.9	38.0	49.3	42.6	44.6
1954-55	36.9	35.1	35.7	36.2	32.1	33.1
1955-56	32.7	40.8	35.1	30.5	37.0	32.3
1956-57	40.8	44.1	41.6	36.5	42.9	39.6
1957-58	41.1	37.9	39.2	41.9	41.3	41.4
1958-59	36.8	56.8	45.2	44.5	61.6	55.2
1959-60	41.9	42.5	41.9	45.6	47.0	47.0
1960-61	38.1	41.0	40.0	43.2	44.1	43.7
1961-62	40.3	48.2	43.2	38.9	43.7	40.9
1962-63	43.8	41.7	42.8	38.1	39.5	38.5
1963-64	40.7	58.9	47.5	38.3	57.3	46.0
1964-65	47.1	64.2	55.0	56.7	91.3	79.7
1965-66	57.3	58.3	58.1	70.7	76.9	77.2
1966-67	64.3	93.7	75.8	70.0	103.9	85.1
1967-68	83.7	76.1	80.3	120.6	97.5	113.1
1968-69	75.7	92.8	85.6	74.1	82.0	77.4
1969-70	80.9	95.9	86.7	78.7	100.9	88.1
1970-71	83.2	84.1	83.0	81.8	84.7	83.2
1971-72	80.4	91.0	85.8	73.7	86.5	77.3

Note: These are simple averages of prices for the following markets (the quality of wheat is mentioned in brackets).
Punjab-Haryana:
1952-53 to 1966-67: Abohar (dara) and Moga (farm), 1967-68: Sonepat, Rohtak, Moga and Bhatinda (indigenous white, all markets), 1968-69: Sonepat, Ambala, Moga and Bhatinda (all white), 1969-70 to 1971-72: Sonepat, Ambala Jullundur and Bhatinda (all white).
Uttar Pradesh:
1952-53 to 1963-64: Hapur and Bahraich (quality unspecified), 1963-64 to 1966-67: Hapur (dara) and Bahraich (white), 1967-68 to 1971-72: Hapur and Bahraich (both white).
Source: Same as in Table 2.

Table 9: Pace of Market Arrivals—Punjab-Haryana and UP

(Per cent)

Year	Punjab-Haryana				Uttar Pradesh			
	April-June	July-Sept	Oct-Dec	Jan-March	April-June	July-Sept	Oct-Dec	Jan-March
1958-59	62.6	20.6	12.7	4.1	62.9	17.3	11.9	7.8
1959-60	47.8	23.5	15.1	13.5	44.3	13.8	20.1	21.8
1960-61	60.7	17.6	9.1	12.6	37.8	19.6	26.0	16.5
1961-62	52.5	22.3	15.6	9.6	54.1	14.9	14.5	16.5
1962-63	55.1	18.8	14.8	11.2	46.0	17.7	16.8	19.4
1963-64	59.9	23.4	11.6	5.2	60.2	13.7	16.8	9.3
1964-65	50.3	24.9	13.6	11.2	60.2	15.3	12.6	11.9
1965-66	71.1	17.4	7.6	3.8	41.9	16.1	25.2	16.8
1966-67	62.9	19.3	10.5	7.3	43.6	14.9	18.3	23.1
1967-68	48.2	21.3	16.7	13.8	49.4	17.3	16.2	17.1
1968-69	77.8	16.3	3.6	2.3	49.5	22.2	15.2	13.1
1969-70	82.7	10.6	5.0	1.7	57.5	17.1	14.7	10.7
1970-71	75.7	19.1	3.6	1.6	47.6	24.5	17.2	10.7
1971-72	76.5	14.8	6.3	2.3	51.4	28.6	13.6	6.4

Source: Same as in Table 2.

arrivals. In recent years, in the Punjab-Haryana region, market arrivals in the lean season (January-March) have barely constituted 2 per cent of the year's total (Table 9); the Punjabi farmer, is able to unload as much as 75 per cent of his surplus in the post-harvest period at—thanks to the government—what is described as an incentive price.

Our Punjab analysis has highlighted how policy measures contribute to the enhancement of interregional inequalities. We shall examine how far the UP data support this conclusion. For analysing UP prices we have used net imports of wheat into UP by rail and river[11] as a proxy for excess demand. This is not very satisfactory because of possible year-to-year variation in the proportion of grain moved by road but, perhaps, is the best choice from the available data. Also, the zoning status for UP is different from the all-India pattern in one important respect: under the large zone system UP continued to constitute a zone by itself in all but one of the years (1966-67) when this system was in force. In 1966-67 UP was merged with the northern wheat zone.[12] Since large zones are ineffective we have introduced one single dummy for zoning, Z_t, which assumes the value 1 for 1953-54, 1954-55, 1957-58 to 1960-61, 1964-65, 1965-66, 1967-68 and 1968-69 and 0 for the rest of period. (Our analysis of UP is restricted to the period 1953-54 to 1969-70 for want of data on UP's imports for the other years.) The results of the analysis will be found in Table 12.

To make these coefficients comparable with those in Table 6 we must convert these into index terms with 1952-53=100; since the average price in 1952-53 in UP was Rs 50.9 per quintal this implies multiplication of the entries in Table 12 by approximately 2.

The results present a mixed picture partly because of the unsatisfactory nature of i (imports into UP by rail and river) as an indicator of shortage. However, some tentative conclusions can be drawn. Support operations raise average annual prices by about 40 points in contrast to a similar rise in the Punjab-Haryana region by 80 points. The policy of support appears to raise the harvest prices and leave the off-seasonal prices undisturbed at their normal levels. This could be a reason why in UP market arrivals in the lean season have not slackened off to such a great extent as in Punjab-Haryana (Table 9).

None of the coefficients of Z are significant at the 5 per cent level but the one in respect of harvest prices is significant at the 10 per cent level. If at all anything is implied in this, it is that zoning raises harvest prices in UP which may indeed be true.

All these are factors that promote inter-state inequalities. Relaxation of movement restrictions is a policy that favours the farmers of Punjab but not of UP, while support prices favour farmers everywhere but they favour the Punjabi farmer more than the others.

It is possible now to use our estimated equations to evaluate the net effect of various combinations of support and zoning policies on the trend and seasonal variation in Punjab-Haryana as well as UP. However, we shall restrict ourselves to just two alternative policies and evaluate their implications for the period 1968-72. The two policies are: support combined with unfettered movement, the actual policy that prevailed during this period, which we shall call policy A; and the policy of withdrawing support combined with the single state zoning system everywhere, which we shall call policy B. Now, it is obvious that policy B will bring down prices; in particular for the period 1968-72 this policy would have seen prices dropping to the floor levels—or the currently notional support prices—which would have enabled the government to procure large quantities of grain at these depressed price levels. For evaluating policy B it would thus be necessary to bring in such considerations as support prices that would cover costs and normal profits. We are not attempting this here but merely using our equations which are based on the working of the single state zoning system of the early fifties and hence our estimates corresponding to policy B would merely reflect the 1951-55 pattern so far as the impact of zoning is concerned,

Table 10: Procurement of Wheat

(Thousand tonnes)

State	Marketing Season (April-March)				
	1967-68	1968-69	1969-70	1970-71	1971-72
Haryana	49	214	271	482	710
Punjab	503	1358	1873	2369	2938
UP	156	516	199	322	1144
Rest of India	107	185	42		308
Total	815	2273	2385	3192	5100

Source: Reports of the Agricultural Prices Commission.

Table 11: Estimated Price Equations—Punjab-Haryana

Dependent Variable (Price)	Estimated Coefficients of						Constant	R^2	Period of Study
	I	D	L	S	A_h	A_o			
Annual	2.68 (0.37)	27.07 (2.84)	-2.09 (2.44)	-11.80 (2.80)			33.77	0.964	1952-53 to 1971-72
Harvest	2.24 (0.36)	28.36 (2.80)	-3.04 (2.40)	-7.51 (2.76)			32.93	0.961	-do-
Off-seasonal	3.31 (0.76)	23.44 (5.80)	-2.97 (5.02)	-16.46 (5.71)			42.14	0.872	-do-
Harvest	2.13 (0.99)	21.68 (9.45)			0.08 (0.42)		38.82	0.808	1958-59 to 1971-72
Off-seasonal	3.69 (0.78)	18.76 (6.72)				-1.10 (0.74)	40.97	0.906	except 1967-68

Note: A_h and A_o stand for per cent of arrivals in Punjab-Haryana in the harvest and off-seasonal periods, respectively.

Table 12: Estimated Price Equations—Uttar Pradesh

Dependent Variable (Price)	Constant	Coefficient of				R^2	Period of Study
		i	D	Z	A_h	A_o		
Annual	35.00	22.32 (8.69)	20.70 (12.73)	10.27 (7.71)			0.672	1953-54 to 1969-70
Harvest	34.76	11.45 (8.04)	33.65 (11.52)	10.75 (7.13)			0.692	-do-
Off-seasonal	38.22	31.24 (9.18)	9.37 (13.56)	5.15 (6.16)			0.668	-do-
Harvest	106.16	5.65 (6.12)	38.29 (7.21)	4.71 (5.15)	-1.23 (0.31)		0.912	1958-59 to 1969-70
Off-seasonal	88.77	25.63 (8.03)				-2.54 (0.91)	0.725	-do-

Note: A_h and A_o represent arrival rates in UP in the harvest and off-seasonal periods, respectively.

without reference to the rational concomitants of the policy like, for example, a properly planned regional allocation of the pro- cured grain. However, for what they are worth, we give these estimates (Tables 13 and 14).

For Punjab we have computed harvest prices on the basis of the second equation in Table 11. We give two sets of estimates of off-seasonal prices, (1) and (2), based respectively on equa- tions 3 and 5 of Table 11. The latter of these has A_0 as one of the variables. We have already argued that the arrival pattern itself is influenced by policy measures. Hence, for estimation in (2) we assumed that the lean season arrivals (A_0) will increase to 5 per cent (in contrast to the current 2 per cent) under the regime determined by policy B. The prices in the second set of estimates are higher than in the first because of this smallness of A_0. Under policy B we can reasonably expect harvest arrivals to diminish very significantly from their current high levels (75 per cent); taking this fact into account we must regard the

Table 13: Prices under Alternative Policies—Punjab-Haryana

(Rs per quintal)

Year	Actual Prices (Policy A)		Policy B		
	Harvest	Off-Season	Harvest	Off-Season (1)	(2)
1968-69	75.7	92.8	48.1	59.2	72.9
1969-70	80.9	95.9	46.6	59.0	70.3
1970-71	83.2	84.1	45.3	55.4	67.5
1971-72	80.4	91.0	42.7	51.2	63.9

Table 14: Prices under Alternative Policies—UP

(Rs per quintal)

Year	Actual Prices (Policy A)		Policy B			
	Harvest	Off-Season	Harvest (1)	(2)	Off-Season (1)	(2)
1968-69	74.1	82.0	53.5	53.5	65.2	68.6
1969-70	78.7	100.9	72.9	63.0	118.3	112.2
1970-71	81.8	84.7				
1971-72	73.1	86.5				

second set of prices as being on the high side. We have estimated UP prices corresponding to policy B for the years 1968-69 and 1969-70 only because of the lack of information on i (import into UP by rail and river) for the later years. These estimates are based on the equations in Table 12. For harvest prices the first set (1) is based on equation 2 and the second (2) on equation 4 with the additional assumption that A_h will be 50 per cent under policy B. The first set of estimates of off-seasonal prices are based on equation 3 and the second set on equation 5 where we assumed that A_o = 15 per cent (as against the actual 13.7 per cent and 10.7 per cent for 1968-69 and 1969-70, respectively).

Our estimates of actual prices for both the regions, for the period 1968-72, are all fortunately based on prices for indigenous white wheat and this, we hope, validates their comparison. It will be seen that actual prices (i e, those corresponding to policy A) in UP were lower than their corresponding levels in Punjab-Haryana (except in respect of the off-seasonal price in 1969-70). It will also be found that policy B will not only reverse this relation but also lower prices everywhere and give rise to declining trends in Punjab in keeping with the rapid increase in production. Since UP has continued to be a net importer even in recent years it is easy to see why policy B will bring in such a change in relative prices and equally easy to see policy A as an instrument responsible for increasing inter-state disparities.

V
INTRA-STATE INEQUALITIES

Recalling that market prices are determined by the combination of the three factors, excess demand, support prices and zoning policies, we may now examine the nature of the contribution of each of these to the fortunes of different rural classes. For this purpose we need to remember the following facts: (a) the choice between selling during the harvest season and holding on to sell later for a price advantage exists to a significant degree only for the large farmers (loosely speaking, the holding power increases with farm size); (b) a phenomenon related to (a) is that market dependence also declines with farm size. At the bottom is the landless labourer who is almost entirely dependent on the market for his consumption needs.[13]

Now, an increase in excess demand enhances both the average

price and the seasonal rise, i e, the increase in the lean season price over the harvest price (Table 6). Given the pattern of selling and buying determined by (a) and (b) above, it is obvious that small farmers and labourers are much better off when production rises faster than demand. The tendency of unfettered grain movement to dampen seasonal variation is a factor favourable to small farmers and landless labourers so far as their buying is concerned, but this same factor gives a very big advantage to the large farmers in their selling operations. But the kingpin is the support scheme which raises prices all round the year by an amount which wipes off any marginal advantage that small farmers and labourers may derive from the other two factors, particularly from a rapidly rising production. Table 15 illustrates the operation of policies A and B on all-India prices.

A superimposition of these two sets of prices on (a) and (b) will yield information on the impact of policies on inequalities between different classes of farmers. Despite the absence of detailed data on (a) and (b) we can see that policy A tilts the income distribution in favour of sellers while the low prices corresponding to B give immense relief to all the rural poor.

VI
CONCLUDING REMARKS

The events of this summer (1973) following the take-over of the wholesale trade in wheat confirm our main finding that prices are made to behave as they do. A good harvest of wheat succeeding a poor kharif season has created the right atmosphere for securing price increases. The procurement price of Rs 76 per quintal made no impression on the farmers and all the well

Table 15: All-India Prices under Policies A and B*
(1952-53 = 100)

Year	Actual Prices (Policy A)		Policy B	
	Harvest	Off-Season	Harvest	Off-Season
1968-69	174	191	111	136
1969-70	179	211	108	131
1970-71	185	190	106	127
1971-72	181	197	99	118

* Computed on the basis of the equations of Table 6.

known devices for enhancing the price are already at work: bonus schemes, subsidies for inputs and so on. The APC has also fallen in line, recommending an increase in the procurement price of paddy for the coming kharif season and the chief ministers have accepted this subject to the proviso that "these would be support prices and not procurement prices".[14] And "the implication of this decision is that the government will have freedom to offer a higher price to the growers, if market conditions necessitated, to fulfil procurement targets".[15]

We have been arguing so far that price policy has been designed mainly to protect the interests of the large farmer and that this form of intervention contributes to the worsening of both inter-state and intra-state inequalities. Given a highly skewed land distribution and the resulting concentration of marketed surplus in the hands of the big farmers it is obvious that any upward movement of the price level combined with seasonal stability will have adverse effects on the income distribution. In the context of this argument it is, however, necessary to examine the relationship between cost and price. Another related question is that of price incentives. Both these issues require detailed study and a beginning can be made by raising the question of how actual cost of production compares with, say, a procurement price of Rs 76 per quintal.

Unfortunately, even the APC has not gone into the question of costs in detail: the commission mainly looks at the increase in the price of some inputs to determine the warranted increase in the procurement price leaving aside the more important question relating to the level of prices. While lack of suitable data could be one reason for this, other difficulties are also likely to arise in the estimation of costs: for example, how does one treat family labour? These questions are being examined and the results will be reported separately.

NOTES

1 Appendix to report of the Agricultural Prices Commission (APC) on the price policy of kharif cereals for 1965-68 season, p 47.
2 Ibid, p 47.
3 Report of the APC on minimum prices for wheat and gram for the 1968-69 crop.
4 'Procurement without Tears', *Economic and Political Weekly*, December 9, 1972.

5 'Rice Zone Policy: A Note of Dissent' by Raj Krishna, report of the APC on the price policy of kharif cereals for 1965-66 season.

6 Table 7, report of the APC on price policy for rabi foodgrains for 1968-69 season, p 19. For 1967 onwards, information on these changes is available in *Bulletin of Food Statistics* (various issues).

7 Report of the APC price policy for rabi foodgrains for 1968-69 season, p 4, and a similar report for 1970-71 season, p 8.

8 Report of the APC on the price policy for rabi foodgrains for the 1972-73 season, mimeo, p 8.

9 The information on zoning policies is collected from the reference quoted in (6) above up to 1967 (p 9) and various issues of *Bulletin of Food Statistics* thereafter.

10 We could have retained 1967-68 but then the estimate of the impact of single zoning will be measured on the basis of just one observation.

11 UP's imports of wheat by rail and river, collected from the *Bulletin of Food Statistics*, are from 1953-54 to 1969-70 in succession 0.12, −0.11, −0.15, 0.16, 0.33, 0.45, 0.52, 0.68, 0.34, 0.30, 0.65, 0.89, 0.69, 1.02, 0.98, 0.70 and 2.39 (all in million tonnes).

12 All this information is collected from sources mentioned in (9) above.

13 Statistics relating to market dependence of rural households for foodgrain requirement in respect of a few states, based on NSS data, will be found in report of the APC on price policy for kharif cereals for the 1968-69 season, pp 49-50.

14 *The Hindu,* June 15, 1973.

15 Ibid.

June 30, 1973.

3

Inter-Regional Disparities in Per Capita Production and Productivity of Foodgrains

I

RELEVANT PARAMETERS

THE 'new agricultural strategy', with its emphasis on the use of modern inputs such as improved seeds and chemical fertilisers in areas of assured water supply, has a built-in bias towards the promotion of inequalities—both between and within different regions of the country. Large farmers have generally greater access to credit, and hence better scope for the adoption of the new methods, than do small farmers. The tendency of disparities in income to widen within given areas, even at the village level, has been traced to this factor in numerous empirical studies.[1] The same factor, together with unevenness in water supplies, promotes inequalities between regions. For, wide inter-regional variations exist at the district and state levels with respect to not only the skewness of distribution of land but also the availability of irrigation facilities. Another, equally important, factor in the process of inter-regional divergence is the crop-specificity of the 'green revolution': only in respect of wheat have *significant* increases resulted in the overall yield, although yield rates of other crops too have risen through the use of the new varieties in some areas of the country.

But has such regional divergence taken place, and if so to what extent? The answers would depend, first, on how a region is defined, and secondly, on how regional concentration in output is measured. Since, in most states, a few small areas have benefited from the adoption of the high-yielding varieties of seeds, if states are taken as regions, the impact of the new technology in inter-regional differences in yields may appear to be insignificant. The only exception to this is Punjab where the use of high-yielding varieties of wheat has been quite widespread as a result of both better irrigation facilities and higher proportion of large farms than in other parts of the country. Consequently, even if the state is taken as the unit for inter-regional analysis, Punjab can be shown to have enjoyed a differential advantage. Indeed, analysis shows that, during the sixties, the inter-state differences in foodgrains productivity have not widened perceptibly. The rise in the inter-state coefficient of variation, whatever be its magnitude, appears to be wholly on account of the differential rise in Punjab's productivity.[2] It is necessary, therefore, to disaggregate states into smaller regions to capture the spatial effects of the new technology.

Turning now to the question of measurement of regional concentration, we may observe that, viewed solely from the point of availability of food, growth in regional disparities in productivity and production of foodgrains would be of no importance if the regional imbalances could be corrected through a workable distribution policy. The Indian experience shows, however, that it is extremely difficult to mop up surpluses to make good regional deficits. A recent analysis, based on the data for 1961-62 when there were no inter-state movement restrictions on foodgrains trade, shows that levels of food intake in general and foodgrains consumption in particular are very closely correlated across the states to levels of foodgrains production. This is largely because trade (i e, inter-state net inflows) was insignificant in relation to what was domestically produced. The economic factors underlying this phenomenon have been examined in detail elsewhere.[3] Even during the sixties when movement restrictions were imposed, and inter-state distribution was handled by the government, the magnitudes of transfer have continued to be small mainly because of government's inability to mop up surpluses through its procurement operations. It is in this context that the question of regional disparities in foodgrains production assumes great importance. And, accordingly, it is more appropriate to measure regional concentration with respect to per capita production, rather than productivity, especially since there are areas—such as in Rajasthan—where the productivity is low but so is the population density per hectare cropped, and consequently the per capita production is high. But to the extent that productivity per hectare is an important determinant of per capita production it is necessary to examine regional variations in productivity also.

It is now obvious that the argument that the new technology

has no tendency to widen regional disparities, based as it is on empirical data on inter-state differences in productivity, falls to the ground on two counts. First, regional concentration should be measured with respect to per capita production and not productivity; and second, the spatial impact of the green revolution is so concentrated that large regional units tend to conceal its nature. The computational exercises reported in this note show that even districts are not adequately small for this purpose. A question that may be asked is, why it is necessary to disaggregate states into smaller units (say, districts), since within the states generally there are no movement restrictions. While data in support are lacking, it appears safe to assume that very little inter-district movement actually takes place, particularly in favour of rural deficit areas. This is clearly reflected in the odd fact that Orissa is a 'surplus state' in spite of being one of the poorest states by any standard. Orissa's 'surplus', small in relation to the total production in the state, originates in a few districts and goes out of the state rather than into the rural areas of the deficit districts in the state.

We approach the question of regional disparities in the above light. We shall be concerned with differences, not only in productivity but also in per capita production; and wherever possible we shall treat the district as the unit of analysis. No further disaggregation is possible for want of adequate data. While making no attempt to identify all the factors which contribute to the regional variations in productivity, we shall attempt to isolate the impact—in however crude a fashion—of irrigation and cropping pattern, which are particularly important in the context of the spatial effects of the new technology.

II

INTER-STATE DIFFERENCES

We begin by analysing inter-state variations in the per capita production of foodgrains as a whole. For this purpose we take the annual averages corresponding to three triennia, viz, 1950-53, 1960-63 and 1970-73. Averages over three-year periods tend to dampen weather-induced fluctuations to a certain extent and hence may be expected to reflect spatial variations resulting from other factors fairly accurately. Wide inter-state differences in per capita production existed and continue to exist (see Tables B1 and B2 in Appendix B).

Since large inter-crop differentials in productivity exist, the cropping pattern is an important determinant of productivity and hence of per capita production of foodgrains as a whole. The effect of the cropping pattern can be captured in a crude way, by classifying the states according to the main crop: this has been done by considering the allocation of area under cereals to rice, wheat and other cereals (as a group). States are thus divided into three regions: mainly rice-growing, wheat-growing, and remaining states where inferior cereals are allocated maximum area. A comparison of the regional averages gives some idea of the variations induced by the cropping pattern.

Table 1, which summarises the trend in inter-state variations in per capita production, clearly shows that the overall inequality—as reflected in the coefficient of variation—hardly changed during the fifties but has sharply increased during the sixties. Calculation shows that the inter-state coefficient of variation for 1964-65 is 0.3667, and hence there is no doubt that the widening of overall inequality has taken place during 1965-70. When the total observed variation is broken up into two parts, viz, between regional averages, and within regions, it can be seen that the former has increased relatively to the latter: as much as 39 per cent of the observed variation in 1970-73 arises out of variation between crop regions while such variation was practically non-existent in 1950-53. Comparing the regional averages for 1960-63 with those for 1970-73, it is seen that this rise in inter-regional variation is entirely because of the rise in per capita production in wheat areas. The regional averages of per capita

Table 1: Inter-State Differences in Per Capita Production of Foodgrains

	1950-53	1960-63	1970-73
Annual average per capita production (kg) (average of states)	157.7	180.1	200.3
Inter-state coefficient of variation	0.3827	0.3818	0.5064
Regional averages:			
Rice regions	158.1	170.2	169.1
Wheat regions	—	216.1	328.6
Other regions	157.4	173.6	172.6
Variation between regional averages as per cent of total inter-state variation	0.004	6.80	39.40

Note: See Appendix B, Tables B1 and B2 for classification of states into regions.

production for the non-wheat areas hardly changed during the sixties, remaining around 170 kg per annum. By contrast, the per capita production in the wheat region increased from 216 kg in 1960-63 to 329 kg in 1970-73. This is a highly aggregative, but nevertheless suggestive, picture of the regional variations which have recently emerged.

The impact of cropping pattern on variations in productivity is analysed in the same manner as in the case of per capita production, i e, by classifying states into crop regions on the basis of the allocation of area to the different cereals. While no attempt is made to fully explain inter-state differences in productivity, the variation accounted for by differences in intensity of irrigation is computed for all the three time-periods. In addition, the variation explained by differences in levels of fertiliser consumption as well as intensity of irrigation is computed for the 1970-73 data. The remainder, which can be termed as the residual variation, includes not only a purely random part but also variations caused by other factors   such as soil fertility, labour and other inputs, and the distribution of land. The computations are carried out in the framework of an analysis of the covariance model explained fully in Appendix A. These calculations enable us, first, to see how large are the cropping-pattern-induced differences in regional productivity in relation to variations within the regions, and secondly, to infer whether such differences, when they are found to be wide, could be attributed to disparities in the level of irrigation (and fertiliser consumption) alone or to other factors. Thus, if differences in regional averages after eliminating the effects of irrigation are found to be insignificant, it implies that such differences are no wider than disparities in productivity within homogeneous crop regions, and hence that any observed variations between the regional averages must be attributed mainly to differences in levels of irrigation.

Table 2 summarises our inter-state analysis of differences in foodgrains productivity. Judged by the coefficient of variation, inter-state differences can be seen to have shrunk during the fifties but widened during the next decade. Large differences in productivity between the areas growing mainly inferior cereals and those growing mainly rice or wheat existed and continue to exist. The difference in average productivity between wheat areas and inferior cereals areas has grown from about 230 kg to 346 kg per hectare. But if we compare these cropping-pattern-induced differences in regional averages to the variations within regions, the former can be seen to have shrunk relatively to the latter (see rows 6, 7 and 8 of Table 2). This is because variations *within* regions have increased at a faster pace than variations *between* regions, and the cropping pattern effect on regional variations has gradually reduced to insignificance. However, we must remember that this insignificance is with respect to variations within the regions; the mean square within regions, reflecting the variability therein, has more than trebled during 1960-63 to 1970-73, in contrast to a rise in overall productivity by a mere 27 per cent. We may conclude that the growth in inter-state disparities in the productivity of foodgrains is largely the result of a rise in intra-regional differences in broadly defined crop regions, although cropping-pattern-induced disparities still persist between such regions.

Table 2: *Inter-State Differences in Foodgrains Productivity*

	1950-53	1960-63	1970-73
Overall average productivity per hectare (kg) (average of states)	565	781	997
Inter-state coefficient of variation	0.3677	0.3002	0.3758
Regional averages:			
Rice regions	723.8	924.4	1055.3
Wheat regions	—	823.7	1191.7
Other regions	477.8	593.3	745.0
Proportion of variation in productivity within regions explained by variations in irrigation rates (per cent)	51.1	41.3	71.52
Proportion of variation in productivity within regions explained by variations in irrigation and fertiliser consumption (per cent)	—		71.53
Mean square between regions	241384.0(1)	180387.0(2)	308895.0(2)
Mean square within regions	29989.8(15)	35737.7(13)	116369.0(14)
Variance ratio (F)	8.04*	5.04*	2.65*
	(1,15)	(2,13)	(2,14)
F statistic for testing regional differences after elimination of effects of irrigation	8.17*	0.007	1.81
	(1,14)	(2,12)	(2,13)

* Denotes significance at 5 per cent level. The degrees of freedom are given in parentheses.

Irrigation (more precisely, the proportion of irrigated area to the total area under foodgrains) accounts for a substantial part of the inter-state variation in productivity. The data for 1970-73 reveal that irrigation alone accounts for 71.52 per cent of the variation in yield rates within regions, and that irrigation and fertiliser consumption (per hectare of area under foodgrains[4]) together explain not much more of the variation. This shows, not unexpectedly, that levels of fertiliser consumption have not yet induced significant differences in state-wide averages of productivity independently of the levels of irrigation. The impact of fertiliser consumption on regional differences in productivity can perhaps be seen only through disaggregation of states into smaller regions. However, to the extent that complementarity exists between intensity of irrigation and fertiliser use, the growth in inter-state disparities during the sixties can legitimately be attributed largely to the green revolution.

We have seen that the cropping pattern effect on inter-state disparities, as reflected in the differences between regional averages, is reduced to insignificance by 1970-73 in comparison with intra-regional differences. This has happened partly because of a higher rate of growth in overall foodgrains productivity in the areas growing mainly inferior cereals but more because of the widening of productivity differentials within the rice and wheat areas. In contrast, the cropping pattern effect is significant in both 1950-53 and 1960-63 (i e, the inter-regional averages differed more widely than intra-regional productivity levels: see row 8, Table 2). The values of the F statistic for testing differences between the regional averages after elimination of the effects of irrigation (row 9) show that this phenomenon could not be entirely attributed to differences in levels of irrigation in respect of the 1950-53 data, while the cropping pattern effect in 1960-63 appears to be entirely due to irrigation. This may well imply that inter-crop yield differentials in unirrigated areas have narrowed during the fifties and irrigation emerged as the most important single determinant of productivity differences. But the same factor, viz, irrigation, along with fertiliser consumption, appears to have caused widening of productivity variations during the sixties largely through the growth of inequalities within the rice and wheat regions. The level of aggregation at which the analysis is done here allows us to put forward this as a hypothesis rather than a firm conclusion.

We may now link up our analysis of productivity differentials with an analysis of variations in per capita production. Since productivity differentials narrowed down but inequalities in per capita production remained stable during the fifties, it is obvious that changes in the land-man ratio (i e, the area cropped per person) took place to neutralise the shrinkage in spatial variations in productivity. In the sixties, along with the growth in inequalities in productivity, variations in per capita production have also widened significantly—again implying that compensating changes in the land-man ratio have not taken place.

III

INTER-DISTRICT DIFFERENCES

The effects of the crop-specificity of the green revolution are thus to be seen in the emergence of significantly larger levels of per capita production of foodgrains in the wheat areas than in other parts of the country. We shall now examine this hypothesis in some detail on the basis of inter-district data. For this purpose, we have taken a random sample of 30 from 302 districts about which detailed data are available not only on different crops but also on irrigation supplies and fertiliser consumption. The data used for the analysis are reproduced largely in Table B3. We follow the same procedure for studying these data as in the case of the inter-state data: the districts are classified into crop regions on the basis of the allocation of area to different foodgrain crops and an analysis is done of the covariance of productivity, along with an analysis of the variance of production of all foodgrains combined.

Analysis of the productivity of all foodgrains is supplemented by a study of the inter-district variations in the productivity of rice and wheat. For this purpose, random samples of four districts each from seven states growing rice and four each from six states growing wheat have been chosen (see Table B4). This kind of sampling enables us to study both inter-district and inter-state variations simultaneously.

All the conclusions that follow are thus inferences based on random samples and apply to the population at large only with a degree of uncertainty.

The main features of inter-district disparities are given in Tables 3 and 4. Considering foodgrains as a whole first, much of what we said about inter-state variations can be repeated in the context of regional disparities at the district level. In particular, spatial inequalities in per capita production have grown during the sixties mainly because of the rise in per capita production of foodgrains in the wheat areas (see Table 3, rows 3 and 4).

Table 3: Inter-District Differences in Per Capita Production and Productivity of Foodgrains: Random Sample of 30 Districts

	1950-53	1960-63	1970-73
Per capita production			
Annual average per capita production (average of all 30 districts) (kg/year)	160.0	189.7	197.1
Inter-district coefficient of variation	0.4631	0.4923	0.5703
Regional averages:			
Rice regions	152.0	181.7	165.7
Wheat regions	223.0	277.0	329.7
Other districts	154.0	178.1	189.5
Variation between crop regions as per cent of total variation between districts	8.31	10.07	23.15
Productivity			
Average of all 30 districts' productivity (kg/ha)	603.6	778.6	1000.4
Inter-district coefficient of variation	0.4902	0.4498	0.4552
Regional averages:			
Rice regions	749.9	1003.7	1135.3
Wheat regions	785.7	905.3	1285.5
Other districts	428.8	506.8	748.0
Variation explained by irrigation (per cent)	17.4	14.2	39.2
Variation explained by irrigation and fertilisers (per cent)	—	—	52.8
Mean square between crop regions (2 degrees of freedom)	402810.5	859078.2	672157.6
Mean square within crop regions (27 degrees of freedom)	63983.9	68097.2	172941.1
Variance ratio $F(2, 27)$	6.29*	12.61*	3.88*
F for testing differences after elimination of effects of irrigation (and fertiliser use in 1970-73)	5.49* (2,26)	7.25* (2,26)	2.61 (2,25)

* denotes significance at 5 per cent level.

But, unlike inter-state differences, foodgrains productivity differentials between districts have not grown perceptibly during the period 1960-63 to 1970-73. The apparent anomaly arises partly because the green revolution is localised to Punjab and hence its effect cannot be captured adequately through a random sample of 30 districts but also because of other factors to be discussed presently. However, notwithstanding the absence of change in the overall inequality in productivity of foodgrains, the relationship between its two spatial components, viz, inequality between crop regions and that within, has radically changed: Whereas the former declined, the latter has more than doubled itself during the sixties (see rows 6 and 7 of Table 3). This agrees

Table 4: Regional Variations in the Productivity of Rice and Wheat
(Based on Random Samples of Districts)

	1961-62	1971-72
Rice (28 districts)		
Average productivity per hectare (kg) (average of 28 districts)	1106.2	1348.5
Coefficient of variation (inter-district)	0.3566	0.4695
Variation between districts within states (per cent of total)	34.05	16.30
Mean square between states (6 degrees of freedom)	461701	1504950
Mean square between districts within states (21 df)	68131	84028
Variance ratio F (6, 21)	6.77*	17.96*
Variation explained by irrigation	50.0	—
F for testing inter-state differences after elimination of the effects of irrigation (6, 20)	2.62*	—
Wheat (24 districts)		
Average productivity per hectare (kg)	931.8	1554.1
Inter-district coefficient of variation	0.3165	0.4562
Variation between districts within states (per cent of total)	21.6	33.1
Mean square between states (5 df)	314200	1546892
Mean square within states (18 df)	23920	212033
Variance ratio F (5, 18)	13.13*	7.29*
Variation explained by irrigation (per cent)	42.6	
F for testing inter-state differences after elimination of the effects of irrigation (5, 17)	8.64*	

* denotes significance at 5 per cent level.

with the conclusion already arrived at, on the basis of inter-state data, that the new technology is associated with among other things growth of inequalities within broadly defined crop-regions.

Turning now to the impact of the cropping pattern on inter-district differences in productivity, we see that the variations in the regional averages continue to be significantly wider than intra-regional disparities (row 8, Table 3). These differences, induced by the cropping pattern, were not entirely due to variations in levels of irrigation in 1950-53 and 1960-63, since, the F statistic for testing regional differences in productivity after the elimination of the impact of irrigation is significantly high in both these cases; but the data for 1970-73 imply, on the surface, that the observed wide variation in regional averages must be attributed entirely to levels of irrigation and fertiliser use[5] since the corresponding F value is insignificant (see row 9, Table 3). But this significance between the regional averages (after the elimination of effects of irrigation and fertiliser use) is only in relation to the intra-regional variations which have considerably widened by 1970-73, and hence is no true guide to the nature of the effect of the cropping pattern on yield rates and its relationship to irrigation and fertilisers. We must accordingly conclude that the cropping pattern still plays an independent role in the determination of spatial inequalities in the productivity of foodgrains.

The absence of change in the inter-district productivity differentials, together with growth of inequalities in per capita production during the sixties, implies that the latter was brought about by changes in regional pattern of the land-man ratio; however, we shall not pursue this theme here. Instead, let us first examine how this absence is to be reconciled with the observed widening of inter-state disparities in foodgrains productivity during the sixties and then try to see if it supports the contention that the green revolution has no tendency to increase inter-district inequalities.

We have already noted that the inter-state coefficient of variation in foodgrains productivity increased from 0.3002 for 1960-63 to 0.3758 for 1970-73. If we exclude Punjab from the reckoning, the latter coefficient gets reduced to 0.3151. The absence of change in the overall inequality between districts is thus partly explained by the fact that our random sample fails to capture the inter-regional variation in full since Amritsar (the only district of Punjab in our sample) receives a weight of only 1 in 30 in the sample, whereas Punjab gets the higher weight of 1 in 16, in the inter-state analysis. Indeed, if we exclude Amritsar, the inter-district coefficient of variation for 1970-73 gets reduced from 0.4552 to 0.4200, which is lower than its 1960- 63 level (0.4498). While adequately demonstrating the regional specificity of the spread of the new technology, this by no means implies that the green revolution has not accentuated regional inequalities in other parts of the country. To substantiate this we now examine data relating to different foodgrains separately.

Table 4 contains the results of our analysis of the samples of rice and wheat districts (see Table B4 for the basic data). It can be seen that spatial differentials in the productivity of both these crops have widened considerably during the sixties. But the regional components of the overall variation have moved in a significantly different way as between the two crops. Although the state averages have continued to differ significantly more widely than productivity levels within the states in respect of both rice and wheat, the mean square within the wheat states has increased almost nine-fold (from 23,920 to 212,033) during the sixties. The most significant aspect of the change in productivity therefore appears to be the sharp increase in the intra-state inequality in wheat yields. A last point is that our analysis of the 1961-62 data shows that irrigation alone does not explain inter-state differentials in the yield rates of the two major cereals.

Since inter-district disparities in the productivity of the two major foodgrains are clearly shown to have widened, we may now ask why such a widening did not take place in the case of the productivity of all foodgrains combined. An analysis of the data on productivity differentials of inferior cereals and pulses taken together (see Table B5) shows that the inter-district coefficient of variation (for the same sample of 30 districts referred to earlier) has decreased from 0.4267 for 1960-63 to 0.4030 for 1970-73. If Amritsar is excluded from the sample, the decline is quite sharp: from 0.4294 to 0.3500. While this narrowing down of the inter-district differentials in the productivity of inferior cereals and pulses neutralised, to a certain extent, the growth in disparities in the yield rates of rice and wheat, an equally important neutralising factor appears to be the significant shift of acreage in favour of superior cereals which has taken place in low productivity regions. It will be seen from Table 5 that such shifts have occurred to a greater extent in the districts where the

1960-63 levels of foodgrains productivity were relatively low. The table also shows that high productivity is associated with greater allocations of area to the major cereals. Thus the cropping pattern is clearly identified as an important source of spatial variations in productivity and, accordingly, both the factors discussed must have contributed to the absence of change during the sixties in the inter-district differentials in productivity of foodgrains.

It will be rash either to blame or to praise the green revolution for all these changes. However, what stands out quite clearly as the net effect of the new technology is the rise in regional differences in productivity within the wheat areas combined, somewhat paradoxically, with a differentially large rise in the per capita production of foodgrains in the wheat regions as a whole. To say more on the spatial impact of the green revolution would require data relating to regional units much smaller than a district.

IV

CONCLUDING REMARK

Turning back to inter-state variations in per capita production, we may recall that they have remained stable during the fifties but have widened during the next decade. However, since

Table 5: Changes in Cropping Pattern

(A Random Sample of 30 Districts)

Districts Ranked in Ascending Order of Foodgrains Productivity, 1960-63	Proportion of Rice and Wheat in Area under All Foodgrains (Per Cent)	
	1960-63	1970-73
Churu, Jamnagar, and Jodhpur	3.01	3.86
Chitradurg, Jalore and Junagarh	9.58	13.74
Anantapur, Ganganagar and Yeotmal	11.72	19.63
Baroda, Surguja and Pulamau	54.36	64.48
Chattarpur, Rohtak and Vidisha	37.62	42.13
Goalpura, Monghyr and Sultanpur	72.98	71.90
Darbhanga, Nizamabad and Shimoga	64.51	67.60
Amritsar, Kolhapur and Muzaffarpur	60.37	76.30
Bankura, Chingleput and Thana	89.10	92.95
East Godavari, Kolaba and Tirunelveli	74.08	77.84

Source: Listed under Table B3.

APPENDIX A

The analysis of covariance model used in the text is of the following form:
$Y_{ij} = a + b_i + c X_{ij} + e_{ij}$ where Y_{ij} denotes the yield of the ith state (or district) in the ith crop region, X_{ij} the corresponding intensity of irrigation and b_i is the region effect. The usual assumptions are made about the residuals e_{ij}

The full computational layout in respect of the 1960-63 data on inter-state differences in foodgrain yields is given below:

Sums of Square and Products

Source	Degrees of Freedom	YY	YX	XX
Between regions	2	360774.04	17996.81	302.20
Within regions	13	464577.71	23024.78	2761.29
Total	15	825351.75	41021.54	3063.49

Test for Regression

Source	df	SS	MS	F
Regression	1	191989.41		8.45*
Residual	12	272588.30	22715.69	
Within regions	13	464577.71		

Test for Regional Differences after Elimination of the Effects of Irrigation: H_0

Estimate of c under H_0 : 41021.54/3063.49 = 13.3904
and the corresponding residual SS = 276056.92 (14)

Test for H_0

Source	df	SS	MS	F
Deviation from H_0	2	3468.62	1734.31	0.076
Unconstrained residual	12	272588.30	22715.69	
Residual under H_0	14	276056.92		

productivity differentials narrowed down somewhat during the earlier period, it is obvious that changes in the regional pattern of the land-man ratio neutralised the dampening effect of productivity differentials. These changes depend on the spatial pattern of the growth of acreage under foodgrains in relation to the growth in population; and the net effect of the changes was not in favour of low productivity regions. Our inter-district analysis

APPENDIX B

Table B1: Per Capita Production and Productivity of Foodgrains and Intensity of Irrigation, 1950-53
(Annual Averages)

Region/State	Per Capita Production of Foodgrains (Kg/Year)	Productivity Per Hectare (Kg/Ha)	Proportion of Area under Foodgrains Irrigated (Per Cent)
Rice			
Assam	171.3	876	26.7
Bihar	125.8	515	18.7
Travancore-Cochin	39.7	901	73.0
Orissa	184.9	620	21.0
Madhya Pradesh	253.2	530	7.2
West Bengal	174.2	921	20.3
Other States			
Madras	121.9	708	38.9
Bombay	109.9	356	5.2
Uttar Pradesh	183.9	685	25.0
Punjab	264.7	653	33.8
Hyderabad	110.5	294	8.3
Madhya Bharat	129.1	301	4.1
Mysore	99.5	417	15.9
Rajasthan	111.4	311	17.4
PEPSU	246.5	620	40.1
Himachal Pradesh	169.5	507	17.7
Vindhya Pradesh	185.0	404	4.6

Note: States are classified into regions on the basis of allocation of area to rice, wheat and inferior cereals. The criterion is maximum allocation between the three groups. No state could be classified as a wheat area according to this criterion.

Sources: Compiled from various issues of *Estimates of Area and Production of Principal Crops in India*, and *Indian Agricultural Statistics*, Directorate of Economics and Statistics, Ministry of Agriculture.

Table B2: Per Capita Production and Productivity of Foodgrains and Intensity of Irrigation and Fertiliser Use, 1960-63 and 1970-73
(Annual Averages)

Region/State	1960-63			1970-73			
	Per Capita Production (Kg/Year)	Productivity (Kg/Ha)	Area under Foodgrains Irrigated (Per Cent)	Per Capita Production (Kg/Year)	Productivity (Kg/Ha)	Area under Foodgrains Irrigated (Per Cent)	Fertiliser Consumption Per Hectare (Kg)
Rice							
Assam	136.2	874	30.3	143.2	988	24.8	3.9
Bihar	159.0	749	20.5	154.4	881	25.7	10.2
Kerala	64.5	1313	43.0	63.0	1458	52.9	57.9
Madhya Pradesh	285.1	602	5.1	263.4	652	7.7	5.7
Orissa	228.4	843	21.7	220.3	826	24.9	6.9
Tamil Nadu	165.1	1102	54.0	169.6	1365	54.2	49.3
West Bengal	153.2	988	24.0	170.1	1217	23.1	13.0
Wheat							
Punjab (incl Haryana)	340.6	892	34.4	510.4	1535	58.6	32.3
Himachal Pradesh	117.7	819	15.7	267.3	1097	16.4	7.0
Uttar Pradesh	190.0	760	21.4	208.0	943	34.9	19.6
Other states							
Andhra Pradesh	180.3	724	37.6	149.1	766	42.2	28.5
Gujarat	104.8	473	8.9	135.4	755	12.4	16.6
Jammu and Kashmir	174.1	850	36.6	207.7	1211	34.7	7.4
Maharashtra	166.9	525	6.2	89.9	382	4.9	8.1
Mysore	164.7	536	10.8	189.2	817	14.3	18.4
Rajasthan	251.1	452	12.1	263.4	539	14.5	3.6

Sources: Same as for Table B1. Fertiliser consumption figures are collected from *Fertiliser Statistics* (see footnote 4 to the text for method of estimation of fertiliser consumption per hectare).

Inter-Regional Disparities 57

Table B3: Per Capita Production (Z) and Productivity (Y) of Foodgrains, Area under Foodgrains Irrigated (I) and Fertiliser Consumption Per Hectare (F), Random Sample of 30 Districts (Units: Z: Kg/Yr, Y: Kg/Ha, I: Per Cent, F: Kg/Ha)

District	1950-53 Z	Y	I	1960-63 Z	Y	I	1970-73 Z	Y	I	F
East Godavari	161	1120	72.7	201	1415	79.4	162	1410	54.0	57.8
Anantapur	160	385	14.6	181	508	15.6	115	779	12.3	14.8
Nizamabad	123	554	52.5	238	974	49.2	157	922	35.5	79.2
Chingleput	98	682	57.6	201	1173	74.7	209	1673	55.5	85.8
Tirunelveli	95	841	65.3	151	1300	67.3	149	1716	34.2	70.8
Chitradurg	126	406	18.4	161	493	7.6	245	1294	19.9	52.2
Shimoga	174	749	42.9	203	980	56.3	304	1718	48.3	37.1
Baroda	77	380	1.2	85	655	2.4	63	836	10.3	121.5
Junagarh	67	200	0.0	61	415	28.5	104	1071	8.5	95.3
Jamnagar	96	169	16.8	55	236	7.4	106	523	15.3	50.6
Thana	126	1047	0.0	147	1248	0.4	93	1258	1.4	32.9
Kolaba	192	1119	0.0	208	1335	0.9	170	1363	2.2	36.5
Kolhapur	106	680	1.6	153	1079	2.6	83	930	11.9	79.3
Yeotmal	313	801	0.0	179	587	0.1	115	447	0.8	18.0
Surguja	220	571	0.4	253	605	0.2	195	715	1.0	2.3
Chattarpur	193	499	20.0	266	735	20.6	252	844	19.5	12.7
Vidisha	332	534	0.0	480	669	0.1	408	695	0.4	1.2
Churu	85	128	0.0	122	212	0.0	95	238	0.1	0.1
Ganganagar	286	469	31.8	452	542	28.1	442	717	46.7	11.9
Jalore	150	211	11.7	214	303	9.5	370	546	11.7	0.5

Table B3: (Contd.)

	1950-53			1960-63			1970-73			
	Z	Y	I	Z	Y	I	Z	Y	I	F
Jodhpur	150	226	5.4	123	151	2.9	186	299	2.8	0.7
Muzaffarpur	154	875	55.2	145	991	46.1	195	1409	69.5	92.2
Sultanpur	159	676	34.1	180	809	30.6	170	838	39.3	25.5
Rohtak	253	608	35.9	266	673	24.0	345	930	48.3	9.9
Amritsar	183	948	85.7	206	1056	79.4	464	2194	91.3	76.0
Goalpara	186	890	28.0	139	809	27.4	137	834	32.2	2.1
Monghyr	83	453	17.3	130	776	25.8	111	889	26.3	22.1
Darbhanga	74	437	5.0	109	810	2.0	107	918	7.3	11.8
Pulamau	90	360	0.6	140	609	26.5	100	666	26.1	22.4
Bankura	290	1091	47.9	245	1210	36.3	261	1340	37.5	16.4

Note : The data for 1970-73 on irrigation and fertiliser use are not available crop wise. These represent proportion of irrigated area in total under all crops and fertiliser consumption per hectare under all crops (see foot note 5 to the text) compiled from *Fertiliser Statistics*. The irrigation data refer to 1968-69.

Sources: Data for 1950-53 and 1960-63 have been collected from the publications of the Directorate of Economics and Statistics listed under Table B1. Data for 1970-73 are collected through the kind courtesy of Yoginder Alagh.

Table B4: Productivity and Intensity of Irrigation: Rice and Wheat
(Random Samples of Districts)

State/District	Wheat			State/District	Rice		
	1961-62		1971-72		1961-62		1971-72
	Productivity (Kg/Ha)	Proportion of Area under Wheat Irrigated (Per Cent)	Productivity (Kg/Ha)		Productivity (Kg/Ha)	Proportion of Area under Rice Irrigated (Per Cent)	Productivity (Kg/Ha)
(1)	(2)	(3)	(4)	(5)	(6)	(7)	(8)
Bihar				Andhra Pradesh			
Champaran	599	2.1	1149	Srikakulam	1208	85.4	1445
Gaya	600	29.5	2059	Krishna	1605	97.4	1666
Purnea	563	0.0	1604	Nellore	1283	93.6	1458
Saran	908	42.2	3511	Medak	940	94.4	1119
Haryana				Bihar			
Ambala	1162	9.3	1606	Champaran	847	27.9	819
Hissar	1307	71.1	1700	Muzaffarpur	645	6.1	651
Karnal	1391	40.7	2492	Saharsa	504	0.7	785
Rohtak	1395	54.8	2070	Purnea	704	0.2	700
Madhya Pradesh				Madhya Pradesh			
Guna	611	3.3	685	Mandla	578	0.0	643
Hoshangabad	506	1.8	745	Bhind	1385	90.4	1467
Sagar	594	1.1	806	Shivpuri	861	9.1	1010
Vidisha	756	0.1	854	Schore	537	0.6	562

Table B4: (Contd.)

(1)	(2)	(3)	(4)	(5)	(6)	(7)	(8)
Punjab				Mysore			
Bhatinda	1416	75.4	2513	Bangalore	1176	96.4	1620
Ferozepur	1202	64.5	2360	Chikmagalur	1226	95.6	1830
Gurdaspur	885	24.4	2078	Mandya	1660	100.0	2656
Patiala	1281	54.9	2066	Bidar	834	3.3	1625
Rajasthan				Tamil Nadu			
Chittorgarh	894	45.7	1244	S Arcot	1620	89.3	2441
Ganganagar	770	69.5	1196	N Arcot	1493	97.6	1987
Kota	674	12.7	1268	Coimbatore	1865	100.0	2593
Sawai Madhopur	1042	43.9	1160	Tirunelveli	1838	99.3	2369
Uttar Pradesh				Uttar Pradesh			
Basti	938	83.7	978	Aligarh	1004	11.1	923
Deoria	981	60.6	1080	Farrukhabad	1122	12.4	816
Hamirpur	1111	16.3	1122	Jalaun	755	32.9	528
Kheri	779	2.6	954	Unnao	740	21.5	713
				West Bengal			
				Burdwan	1360	57.8	1513
				Bankura	1267	35.2	1407
				Midnapur	1035	28.4	1230
				Malda	884	8.5	1183

Sources: Same as those listed under Table B1 for the 1961-62 data. The 1971-72 data have been compiled from the *Agricultural Situation in India.*

Table B5: Productivity of Inferior Cereals and Pulses

(Kg per hectare)

District	1960-63	1970-73	District	1960-63	1970-73
East Godavari	620	498	Surguja	210	830
Anantapur	408	497	Chattarpur	465	793
Nizamabad	671	682	Vidisha	194	649
Chingleput	697	979	Churu	130	236
Tirunelveli	853	809	Ganganagar	719	530
Chitradurg	434	1092	Jalore	1065	262
Shimoga	586	1306	Jodhpur	1065	262
Baroda	788	817	Muzaffarpur	650	776
Junagarh	175	827	Sultanpur	653	891
Jamnagar	284	402	Rohtak	447	532
Thana	638	814	Amritsar	932	1576
Kolaba	655	764	Monghyr	770	580
Kolhapur	895	773	Darbhanga	1063	673
Yeotmal	591	449	Pulamau	473	623

Note : Goalpara and Bankura which appear in Table B3 are omitted here because they do not have much area under inferior cereals and pulses.

Sources: Compiled from the same sources as those listed in Table B3.

also reveals a similar phenomenon: regional disparities in per capita production have widened during the sixties, in spite of the fact that productivity differentials did not. Again, changes in the land-man ratio have not favoured a reduction in inequalities in per capita production; they worked rather in the opposite direction. These facts may well imply that there is perhaps no tendency for the growth in population (relatively to the growth in area under foodgrains) to be higher—either through a higher natural rate or through greater immigration—in the high productivity regions of the country. In any case, such compensatory changes in the land-man ratio which can neutralise the wide inter-regional variations in productivity per hectare can take place, if at all, only in the very long run. Inter-regional inequalities persist, promoted by the concentration of modern inputs in areas favourably located for their use.

NOTES

[The author is extremely grateful to Chandan Mukherji and Yoginder Alagh for much help in the writing of this note.]

1 See Keith Griffin, *The Political Economy of Agrarian Change,* p 90, for some references on the subject.

2 V S Vyas, 'Regional Imbalances in Foodgrains Production in Last Decade', *Economic and Political Weekly*, December 29, 1973.
3 See Chapter 2 of *Poverty, Unemployment and Development Policy*, United Nations, March 1975.
4 Data on crop-wise allocation of fertilisers are not available. We have assumed that the allocation between foodgrains and other crops is in the same ratio as the allocation of irrigated area to these crops. The fertiliser use for foodgrains, thus obtained, is divided by the acreage under foodgrains to obtain the intensity of fertiliser use. Irrigation data refer to 1969-70.
5 For 1950-53 and 1960-63, data on irrigated area under all foodgrains are available and are used for calculating the intensity of irrigation, i e, proportion of area under foodgrains irrigated. For 1970-73, data on irrigation are not available. For each district, we have used the proportion of area irrigated in total (under all crops) as a proxy for the intensity of irrigation. Total consumption of fertiliser per hectare cropped is used as a proxy for intensity of fertiliser use. Irrigation data refer to 1968-69.

Special Number, August 1975

4

Agricultural Price Policy

A Survey with Reference to Indian Foodgrain Economy

I

INTRODUCTION

BEFORE the mid-nineteen sixties the activities of the government in the foodgrain economy were limited in scope to the import of grain and its distribution—mainly in the urban areas under various forms of rationing—during periods of food scarcity following poor harvests.[1] Thereafter, however, with the adoption and promotion of the 'new agricultural strategy', based on the cultivation of high yielding varieties of seeds with the use of 'modern' inputs—fertilisers, pesticides, etc—in areas of assured water supply, the government began to play a major role in the transformation of the agricultural sector. This led to the involvement of the state in diverse activities such as the development of infrastructural facilities, provision of subsidies of different kinds, supply of inputs and credit, and the promotion of agronomic research for the adaptation of exotic crop varieties to Indian conditions.[2]

The agricultural price policy which evolved subsequently must thus be seen as an essential part of a larger 'package' of policies designed to promote rapid growth in a few regions endowed well with irrigation facilities, and to encourage private investment in the necessary means (modern inputs, tubewells, farm machinery, etc) for the cultivation of the new varieties. It can be argued that, given the highly skewed distribution of land and assets and a marked regional concentration of irrigated areas, the policy package was bound to promote both inter- and intra-regional inequalities. For this reason, one can perceive a built-in regressive character in the price policy and locate it within the overall policy of promoting growth through various production incentives, a policy not based on sufficient consideration of its likely distributional consequences.

Both before and after independence the government of India had been constituting 'committees' and 'commissions' with a fair regularity to investigate the 'food problem' and suggest ways to solve it. But all these were bodies formed *ad hoc* in response to periodic scarcities. The work and recommendations of these various bodies probably had no lasting impact on the Indian agrarian economy.[3]

It was only in 1965 that a permanent body, viz, the Agricultural Prices Commission (APC), was set up with presumably long-run goals in view. The APC, like the Planning Commission (a national body concerned with growth and development in general), is only an advisory body, with all the decision-making powers resting unquestionably with the government. The APC was charged with the responsibility of evolving a balanced and integrated price structure "in the perspective of the overall needs of the economy and with due regard to the interests of the producer and the consumer". The terms of reference of the commission refer not only to the need for providing price incentives for promoting agricultural growth but also to the need to "ensure rational utilisation of land and other production resources" and to the "likely effect of the price policy on the rest of the economy, particularly on the cost of living, level of wages, industrial cost structure, etc".[4]

Wide-ranging as these terms of reference were, they have since been modified and expanded in 1980 in response to the changes in the agrarian economy that have taken place during the late sixties and the seventies. An important addition is the directive that price fixation should "take into account the changes in the terms of trade between agricultural and non-agricultural sectors": the original terms of reference did not cover any principle of pricing in relation to costs or parity between sectors, barring a reference to marketing costs and margins. We shall discuss the specific political context of this directive later but note here that the underlying concern with agricultural input costs in relation to output prices, and, more generally with parities of different kinds, have been given further and explicit recognition in 1985 with the commission being renamed as the Commission for Agricultural Costs and Prices (CACP).[5]

The composition of the commission has undergone some change in character over the years. It was headed in succession by several distinguished economists and originally composed of economists and civil servants with experience in matters relating to the working of the food economy in the country. However, after 1974, one or more representatives of the farmers have been functioning as full-time members in the commission, with obvious implications for the evolution of policy.[6]

The objectives as laid down in the terms of reference of the APC are to some extent mutually conflicting, and difficult to realise for other reasons as well. One may thus say that the APC was given an impossible task. Let us elaborate.

(a) If the sole objective is to promote agricultural growth—whether or not broad-based with respect to crops and regions—through subsidies and price incentives, there is a clear possibility that the implied policy would hurt the interests of the buyers of food and agricultural raw materials. A resolution of the conflict of interests between producers and consumers—or between net sellers and net buyers, and between 'surplus' and 'deficit' areas, as some have described it in the case of foodgrains—thus becomes a necessary element of overall policy-making. It is a recognition of this necessity that is reflected in the expressed concern about the impact of policy on cost of living, etc, and has led to the conversion of price policy into an approach which seeks to integrate in some measure production objectives with those of distribution. In the case of foodgrains this meant that price policy had to be combined with the operations of a public distribution system (PDS) to ensure supply of foodgrains at subsidised prices to at least some of the poorer sections of the population. However, to the extent that subsidising both the producer and consumer is severely limited by financial constraints, it cannot be sustained on either a short- or long-term basis without being supplemented by compensating measures of taxation. All this makes the design of price policy difficult, especially by a body with no decision-making powers; more importantly, the difficulty leads to politically expedient measures which exacerbate rather than resolve conflicts.

(b) The difficulty is compounded by two other obvious factors. First, if relative prices are to play an efficient allocative role and not lead to undesirable cropping pattern shifts, policies must be designed to cover all the major crops on a country-wide basis, an impossible task to accomplish.[7] Second, since public distribution of subsidised grain cannot hope to meet the entire market demand (of both the rural and urban consumers), the impact of policies on market prices assumes importance. Thus, with the government handling only a fraction of the marketed surplus, the pricing objectives may in the end be defeated by market forces. The design of price policies with only a limited control over the market thus not only requires an appropriate combination of procurement, stock accumulation and depletion policies but must necessarily be based on a sound knowledge of the implied working of dual markets. The biggest hindrance in this respect is not lack of knowledge about production trends and demand elasticities but our virtual ignorance about the operations of private traders at the different tiers of the grain markets and their impact on prices.

(c) Finally, it must be noted that the objectives are not only conflicting—the fact that there is no indication in policy formulations whether it is only in the short run but also in the long run these conflicts could be left unresolved is also important—they are also incomplete and imprecise in some respects. For example, income and price stabilisation are common objectives of price policy; maintenance of some form of parity between the agricultural and industrial sectors and prevention of the erosion of purchasing power of agricultural incomes is a related concern, and all these are adequately discussed in the literature. Indeed, they can be stated with some precision: unlike the vague 'protection' of producer and consumer 'interests'; but, it is doubtful if multiple objectives are realisable.

Given the all-embracing but vaguely set out nature of the objectives of price policy, the APC had to recommend not one but several sets of prices; its recommendations had also to cover issues relating to the procurement and distribution of foodgrains by governmental agencies. It had to develop notions about: 'support' prices to prevent farmer distress,[8] 'incentive' prices to promote investment and growth in agriculture, 'procurement' prices—possibly involving an element of tax—at which grain could be procured by the government under varying degrees of compulsion (or none), and 'issue' prices—involving an element of subsidy—at which grain could be distributed under the public distribution system whatever be its coverage.

The following discussion attempts to cover the different instruments of policy adopted by the APC, more factually by the government, their rationale as well as how they have worked in terms of the stated objectives.

II
PRINCIPLES

Given large output fluctuations arising out of the vagaries of the monsoon (see below) and given the low price elasticity of demand for foodgrains in the country, prices tend to fluctuate a lot from year to year: changes in the supply induce disproportionately large changes in the market prices.[9]

A notion of a support price can be seen to acquire meaning in this context.[10] Such a price may be regarded as an offer price at which the government is willing to buy any amount of grain from the farmers in years of good harvest when, in the absence of a support operation, the market price may fall below the cost of production; it has therefore to be above that hypothetical market price, and, has a built-in element of subsidy to the producer. Some economists have argued, however, that support prices conceptualised in this manner need bear no relation to costs, at least in the short run: as long as it is above the low market price that will be realised in the absence of intervention, there is an element of subsidy, and the government absorbs a part of the loss and neutralises in some measure the effects of output fluctuations.

A logical corollary to the concept of the 'minimum' support price is that of a maximum or ceiling price, the rationale for which lies in two factors.[11] First, protecting farm incomes in years of abundance through purchases by the government at minimum prices implies building up of stocks; and for viability—at least over the long run—such a policy requires stock depletion as well. Second—this is a related factor—a maximum price would imply protection of consumer interests in years of crop failure; without it a support programme unilaterally favours the farmer and is clearly undesirable because the effects of agricultural output fluctuations in India are not restricted to the farm sector alone but are quickly transmitted to the other sectors of the economy, especially in periods of scarcity, through high food prices. In a sense the food price acts as a base price in the determination of both agricultural and industrial costs.

We thus see that the two notions, one of price stabilisation—or, rather, price control within a certain range—and the other, of support of farm incomes along with some degree of protection of non-farm interests, are interrelated. This, however, still leaves some asymmetry, for the question remains whether in poor crop years corresponding to a disproportionate price rise, farmers and traders should be left free to sell all the surplus on the market to earn super-normal profits. Of course the policy of stock depletion by the government tends to depress the market prices to some extent and holds these profits in check but it can be obviously more efficacious in combination with a policy of compulsory procurement at lower-than-market prices in lean years.

Thus the logic of a support price leads to the notion of a price range, especially in relation to the objective of dampening price and income fluctuations arising out of unpredictable monsoons. Supporting agriculture in this context is clearly different in nature in India from, for example, that in the US where it has more to do with the preservation of the purchasing power of farmers in relation to manufactured goods under conditions of abundant and growing farm supplies than with weather-induced fluctuations in farm output. (The US has been able to successfully pursue this policy because of her dominance in the international grain markets.)

In contrast to the support price, it is not easy to settle what constitutes an incentive price. The rationale of a price incentive lies in the promotion of growth. In the case of a single crop such as wheat—hindsight enables us to cite this as an example—a support price covering costs and some profit during a period of rapid growth in production is in effect an incentive price, with the government standing by to lift surpluses and ensure profit margins irrespective of output growth. Clearly, such a policy cannot be adopted except in the short run without undesirable consequences (including political tensions) bound to arise because of the regional concentration of surpluses. On the other hand, a price incentive policy is not viable if the objective is to promote a balanced growth with respect to all regions and crops because there are obvious limits to the provision of incentives.

It must also be noted that incentives need not cover output prices alone but may be extended to include subsidies in the supply of inputs and credit. It is possible to analyse the growth and welfare effects of the different underlying choices, but it is generally agreed that input price subsidisation may be cheaper only in the very short run—an immediate increase in food and raw material prices being avoided; in the long run, with price adjustments taking place across the board, the effects may be

similar to those of producer price subsidies.[12] More importantly, as it has been repeatedly stressed in the literature, the promotion of technological improvement through, for example, the
development of irrigation may at all times be a better alternative
than the provision of price incentives to secure agricultural
development. This belief is firmly grounded in the empirical finding that generally the elasticities of supply (in terms of output)
with respect to such technological change variables as the irrigation ratio exceed price elasticities: greater gains can be secured
through upward shifts in the production function than from
movements along the supply curve. In other words, if price policy
is to be the only instrument for agricultural development, the
low supply response would require a tilting of the terms of trade
in favour of agriculture to a degree the economy cannot bear
except over a very short period.[13] Finally, given the uneven
spatial distributions of irrigation and other resources, the scope
for achieving desired levels of overall growth through even
marginal increases in per-hectare yields in the unirrigated tracts
of the country (covering about two-thirds of cultivated area) must
indeed be enormous; the means for such a raising of the yields
are without doubt technological in nature.

Given the structure of the Indian economy and the decisive
role of drought-induced agricultural output fluctuations within
it, the operation of a support programme is inextricably linked
with that of a public distribution system for the supply of grain
at subsidised prices. It is clear that a system of subsidies at both
ends (production and consumption) can be financially viable only
if there are compensatory measures of taxation within the
agricultural sector itself or elsewhere: subsidies beyond a certain quantum without taxes will cripple the economy in the long
run.

This leads to the concept of procurement as a tax on surplus
producers, especially in years of poor harvest when market prices
and hence profit margins tend to be very high.[14] And it is
obvious that a degree of compulsion is inevitable if producers
are to be made to surrender a part of the surplus at prices lower
than those prevailing in the market. While both the support and
procurement operations involve the government in the acquisi-
tion of stocks, they can thus be seen to be analytically quite
distinct in character—one, a mode of subsidisation and the other,
a form of taxation.

This important analytical distinction was, however, lost sight of in the academic debates as well as in policy implementation, after some initial consideration.[15] The reasons are many. Soon after the procurement and distribution programmes began to gather momentum by the late sixties, the procurement price emerged as a guarantee price, announced well ahead of harvest time, at which the government was committed to make purchases. More decisive, of course, was the concern of the government to promote growth in the production of wheat through the new technology. All in all, the price guarantee scheme was a hasty response to a combination of several factors: the need to recover from an environment of shortages resulting from two consecutive years of severe drought (1965-67), the possibility of such a recovery at a rapid rate through the cultivation of the newly emerging high yielding varieties and finally the purely localised and limited nature of the support operation which made it eminently feasible. However, neither the subsequent emergence of surpluses on a wider scale nor the greater involvement of the government in the markets it entailed led to any basic revision of the policy with regard to the rationale of procurement and its pricing.

The policy had predictable consequences. While the support operation was satisfactorily served by the levels of procurement prices whenever and wherever support was needed in response to bumper harvests, procurement of grain became increasingly difficult under conditions of scarcity, local or global. This meant that procurement prices had to remain close to, even if slightly below, market prices at all times. Since procurement prices were being announced in advance of the harvest and could be based at best on insufficient knowledge of the crop prospects and market conditions expected to prevail in the coming season, this in turn required the upward revision of prices[16]—secured in practice through diverse means—for meeting procurement targets with varying degrees of success. (Section IV discusses further details about price movements.)

Returning briefly to the question of compulsion which could have been the basis of procurement under conditions of relative scarcity, we may note that the government did employ a number of instruments incorporating a coercive element. These range from direct compulsory levies on producers, traders and millers to the zoning or cordoning off of supplies to facilitate procurement. But the measures proved to be ephemeral in character and ineffective in execution, whether it is the lack of 'political will' or some other factor that could be held responsible for the failure of policy. Take, for example, the constitution of zones comprising one or more regions. The usefulness of zoning has been much discussed in the literature. Let us note however that movement restrictions generally amplify the changes in prices in any region as they occur in response to variations in domestic production. Hence, to the extent that a normally surplus region can be kept immune to short-falls occurring elsewhere in order to create conditions favourable to the procurement agency, zoning may be seen to be consistent with the principle of procurement below market prices in lean years. However, the net impact of zoning on prices, both in terms of the all-India average and the range of regional variation, would crucially depend not only on the coverage of zoning but also on how much, where and at what prices grain is procured and subsequently distributed. In practice, movement restrictions have been imposed and relaxed in an arbitrary manner, sometimes in dissonance with stated objectives.[17]

Let us now consider the relevance of costs of production to the fixation of prices. The general consensus is that minimum support prices—now indistinguishable from procurement prices—must fully cover the average cost production, but the question what elements of cost should be included in the calculation of the average total cost continues to be debated.[18] Specifically, the debate refers to the appropriateness of the inclusion of not only the so-called paid-out costs but also the imputed values of the services of family land and labour inputs in the calculation of the 'complete' average cost. A price covering such a complete cost has been described as a 'forward-looking' floor because it ensures cash incomes to farmers over and above the actual money expenditure incurred. Moreover, it is seen to incorporate at least one principle of parity, viz, input return parity, since the family inputs are given the same remuneration that they could notionally earn outside the family farming activity.[19]

(Even if one accepts this complete cost principle of pricing, it is beset with many operational difficulties arising from the fact that even for a single crop the cost of production varies a lot not only from region to region but also within regions across different farms.[20] A solution suggested in this respect recommends the use of a bulk-line cost, the minimum cost that covers the costs of farmers producing a major part of the output, weeding out the very 'inefficient' farmers. But then the derived price would cease to have the same meaning as that based on the average cost in standard economic theory. It is equally difficult to grapple with the question of regional variation in costs. The actual practice of fixing a uniform price for all regions is obviously defective. For example, the adoption of a price that covers the costs in a high cost region, where, say, traditional methods of cultivation are used, results in abnormal profits to farmers of other regions using the cost-reducing new technologies. Thus the principle may be consistent with the objective of growth but not with that of the reduction of inter-regional disparities.)

Two important points have been made in relation to the imputation of values at market prices to the use of family land and labour resources. Since the price of produce is raised by the inclusion of these elements in the total cost, agricultural labourers—and other net buyers of food for whom wages constitute a major element of income—lose because wages actually paid generally tend to be below the statutorily fixed minimum levels (which in principle could be in line with output prices fixed by the complete costing principle) while employers of hired labour earn an abnormal profit for the same reason. In simpler terms, money incomes of net buyers (especially of wage earners in rural areas) generally lag behind food prices and the total cost principle reinforces the tendency. Regarding the imputation of market rental values to the use of owned land, it has been argued that there has been a continuous increase in these values arising from increasing productivity as well as demographic pressure. Regions well-endowed with, say, public irrigation resources are also, in general, regions of high productivity and it is debatable whether such regions should be allowed to enjoy high economic rents through the enhancement of product prices resulting from the inclusion of rental values in the total cost.

Similarly, it is arguable whether the increase in rental values arising from exogenous factors such as demographic pressure or insufficient expansion of non-agricultural employment should automatically be transmitted as additional costs to the product price. Thus the debates in the literature demonstrate that even a well-defined cost-based principle for price fixation can become meaningful and reasonably operational only in relation to a clearly specified policy goal (such as the reduction of spatial disparities in incomes earned from the cultivation of the same crop).

The parity with input costs is only one among different kinds of parity one can think of in the context of product pricing. For example, there is the parity between farm incomes and incomes earned in other sectors of the economy. A little reflection shows that in India, with large output fluctuations the rule rather than the exception, it is difficult to maintain such a parity through a product pricing policy alone: here again a system of subsidies and taxes is needed to limit the range of fluctuations in farm incomes and ensure their parity with incomes in other sectors. Also, because of the stickiness of nominal wage incomes over the short period, product price adjustment can at best protect incomes from cultivation only. Thus, upward adjustments in agricultural prices made in response, for example, to increases in the prices of some manufactured consumer articles may fail to maintain the purchasing power of all rural classes uniformly; wage earners may in fact suffer a loss in real income following the rise in the price of food because food absorbs most of their expenditure. A uniform output price consistent with the income parity criterion cannot be calculated simply because the commodity baskets of consumption vary as between the different rural classes.

III
POLITICS

Political factors behind the making of economic policy are generally ignored in what may be described as 'mainstream' economics but constitute an important element of discussions of economic problems in the growing literature on Indian political economy. The general concern in the alternative stream is with production relations (such as those between landowners and labourers) and how they influence processes of change in the spheres of production and accumulation. However, the politics of price-fixing in the Indian context has received a lot of attention from both the camps.[21]

In the agrarian economy, the importance of politics with respect to policy-making arises from two basic factors. First, policies are formulated by governments at the state and the central levels, the constitution and working of the government depend very much on the configuration of class forces. (For example, the failure of land reforms for imposing ceilings on landholdings and for redistribution of land, despite much legislation and endless rhetoric in day-to-day politics and plan documents, cannot be explained without a consideration of the balance of class forces and the manner in which it has influenced the implementation process.) Second, and more readily seen, is the very large disparity in landholdings in all regions of India, with big landowners constituting a small proportion of rural households but controlling the major share not only of land and assets in general but also, consequently, marketed surpluses.

Rural disparities have grown further with the introduction of the new agricultural technology which has strengthened the economic and political power of the class of surplus producers. Described as the rural oligarchy, this class had appropriated a disproportionately large share of the benefits generated by the policy of incentives and subsidies to the agricultural sector since the late nineteen sixties. The political strength of the class is seen to lie, moreover, in its control over the rural vote in the electoral process, which enables it to further its own interest through bargaining with the other major ruling group, the industrial (urban) bourgeoisie. As a result there is in existence a politically powerful 'farm lobby' which influences policy-making in agriculture with a fair degree of success.[22]

The success is derived from two factors: First, given the nature of the electoral process and the decisive role of the rural vote in its outcome, there is a heavy representation of the 'farmer interest' in the state legislatures and governments. We should note that in reality the farmer interest relates to the amassing of incomes and wealth by the surplus-producing big farmers, although the political rhetoric refers always to the 'peasant cause' in general, as if the peasantry constitute an undifferentiated mass; small, poor farmers and agricultural labourers have hardly any representation in any tier of the decision-making process. Second, practically all political parties accord support to the 'peasant cause' and to rural agitations on a variety of issues such as demands for 'remunerative' prices for the products of agriculture; for provision of inputs like water and electricity, and credit, at cheap rates; for cancellation of rural debt in hard times; and in general for all-round support at all times.

For most political parties, slogans about the rural poor are a necessary means to secure political power through the electoral process. The basis of leftist support for the farmer interest has another dimension however. The communist parties, for example, recognise landlords and capitalist farmers as constituting an exploiting class but seek to mobilise not only poor peasants and labourers but also the middle and richer sections of the peasantry in order to secure peasant unity considered necessary to carry forward the struggle against exploiting classes in general. These parties recognise the fact, for example, that the benefits from increases in agricultural prices flow in a disproportionately large manner, if not wholly, to the surplus-producing big farmers (and therefore suggest measures of taxation on the rich and for relief for the poor to counteract the growth in inequality that price increases entail) but support the struggles for 'remunerative prices' perhaps because of the priority accorded to the necessity for securing peasant unity from a long-term perspective.[23]

The course of events relevant to foodgrain price policy since the mid-sixties can now be described in brief. The heralding of the green revolution with the introduction of new seed varieties of wheat and the unequivocal commitment of the central government to the new agricultural strategy led to the support of wheat prices at levels prevailing during 1966 and 1967—a period of extreme scarcity—without any reference to principles of cost or parity or to the demand and supply conditions in a period of abundance resulting from the wheat surpluses in the north-west. The sole aim was to promote growth at any cost. During this period policy-making was wholly the prerogative of the chief ministers of the surplus states. Such attempts as were made by the APC to introduce some principles into the setting of relative prices and procurement targets proved to be futile.

The most important concern of the farm lobby till about 1973 appears to be the prevention of a fall in the price of wheat which the bumper harvests of 1968-72 would have normally entailed. It must be noted in this context that during this period rice surpluses and quantities procured were marginal; further, some cost comparisons show that the margins of the procurement prices over the costs of production were far higher in the case of wheat than in that of rice (see below). The parity between rice and wheat seems to have been established only from about the mid-seventies,[24] following both the greater quantum of rice being procured and the conditions of relative scarcity prevailing in 1973 and 1974.

At any rate, the terms of trade moved generally in favour of agriculture during 1965-73. The trend has reversed since then, with the prices of manufactured articles and agricultural inputs rising at rapid rates and stocks of foodgrains piling up with the government as a consequence of a succession of good harvests. This adverse movement in the terms of trade is the background to numerous farmers' agitations for remunerative prices. An incidental factor behind the struggles is the emergence in 1977 of peasant leaders like Charan Singh at the centre. The eighties saw not only a reconstitution of the APC (to allow for explicit representation of the farmer interest) but also its renaming as the Commission of Agricultural Costs and Prices, enshrining the cost principle in price fixing. The farm lobby has in recent years been growing further with the mushrooming of self-styled 'non-party' peasant organisations such as the one led by Sharad Joshi. The rhetoric of Joshi's movement refers to the exploitation of agriculture (Bharat) by industry (India) and the goals may therefore look broad-based but the programme has been aptly described as a one-point programme for securing higher agricultural prices in all seasons.[25]

IV
PRICE MOVEMENTS AND RELATIONS

In per capita terms the output of foodgrains in India as a whole has stagnated since the beginning of the sixties, implying thereby that the growth rate in foodgrain production just about equalled that of population.[26] However, different crops exhibit different trends: for example, there has been an impressive increase in the output of wheat but a distinct decline in that of coarse cereals and pulses (both in per capita terms). The impact of these differential trends on relative price movements as well as consumption levels, especially of the poor, has still to be studied in detail.

But more important perhaps is the fact that both at the specific crop level and in the aggregate there have been considerable year-to-year fluctuations in yield per acre as well as production. Since the production of foodgrains as a whole has stagnated in per capita terms, output fluctuations are clearly relevant to price movements in a period characterised by a growth—albeit modest—in real incomes per capita. Some early studies show that the price flexibility coefficient tends to be very high (more than two in absolute value) for cereals such as rice and wheat.[27] Of course, availability is not determined by levels of production alone: the operations of the government (through imports and distribution) and of surplus-holding farmers and traders at the different tiers in the market economy are equally relevant. A good part of the price flexibility may be due to the speculative activities of the traders (singularly absent in studies of price trends), but output fluctuations contribute also to the quantum of grain that could be procured by the government at given prices, to amounts that have to be distributed through the public distribution system, etc, and thus are of central importance to the interaction of private and public agencies in the foodgrain economy, i e, to the dual market economy.

From this perspective, the recently well-documented increase in fluctuations—with much inter-regional and inter-crop variation—in productivity and production of foodgrains in the post-green revolution period assumes importance[28] but is not adequately reflected in policy-making with reference to pricing, building up of stocks and distribution. The studies which demonstrate this increase in instability argue that the improved technologies are not responsible *per se* for this trend in variances and point to a number of concomitant factors such as the sub-optimal use of irrigation and fertiliser, simultaneous increases in year-to-year variability in areas sown as well as an increase in the covariance between yields obtained and areas sown and so on; all this requires more detailed study at a greater level of disaggregation with respect to both crops and regions than has been attempted in the literature so far. A recent study on output fluctuations comes to the conclusion that "aggregate production instability is an inevitable consequence of rapid agricultural growth and there is little that can be effectively done about it" and suggests that policies addressed to the stabilisation of consumption through storage and trade policies may be more promising.[29] This conclusion is, however, contestable because a broad-based strategy for the improvement of yields and stability in output in the dry and rainfed tracts of the country is a clear alternative, admittedly not yet spelt out in detail on the basis of existing knowledge.

The supply of grain is more relevant to price movements than domestic production. If one takes net production augmented

by changes in stocks with the government as a first approximation to supply (designated usually as availability), this variable
exhibits characteristics similar to those of production: since the
early sixties net availability of foodgrains in per capita terms has
virtually stagnated but year-to-year fluctuations have been fairly
wide—although distinctly less wider than in output, with the
government distributing somewhat higher amounts in years of
crop failure.[30] The good harvests of the late seventies and early
eighties have been utilised more for stock-building than for improving levels of availability. Indeed, levels of stocks which were
about three million tonnes in the early seventies grew close to 30
million tonnes by 1985 (more on this later). The fluctuations in
actual availability in the market might have been wider than these
first approximations indicate, because of the possible speculative
hoarding by the private trade.

In this and the following sub-sections we shall discuss the working of the dual markets in the foodgrain sector, especially in relation to the period after the mid-sixties marked by a significant
intervention by governmental agencies in the market. Apart from
procurement and distribution of certain quantities of grain at
set prices, the government was involved also in stock-building
operations. This is the basis for dual market models which seek
to capture the interaction between the operations of the government and the functioning of the open market.[31] It must be
noted, however, that a realistic formulation of such models in
their fullest complexity is not an easy task, for it would require,
apart from the specification of supply and demand functions
under the dual price structure, an explicit consideration of the
role of exogenous output fluctuations and of the complexity introduced by different policy instruments such as zoning and stock-
piling. Perhaps, it is for this reason that most available analytical
models are addressed to narrowly focused issues such as the impact of price and other instruments on levels of procurement.

Let us begin with a descriptive account of the trend in prices
and costs. Although procurement prices have generally been lower
than market prices, both series exhibit a strong upward trend
since 1960-61, characterised in the case of foodgrains as a whole
in India, by a clearly visible staircase type of movement with
prices rising significantly in poor crop years but remaining steady
or increasing moderately in years of good harvest. The only
exceptions to this type of movement—with prices declining in

response to good crops—were in 1968-69, following the initial spurt in wheat production, and in 1975-76, the period of Emergency and all-round 'discipline'.[32]

Two factors appear to underlie this type of price behaviour: first, weather-induced output fluctuations (especially in per capita terms) of a wide order, combined with high price flexibility coefficients; and second, the bounty of good harvests being used more for stock-building than for price reductions. (The asymmetry between the protection of producer interests through price support—inherent in withholding supplies in good years—and the protection of consumers is perhaps most clearly seen in this aspect of government operations. The question of optimal level of stocks is discussed below.)

It must be added, however, that the nature of both the trends in prices and the order relations between procurement and market prices, portrayed above in the case of foodgrains as a whole for all-India, may not hold uniformly across regions and crops.

Turning now to a comparison between procurement prices and costs to see whether procurement has operated as a disincentive to production, let us recall that the comparison is beset with difficulties arising from the conceptualisation of cost. Studies in this regard rely on the average cost at the state level (estimated on the basis of sample surveys) with cost C as the relevant concept. This cost includes the imputed value of family labour as well as the imputed rental value of owned land. The conclusions are that in the case of wheat, since the early years of green revolution, procurement prices have been higher than—well above, in the initial part of this period—costs of production and in some years close to the open market prices. For rice, until the mid-seventies support prices did not cover costs in West Bengal and the southern states but they did in the case of northern states. Thereafter, however, procurement prices of rice have been raised substantially so as to cover costs uniformly in all the producing regions.[33]

It is possible to argue that uniform purchase prices (generally fixed in relation to costs prevailing in a high cost region) are likely to have promoted inter-regional inequalities because of the wide variation in costs (howsoever defined). For example, in 1978-79 while the cost per hectare for paddy was higher in Punjab than in Andhra Pradesh (by about 11 per cent), the cost per quintal of paddy was lower (by about 22 per cent) because of the higher yields per unit area and more favourable conditions for the cultivation of high yielding paddy varieties in Punjab.[34] It must be noted in this context that in the Punjab region paddy is produced almost exclusively as a commercial crop and the region contributes significantly to the rice procured by the government.

To the extent that farmers are free to sell on the open market, prices received by farmers (a weighted average of procurement and market prices, with the relevant quantities as weights) are more relevant than procurement prices alone to a judgment about disincentives. At a hypothetical but more sophisticated level one might compare costs with the prices that would have ruled in the open market in the absence of purchases and distribution by the government. The determination of such prices would require a properly specified supply-demand-prices model but crude calculations can be done on the basis of available demand elasticities and price flexibility coefficients under the assumption that output levels are exogenously given. At any rate, the few studies involving such price-cost comparisons show once again that procurement prices have in general been 'remunerative' in relation to cost.[35]

As noted before, the parity in relation to cost is only one among the different kinds of parity which can form the basis for price fixation. Although the APC has from time to time taken into account, apart from costs of production, prices of specific inputs such as fertilisers or the general price level in the price fixation process, presumably in conformity with some principle of parity, it is difficult to discern from data the working of any particular parity principle (such as that between crops, between input and output prices, or between prices paid and received) possibly because of the arbitrary manner in which elements relevant to different types of parity have in practice entered price fixing in different combinations over the years.[36]

The arbitrariness has made it easy for those who argue for price increases to invoke this or that principle of parity as the occasion demands. For example, if the prices of fertilisers are raised by the government, that alone is sufficient to ensure political mobilisation in favour of the demand for remunerative prices regardless of the *total* cost of production or market conditions. If in the following season the prices of fertilisers are reduced but the general price level rises (for whatever reason), the basis for the demand for price increases may change; for example, it may shift to the cost of living or the real income of poor farmers. The point is important because of the differential trends in prices of commodities covering different crops, agricultural inputs and articles of consumption; it is easily illustrated: the demands for high support (procurement) prices of wheat were based on an appeal to the level and changes in market prices till about the mid-seventies but later, with the prices of some inputs and manufactured articles increasing in general at rates faster than those of agricultural commodities (including wheat), slogans for political mobilisation began to be centred more and more around input prices and costs. It will be interesting to analyse in this light the shifting ground of the farm lobby in response to the changing economic environment.

At a different level, among the academics, questions relating to the terms of trade (TOT) between agriculture and industry have received much attention.[37] They include questions about the relevance of TOT to price policy and mobilisation of rural surpluses in the specific Indian context as well as those relating to the actual movements of relative prices. In contrast to the first set of these questions, the second has generated much controversy in the literature. This is probably a fall-out of the political process in which slogans based on relative prices have, as remarked before, assumed much significance. In any case, the shift in the focus is unfortunate because what is relevant to policy-making concerned with welfare is not so much the actual movement in the net barter TOT as its impact on aggregate farm output, farm incomes and their distribution. It must be pointed out in this context that generally the supply response is low and, therefore, the question to what extent agricultural growth can be stimulated through changes in TOT brought about by policies with a limited coverage of crops and regions becomes crucial to our understanding of such policies.

The picture of actual movements in the TOT (whether in net barter or in net income terms) depends on how the relevant indices are constructed, the commodity compositions taken, the weights assigned, the price data employed, the base year chosen and so on. Indeed, the studies in this area demonstrate, if anything at all, that constructed series are extremely *sensitive* to methods of construction, yielding as they do sometimes opposing conclusions about the direction in the movements. A continuation of this debate can be fruitful only if this sensitivity is examined more closely and in relation to the impact of the TOT on the different aspects of the farm sector.

One of the objectives underlying the promotion of high yielding varieties and the new technology was the attainment of self-sufficiency in foodgrain production, i e, a drastic reduction in the dependence on imports. Indeed, the role of imports in maintaining supplies has become insignificant from about the mid-seventies.

Both imports and internal procurement enable the government to build up stocks needed to maintain supplies at given levels and stabilise the prices, i e, to curb price movements arising out of the output fluctuations characterising Indian agriculture. Two questions arise in this context, the first about the optimal level of stocks to be held by the government and the second relating to the possibility of choice between imports and domestic procurement for the purpose and the conditions governing such a choice. It is obvious that for meaningful analysis the questions have to be set within a framework that includes not only the dual domestic markets but also the international market for foodgrains.

But let us begin with a brief review of the facts. There were broadly two phases, covering 1968-72 and 1975-85, during which stocks held by the government have been allowed to increase, from 2 to 8 million tonnes during the first and from 8 to roughly 30 million tonnes during the second phase respectively. Both these phases cover strings of good harvest, with peak and record levels of per capita production during the early eighties. While both imports and procurement contributed to this stock-piling during the first phase, it was almost wholly the internal effort that enabled the government to accumulate stocks during the second phase. (The droughts of 1986 and 1987 have led to a depletion of stocks.) As noted before, the government has generally been releasing somewhat larger amounts, in per capita terms, for distribution through the PDS under distress conditions, but these amounts have only marginally augmented the fluctuating production levels. Generally, the levels in per capita availability have fluctuated along with those in production, although the year-to-year variations were smaller in the former. It is clear that the government's stock management has not been successful in bringing about a stability in supplies, a fact readily seen from the low levels of per capita net availability in years such as 1975 and 1980 corresponding to poor harvests (406 and 410 gms per day respectively, in contrast to an average of 447 gms over the whole period 1961-84). More importantly, the precedence accorded to the policy of accumulation of stocks over that of depletion in adequate amounts led to the expected price changes: large increases in years of crop failure and moderate changes during times of good harvest following the use of procured grain for accumulating stocks to prevent prices falling. It can be seen thus that the stock management policy of the government has contributed in some measure to the inflation in grain prices and to the disadvantage of consumers.[38]

The question of optimal level of stocks assumes importance in this context.[39] The gross output of foodgrains per capita per day has over the period 1961-84 stagnated around an average of 494 gms with a coefficient of variation of 8 per cent. (The computation includes the worst ever years, 1966 and 1967.) This means that actual output levels in any year are unlikely to deviate from 494 gms by more than 12.8 per cent, i e, 63 gms per capita per day (1.6 times the standard deviation corresponding to a 5 per cent chance for larger deviations, under the assumption of a normal distribution). For a population of 800 million this corresponds to a predictable shortfall not exceeding 18.4 million tonnes (with a probability of 95 per cent) in a single year. The technical committees constituted by the government during the sixties and seventies have recommended buffer stocks in the range of 10 to 15 million tonnes (for lower levels of total population) on a basis of probability calculations similar to the one above.[40]

An insurance cover against two consecutive poor harvests would of course require a much larger buffer stock but the policy is likely to be extremely costly and economically crippling. In any case, it is difficult to argue in favour of a stock-holding in excess of 20 million tonnes at the current population level, especially if the possibility of imports (during a second consecutive year of poor crops) is kept in mind. Indeed, some studies show that the government's stock policies have been sub-optimal in many ways: they demonstrate that higher level of per capita supplies than in the past could be maintained with appropriately designed and coherent policies for fixing prices, accumulating and depleting stocks, determining import levels and so on.

Above all, if the range of price variation is to be limited so as to benefit both producers and consumers, any sensible policy must include the depletion of stocks in adequate amounts when necessary as well as accumulation to the desired extent. The point is important because the increase in inventories beyónd optimal levels not only imposes a crippling burden on the economy but is also regressive in character. For example, the so-called food subsidy—mounting and accounting for a big proportion in the budget deficits of the central government in recent years, and usually interpreted as a subsidy to the poor covered by the PDS—includes the costs of holding stocks; it can be argued that the poor would be better off if prices are allowed to decline in response to good harvests especially when the stocks held by the government are already adequate to meet contingencies such as drought. Accumulation of stocks beyond the level needed to cover contingencies benefit the surplus producers only at the cost of the consumers, especially the rural poor who have no access to the PDS.

The highly correlated movements in costs, procurement prices and market prices, both contemporaneously and with lags in the variables, are not very useful for assessing the impact of state intervention in foodgrain markets. Given the limited coverage of government operations with respect to crops and regions on the one hand and quantities procured and distributed on the other, it would appear *prima facie* that the impact of these operations, for example on market prices, would also be limited with regard to regions and crops. On this understanding, the impact of operations in the wheat market would be limited to regions in the north-west where the procurement effort is concentrated and the regions—mainly large urban areas—where subsidised wheat is distributed in large enough quantities to influence the open market prices. This is questionable, however, because to an unknown extent the markets for different cereals are integrated, with demand, supply and price conditions in the market for one cereal influencing those in the markets for other cereals. The explanation for a strong correlation between market prices and support prices in the case of foodgrains as a whole may lie in such an integration, not addressed adequately in the literature. Our ignorance in this respect is attributable in part to the lack of relevant data, for example, on prices in the rural areas of both the surplus and deficit regions; but also to the absence of analyses of the required nature, for example, of how prices of inferior cereals are influenced (in the different regions of the country) by those of rice and wheat, of trends in the regional dispersion in price levels and so on.

In contrast, the phenomenon of increases in market prices leading on, with some lags, to increases in procurement and issue prices analysed in some detail is perhaps easier to understand.[41] In general, a rise in foodgrain prices can be expected to lead to a rise in wage costs, albeit with time lags in adjustment. More importantly, the burden imposed on the government by its own operations in the foodgrain markets is relieved in practice, although only in part, through increases in the so-called administered prices, for example fertiliser prices, and these increases have a direct bearing on the movement of agricultural costs. Finally, increases in costs of production lead to pressure on the government through the political process to raise support prices. Observed correlations between procurement prices and lagged market prices (and costs) notwithstanding, the chain of causation in this respect requires further study on the support of available documentation on the disposal of subsidies and the budgetary transactions of the central government.

In sum, the elaboration of the means for achieving some form of inter-crop parity and reducing inter-regional disparities in prices, in consistence with a set of well-defined welfare goals, remains elusive in Indian economic literature.

V

NET IMPACT

What is the net impact of foodgrain price policy on the economy in general, on the processes of inflation, investment, growth and distribution, and more particularly on growth rates in agricultural production, the levels of prices and consumption of foodgrains of different types in the different parts of the country?

The question cannot be answered easily, and not merely because it encompasses many interrelated issues. Three other reasons are pertinent: first, the quantitative significance of the limited nature of state intervention in the foodgrain markets is still to be assessed in meaningful analytical terms. (For example, we know practically nothing in this context about rural-urban price differentials.) Second, while there is no doubt that relative prices, irrespective of the extent to which they have been influenced by actually implemented price policies, have played a significant role in shaping the economy, it is necessary to take into account the working of taxes and subsidies of different kinds for understanding this role. And third, there is a need to incorporate into the analysis the experience with non-price instruments such as direct public investments in irrigation development, etc.

What follows covers a limited ground only.

Numerous studies deal with supply response—grist to the agricultural economics mill.[42] Barring a few exceptions they are concerned with the response in terms of the allocation of areas of different competing crops corresponding to relative prices and profitability. These seek to demonstrate, in general, that the Indian farmer is a rational economic animal. The exceptions consider also the response in terms of the increase in input use, especially of modern inputs such as fertilisers, relevant to the generation of higher profits through increases in the productivity per unit land area. We thus have some plausible estimates of the overall output response (combining both the area and input responses). The long-run elasticity of output with respect to the lagged output-input price ratio is in the range of 0.4 to 0.6 for the major cereals: rice and wheat, and the supply response, reckoned thus, is lower than the response of output to increases in the levels of irrigation.[43] These estimates based on past data summarise the Indian experience in some fashion and show therefore that agricultural growth has been promoted more by the development of irrigation than by the price factor.

This is not to deny the very significant role support prices and subsidies (and hence the terms of trade) have played in the promotion of agricultural growth in certain areas of the country. In general, only some crops and some regions have benefited from the mix of policies (pricing, fiscal and other) and this has promoted both inter-crop differences in growth and inter-regional inequalities in agricultural performance. The impressive growth in the production of superior cereals has been brought about to some extent through shifts in the cropping pattern away from inferior cereals and pulses, and in some areas at the expense of commercial crops too. These shifts have been made possible by the policy-mix referred to earlier. In the overall, a substantial part of the increment in production associated with the new technology has originated in five or six advanced states with the eastern region and the semi-arid parts of the country performing poorly. Both price policies and the easy availability of subsidised funds have promoted these developments.[44]

The exacerbation of inter-regional inequalities in foodgrain production and the decline in per capita production of inferior cereals and pulses are strongly suggestive of a general widening of disparities in income and consumption. Let us consider in brief some relevant analytical factors. Procurement prices, farm harvest prices and wholesale market prices are all relevant to the determination of the price producers receive for their surplus crop output. In general, and in the simplest case, price increases are regressive in their impact on the income distribution among the producers because the bigger producers account for the lion's share in the marketed part of the output and therefore appropriate the gains, if any, accruing from a price rise in a larger proportion than do the small farmers. Of further relevance in this context is the fact that small farmers and agricultural labourers are in general net buyers of foodgrain in contrast to the big farmers who are net sellers, so that by virtue of their capacity for retention in full measure of grain for home consumption the latter are not hurt by the rise in market prices. Likewise, the seasonal movements in prices, especially in years of poor harvest, have a regressive impact since the poor as net buyers may depend wholly on market purchases in the lean season when prices tend to be higher.

However, for a more complete assessment of the impact of price increases on income distribution it will be necessary to take into account incomes earned through non-farm activities by wage earners and small farmers. In the absence of detailed research of this type, some analysts have sought to directly relate estimated poverty levels to changing relative prices to see, for example, whether rising food prices hurt the interest of the poor. This effort has also led to some controversy because the same data sets analysed in different ways produce contradictory results. The underlying methodological difficulties have received much attention in the recent literature.[45]

But it is difficult to contest some relevant empirical findings. It has been demonstrated convincingly that at the all-India level poverty ratios (the proportion of people below the so-called poverty line) exhibit fluctuations with no discernible trend—positive or negative.[46] The variations in the ratio are, however, correlated—enough to attract much academic attention—to both real income (inversely) and food prices (directly), suggesting thereby that while agricultural growth contributes to a reduction in poverty, the rising food prices may act independently of levels of output and lead to decreases in the consumption of food and hence to higher levels of poverty.

Regional disparities assume importance in this context. Inter-state differences in the per capita production of foodgrains have widened. But through its operations of procuring grain from the pockets of surplus and distributing it through the PDS the government has ensured that regional disparities in terms of availability have not increased since the mid-sixties. However, except in Kerala and Gujarat (and more recently Tamil Nadu and Andhra Pradesh) the PDS hardly covers the rural areas. An early study dealing with inter-state differences in food intake, covering both the rural and urban parts, is relevant in this context.[47] It suggested that given the magnitudes of regional disparities in incomes and prices, the markets work in such a way that a part of the surplus tends to remain in the surplus-producing regions and deficits left uncovered in other regions. A reason could be that the rural areas in the deficit regions do not attract market supplies, given the range of price differences and the organisation of markets. Therefore, the implied lack of adequate price-quantity adjustments through market forces has generally a greater impact on rural than on urban consumption levels. Of course, the public distribution system reinforces this tendency so that generally while the urban poor are ensured of supplies at given levels, the rural poor eat better only if the local harvest is good.

Price policy refers to the doings of the government, but prices are not determined by policies alone: the markets play a part and so do some non-market factors unrelated to policy. It is not easy then to unscramble observed price trends in relation to the different aspects of the economy to arrive at unambiguous judgments about the correctness or otherwise of this or that policy. Relatively high and rising agricultural prices favour surplus-producing big farmers and may indeed be necessary to promote agricultural growth at a satisfactory rate. But they have adverse effects on the costs and standards of living of the rural and the urban poor, and on a wider stretch, as some have argued convincingly, may also lead to industrial stagnation.[48]

The subject remains controversial and the debate on each specific underlying question is unresolved despite the participation of several eminent economists and political leaders. To some extent there is in all this a loss of perspective resulting from scholarly affinity to hair-splitting. But it has led to a polarisation of sorts.

One school denounces 'cheap food' policies and argues for price-support programmes that give adequate incentives to stimulate supply. On the other hand, it can be argued that aggregate supply response is low, and that, more importantly, price support programmes imply high private and social costs, price incentives fundamentally result in income transfers to the large farmers. Consequently, a well-balanced package of government instruments including promotion of technology, infrastructure investments and production subsidies is preferable to a reliance on the price instrument alone. The literature suggests that public investment, say, in irrigation is better than the provision of price incentives for not only promoting growth but also for 'cost-efficiency' and distributing gains from growth uniformly across the different social and economic classes in India.[49]

These conclusions emerge in part from some well known facts: agricultural growth has remained fairly stable since independence at about 3 per cent per annum; the rates of growth in foodgrain production have been somewhat lower and there is no evidence of an improvement in the levels of consumption; the green revolution has exacerbated inter-regional inequalities in the production of foodgrains, productivity increases having been largely confined to wheat in the north-west; the public distribution system, restricted mainly to the urban areas, has failed to protect the rural poor; and the social costs of public intervention in this sector, including direct subsidies to agriculture and those involved in the operation of the PDS have been heavy and rising. The point is that these subsidies cut into the resources meant for development expenditure, apart from increasing rural-urban inequity since the vast mass of the rural poor are denied access to the PDS.

But the conclusions have been, and continue to be disputed. In some measure the controversies arise from the fact that while the issues can be stated in fairly simple terms (such as whether price policy has contributed to agricultural growth), they cannot be satisfactorily resolved (through, for example, a regression of production on some price variable to measure the supply response) because of the complexity of the structure of economic and social relations within which the questions have to be addressed for a meaningful analysis.[50]

NOTES

1 Internal procurement of foodgrains was generally not high till the mid-sixties; thereafter it gradually increased in quantum from about 4 million tonnes to the current level of about 15 million tonnes a year. For a discussion of the evolution of food policy and data relating to the government operations during the earlier period see Chopra [1981]. Comprehensive data on the foodgrain economy are also to be found in the annual publication, *Bulletin on Food Statistics.*

2 The general economic setting for the adoption of the new technology as a part of overall growth strategy is explained in Chaudhuri [1978].

3 Apart from these bodies, the Americans have also contributed to our wisdom about the food problem. The Ford Foundation compiled a report in 1959 entitled *India's Food Crisis and the Steps to Meet It.* For details see Chopra [1981].

4 The terms of reference are reprinted in the Appendix to the *Report of APC on the Price Policy for Kharif Cereals, 1965-66,* p 47. For some discussion of these terms see Kahlon and Tyagi [1983].

5 The revised terms of reference are contained in a notification of the government of India, No 14011/2/78, ministry of agriculture, dated March 5, 1980.

6 de Janvry and Subbarao [1986], p 17. They add that there is no representation for consumers on the commission.

7 Raj Krishna, who was closely associated with the APC, had written: "A price support programme is unavoidably a disequilibrium programme. The case for it is only that, if effective, it may convert a disequilibrium of shortages into a disequilibrium of supplies in the markets for *selected* commodities", Krishna [1967] p 525 (emphasis added).

8 It must be noted that there are two kinds of distress. Small farmers sell a part of their output, sometimes at a price disadvantage, although they may in general be net buyers of grain. This form of distress is clearly distinct from that underlying farmers—big and small—selling at low prices after bumper harvests. An appreciation of this distinction is absent in the discussion on support prices.

9 The price flexibility coefficient has been estimated at−2.38 for foodgrains as a whole and −2.24 for cereals [see Ray 1972 for details]. Earlier contributions in this respect by Thamarajakshi [1970a and 1970b] also demonstrate high price flexibility coefficients for rice and wheat.

10 The principles for price fixation by the government for its limited intervention in foodgrain markets have been discussed threadbare in the literature published since the mid-sixties. Some relevant references are: Dandekar [1965], Dantwala [1967], Krishna [1967 and 1982] and Thamarajakshi [1977]. Attempts to sum up the debates have been made, for example, in Kahlon and Tyagi [1983], Subbarao [1986] and Rath [1985]. No such attempt is made in the following text. It should be noted, however, that much of the literature is concerned with the efficacy of stimulating growth through price

incentives. Issues relating to distribution are addressed somewhat tangentially.

11 Dandekar [1965].

12 Krishna [1967], pp 526-27.

13 Assuming a realistic estimate of 0.4 for the long-run elasticity of output with respect to the terms of trade, Raj Krishna says: "...a 16 per cent growth over five years [in output] would require a one-shot 40 per cent increase in the real terms of trade of agriculture. This is equivalent to 7 per cent annual increase over this period, which will also, of course, spread out the resulting growth. This order of terms of trade increase is hardly a practical proposition, even assuming that a government can fix terms of trade." In the sequel, he concludes that "...a unit percentage change in the important shifter variable (technology) will yield much greater growth than a unit percentage price shift", Krishna [1982], pp 235-36.

14 Procurement as a tax on farm produce has a long history in the development phase of many countries. This has a bearing on the larger issue (not treated in this survey) of using surpluses from the farm sector to promote industrialisation. See in this context Krishna [1982] and Mitra [1979].

However, in India this has a narrower, more immediate context as recognised, for example, by the APC itself. An early APC report says: "It should be a social obligation on the part of cultivators to surrender a portion of the produce to the state in the wider national interest...While direct taxation involves no *quid pro quo*, in the case of procurement the transactions would still be in the nature of buying and selling and the producers would receive a price, even though this price may be lower than the prevailing market price. The case for such an impost becomes particularly strong in view of the extremely light incidence of agricultural taxation in the country." *Report of the APC on Price Policy for Kharif Cereals (Procurement Prices) for 1967-68 Season*, September 1967, p 5.

15 See Krishnaji [1973] and Nadkarni [1987], p 203.

16 The prices fixed by the state governments were generally higher than those recommended by the APC and the central government. A study making a detailed demonstration of this fact says: "The phenomenon of states fixing prices higher than the recommended prices is explained by the influence exercised by farmer interests on policy at the state level. But it is also due to the realistic economic reasoning that the procurement targets recommended by the centre could not be realised with unattractive purchase prices, especially in bad crop years." Krishna and Raychaudhuri [1980] p 4.

17 Subbarao [1978] summing up the literature on zoning says: "That food zones actually accentuated regional price differences is an empirically well established fact." However, there is some evidence which indicates that the relaxation of zoning in the north-west during the initial spurt of wheat production is a response to the fear that prices would fall and impede growth in that region. Krishnaji [1973].

18 Subbarao (1986). See also Kahlon and Tyagi [1983].

19 Krishna [1987], pp 517-21.

20 What follows is largely based on Subbarao [1986].

21 The debates on price policy are not restricted to professional academic journals: they are conducted also, fairly regularly, in newspapers, at public

92 *Pauperising Agriculture*

22 For a cogent exposition of this view which attracted a good deal of controversy, see Mitra [1979].

23 Representative views of the different parties are explained, for example, in CPI(M)-[1973 and 1981], Nathan [1982] and Sinha [1980].

24 See Krishnaji (1975) and Krishna and Raychaudhuri [1980].

25 The growth of farmers' lobbies and movements has been traced in Nadkarni [1987].

26 The growth rate calculated separately for aggregate output shows a higher value than that of population but the growth in per capita output is found to be statistically insignificant. This is a statistical artefact. The data are given by Roy (1984) and Krishnaji [1988]. See, in particular, the graphical representation of the data in Roy.

27 Ray [1972].

28 Mehra [1981], Hazell [1982] and Ray [1970, 1971 and 1983].

29 Hazell [1982], p 10.

30 Roy [1984].

31 For example, Krishna and Chibber [1983] and Gulati [1987].

32 For the data, see, Roy [1984] and Krishnaji [1988].

33 For cost-price comparisons, see, Krishna and Raychaudhuri [1980].

34 de Janvry and Subbarao [1986], pp 20-27.

35 See, in this context, the discussion in Roy [1984]; also for a case study of rice, Subbarao [1978a].

36 A review of the actual process of price fixation by the APC is contained in Kahlon and Tyagi [1983].

37 For a review of the debate see Vittal [1986]. See, in particular, Mitra [1979] and Tyagi [1979].

38 See Roy [1984] for the data and Krishnaji [1988] for further discussion.

39 Questions relating to stock policies have been addressed in Ray [1970], Krishna and Chibber [1983], Krishnaji [1984] and Reutlinger [1978].

40 For details of these recommendations see Acharya [1983].

41 Krishna and Raychaudhuri [1980] discuss the empirical determinants of procurement prices.

42 Askari and Cummings [1976].

43 Krishna and Raychaudhuri [1980].

44 Subbarao [1985]. See also Mahendradev [1987].

45 For a debate on the poverty-price relationship, see, Mellor and Desai [1986] and for a comment on the statistical methodology, see, Krishnaji [1987].

46 See Bhattacharya et al [1985].

47 See Chapter 1 in United Nations [1975].

48 Mitra [1979]. This important aspect of relative prices is not dealt with in this survey.

49 This section draws heavily from de Janvry and Subbarao [1986].

50 de Janvry and Subbarao [1986] attempt to grapple with this complexity through a computable general equilibrium (CGE) model, which enables them to carry out several simulation exercises. They find that technological change in agriculture and irrigation development with *flexible prices* are essential for alleviating poverty. Price flexibility benefits both rural and urban workers through a combination of employment and deflationary effects.

In general it benefits the net buyers of food through relatively low prices. Generally, they find price incentive policy an inferior alternative to technological development, especially in relation to welfare goals.

REFERENCES

Acharya, K C S [1983], *Food Security System in India*, Concept, New Delhi.
Askari, H and Cummings, J T [1976], *Agricultural Supply Response: A Survey of the Econometric Evidence*, Praeger, New York.
Bhattacharya, Nikhilesh et al [1985], *Relative Price of Food and the Rural Poor: The Case of India*, Indian Statistical Institute (mimeo).
Chaudhuri, Pramit [1978], *The Indian Economy: Poverty and Development*, Vikas, New Delhi.
Chopra, R N [1981], *Evolution of Food Policy in India*, Macmillan India.
Communist Party of India (Marxist) [1973], *Central Committee Resolution on Certain Agrarian Issues and an Explanatory Note by P Sundarayya* (party document).
—[1981], *New Peasant Upsurge: Reasons and Remedies*, Documents and Resolutions at the AIKC meeting at Trichur.
Dandekar, V M [1965], 'Minimum Support Prices for Foodgrains: Guidelines for a Policy and a Programme', *Artha Vijnana*, Vol 7, No 4, pp 272-83.
Dantwala, M L [1967], 'Incentives and Disincentives in Indian Agriculture', *Indian Journal of Agricultural Economics*, Vol 22, No 2, pp 1-25.
—[1976], 'Agricultural Price Policy in India since Independence', *Indian Journal of Agricultural Economics*, Vol 31, No 4, October-December, 9, 37.
de Janvry, Alain and Subbarao, K [1986], *Agricultural Price Policy and Income Distribution in India*, Oxford, Delhi.
Government of India, *Report of the Agricultural Prices Commission*, various issues.
—*Bulletin on Food Statistics*, various issues.
Gulati, Ashok [1987], *Agricultural Price Policy in India: An Econometric Approach*, Concept, New Delhi.
Hazell, Peter B R [1982], 'Instability in Indian Foodgrain Production', International Food Policy Research Institute, Report No 30, Washington.
Kahlon, A S and Tyagi, D S [1980], 'Intersectoral Terms of Trade', *Economic and Political Weekly*, Review of Agriculture, December 27, pp A173-84.
—[1983], *Agricultural Price Policy in India*, Allied Publishers, New Delhi.
Krishna, Raj [1967], 'Agricultural Price Policy and Economic Development' in Herman M Southworth and Bruce F Johnston (eds), *Agricultural Development and Economic Growth*, Cornell, New York.
Krishna, Raj [1982], 'Some Aspects of Agricultural Growth, Price Policy, and Equity in Developing Countries', *Food Research Institute Studies*, Vol 18, No 3, pp 219-60.
Krishna, Raj and Chibber, Ajay [1983], 'Policy Modelling of a Dual Grain Market: The Case of Wheat in India', Report No 38, International Food Policy Research Institute.
Krishna, Raj and Raychaudhuri, G S [1980], 'Some Aspects of Wheat and Rice Price Policy in India', World Bank Staff Working Paper, No 381.
Krishnaji, N [1973], 'Wheat Price Movements: An Analysis', *Economic and Political Weekly*, Review of Agriculture, June 30.

94   *Pauperising Agriculture*

—[1975], 'State Intervention and Foodgrain Prices', *Social Scientist*, Vol 3, Nos 6/7.
—[1987], 'Agricultural Growth, Prices and Poverty', *Economic and Political Weekly*, June 27.
—[1988], 'Foodgrains Stocks and Prices' in Amiya Kumar Bagchi (ed), *Economy, Society and Polity: Essays in the Political Economy of Indian Planning*, Oxford, Calcutta.
Mahendradev, S [1987], 'Growth and Instability in Foodgrains Production: An Inter-State Analysis', *Economic and Political Weekly*, Review of Agriculture, September 26, pp A82-92.
Mehra, Shakuntala [1981], 'Instability in Indian Agriculture in the Context of the New Technology', International Food Policy Research Institute, Report No 25.
Mellor, John W and Desai, Gunvant M (eds) [1986], *Agricultural Change and Rural Poverty*, Oxford, Delhi.
Mitra, Ashok [1979], *Terms of Trade and Class Relations*, Rupa, Calcutta, also published by Frank Cass, London, 1977.
Nadkarni, M V [1987], *Farmers' Movements in India*, Allied Publishers, New Delhi.
Nathan, Dev [1982], 'On Agricultural Prices', *Economic and Political Weekly*, December 25, pp 2101-04.
Rath, Nilakantha [1985], 'Prices, Costs of Production and Terms of Trade of Indian Agriculture', *Indian Journal of Agricultural Economics*, Vol 40, October-December, pp 451-81.
Ray, S K [1970], 'Imbalances, Instability and Government Operations in Foodgrains', *Economic and Political Weekly*, Review of Agriculture, September 26, pp A115-24.
—[1971], 'Weather and Reserve Stocks of Foodgrains', *Economic and Political Weekly*, Review of Agriculture, September 25, pp A131-42.
—[1972], 'Effects of Consumption, Availability, Fluctuations on Foodgrain Prices', *Economic and Political Weekly*, Review of Agriculture, June 24, pp A86-92.
—[1983], *Growth and Instability in Indian Agriculture*, Institute of Economic Growth (mimeo), Delhi.
Reutlinger, Shlomo [1978], 'The Level of Stability of India's Foodgrain Consumption', *India: Occasional Papers*, World Bank Staff Working Paper, No 279.
Roy, Shyamal [1984], 'Government Management of Foodgrains Supplies: A Critical Appraisal', *Towards Continuing Education*, Vol 5, pp 1-19.
Sinha Indradeep [1980], *The Changing Agrarian Scene: Problems, and Tasks*, Peoples Publishing House, New Delhi.
Subbarao, K [1978], 'Rice Price Behaviour and Public Procurement: An Analysis of the Experience of Andhra Pradesh', *Indian Journal of Agricultural Economics*, Vol 33, No 3, pp 1-20.
—[1978a], *Rice Marketing Systems and Compulsory Levies in Andhra Pradesh*, Allied Publishers, New Delhi.
—[1979], 'Producer Levy Evasion and Income Loss', *Economic and Political Weekly*, Review of Agriculture, March 24-31, pp A2-7.
—[1985], 'State Policies and Regional Disparity in Indian Agriculture', *Development and Change*, October.
—[1986], 'Farm Prices: A Survey of the Debate' in M L Dantwala and others

(eds), *Indian Agricultural Development since Independence,* Oxford and IBH, New Delhi, pp 373-84, Growth (mimeo).

Thamarajakshi, R [1970a], 'Determinants of Rice Prices', *Agricultural Situation in India,* March, pp 1075-79.

—[1970b], 'Determinants of Rice Prices', *Agricultural Situation in India,* May, pp 129-36.

—[1977], 'Role of Price Incentives in Stimulating Agricultural Production in a Developing Economy' in D E Ensminger (ed), *Food Enough or Starvation for Millions,* Tata McGraw Hill, pp 376-90.

Tyagi, D S [1979], 'Farm Prices and Class Bias in India', *Economic and Political Weekly,* Review of Agriculture, September 29, pp A111-24.

United Nations [1975], *Poverty, Unemployment and Development Policy.*

Vittal, Nalini [1986], 'Intersectoral Terms of Trade in India: A Study of Concept and Method', *Economic and Political Weekly,* Review of Agriculture, December 27, pp 147-66.

June 30, 1990

5

The Demand Constraint

A Note on Role of Foodgrain Prices and Income Inequality

THE context of this note is the widely documented slow-down in industrial growth in India dating from about the mid-sixties. Many factors have been cited in the literature as being responsible for the poor growth of industry. One of these is the narrowness of the market base for manufactured goods.

If what is produced cannot be sold, the processes of accumulation and investment are held in check and hence growth is retarded. The question of industrial growth has thus been posed essentially as a problem of what determines the level of investment, and the role of demand analysed within frameworks involving sectoral dichotomies such as those involving investment and consumption goods or agriculture and industry.

This note is exclusively concerned with the determinants of the level and composition of household demand for items of consumption other than foodgrains. For this purpose incomes and prices are assumed to be given so that their impact on the structure of demand can be assessed.

This means that questions relevant to the growth problem viewed in intersectoral terms are ignored here. The terms of trade between agriculture and industry are, for example, relevant not only to the growth process in the ultimate sense but also in a direct manner to the determination of income inequalities.[1] However, since this paper deals with ex-post data on aggregate household consumption, the simplifying assumption about prices and incomes being given may not be wholly unjustified.

Moreover, the main objective is to assess the magnitudes underlying the demand structure so that some common notions about the 'restricted home market' may be reviewed. For example, it is held, with ample justification, that extreme inequalities restrict the market base. However, it is not clear from this whether and, more important, to what extent the base will widen if in-

come inequalities reduce. Given (by definition) the inadequate
levels of food consumption among the poor, it is possible that
the widening effects of a redistribution may largely be restricted
to the foodgrain market. Pursuing this reasoning a little further,
it is easy to see that if incomes of the poor rise to a level which
ensures satisfactory food consumption, a redistribution of income
will lead to a significant improvement in the growth of the demand for manufactures. The quantitative significance of
analytical truths can thus be seen to be quite relevant to any
analysis of the Indian industrial growth experience.

In what follows it is argued that cereal prices play an important role in restricting the domestic market for 'other things',
especially manufactured goods. It is only at relatively very high
levels of income that the food constraint becomes inoperative.
Some items in the food basket are non-substitutable for the great
majority of the people. The absolute level of the cereal price has
thus an independent role, quite apart from that of the structure
of relative prices in relation to money incomes, in generating
changes in demand patterns. Likewise, income inequalities are
important not only in the relative sense of the distance between
the poor and the rich but also in terms of the absolute levels of
low incomes (such as those earned by labourers) which have continued to be insufficient for buying the most basic need: food.
Such low incomes are so low that even at higher levels of income
increasing food prices erode the consumption of non-food items
by households usually regarded as those above the 'poverty line'.

I

This section is about income inequality and its influence on
the composition of demand. Since the poor and the rich have
widely differing consumption baskets, there is no need to emphasise the relevance of trends in inequality to the changing patterns of demand.

The most striking feature of differential expenditure patterns
in the Indian economy is that food accounts for the giant share
in total expenditure among all but the top 10 to 20 per cent
households. The National Sample Survey (NSS) data for 1965-66
in this respect are given in Table 1. (The proportion of expenditure on food has been decreasing. But the differential pattern
is likely to have persisted.)

In Table 1, the fractiles refer to households ranked by the level of per capita expenditure. But the average household size systematically decreases from the bottom to the top fractile so that, for example, the top-most rural decile contains only 7.4 per cent of the population and the preceding (80-90) decile accounts for roughly 8.8 per cent of the population. Thus in terms of population fractiles the differences would be wider than what the figures in Table 1 imply.

Besides, there are good reasons to believe that the NSS data do not adequately capture the consumption profiles of the rich. Therefore, these data represent an understated version of the impact of inequality on consumption. In any case, there is no doubt that the market base for manufactured goods is restricted in a large measure to the relatively richer households.

In terms of total expenditure, the distribution among the poor, the middle and the rich households, as exhibited by the NSS data, has not changed much (Table 2). A more detailed study on the trends in inequality confirms the lack of dramatic changes in the distribution of expenditure as revealed through NSS statistics.[2]

However, a few further comments on trends in inequality may not be out of context. Apart from the consumption data referred to above, there are data relating to the distribution of landholdings which also indicate a marginal reduction in inequalities, with the relative importance of very large holdings progressively declining since the fifties.

Table 1: Percentage of Expenditure—All India, 1965-66

Fractile Group	Rural		Urban	
	Food	Non-Food	Food	Non-Food
0-10	84	16	80	20
10-20	87	13	78	22
20-30	82	18	77	23
30-40	81	19	74	26
40-50	70	20	71	29
50-60	79	21	68	32
60-70	77	23	65	35
70-80	75	25	61	39
80-90	70	30	57	43
90-100	55	45	45	55

Source: NSS Report No 201.

However, such a reduction portrayed by these different statistics may not be real at all. Several reasons justify the scepticism about official statistics. First, as already noted, expenditure data do not tell us much about the consumption patterns among the rich. Second, there is a considerable under-reporting of true land-holdings by large owners. Third, there has been a perceptible growth in the proportions of agricultural labourers and small cultivators among workers. Fourth, despite the growth in per capita real incomes, albeit at not much more than 1 per cent per annum, the evidence (as in the rural labour enquiries) shows a decline in the incomes of agricultural labour, arising partly from a reduction in the levels of employment. Fifth, unreported incomes—black money—is acknowledged to be a growing phenomenon, which could have contributed only to the worsening of inequality. And finally, there is a good deal of evidence to show that inter-regional inequalities have increased.[3]

However, taking everything into account, if one accepts the hypothesis that redistribution of income in favour of the poor has not taken place to a *significant* extent—a hypothesis accepted with some equivocation even in the official plan documents—nothing much more is needed to characterise the narrowness of the market for manufactures.

The distance between the poor and the rich, large in absolute magnitude, gives rise to consumption differentials of the type given in Table 1. More detailed data in respect of individual items such as sugar, meat and fish, clothing and footwear are available for exhibiting the extremely large shares the rich account for in

Table 2: Distribution of Household Consumer Expenditure

Share of	1958-1959	1961-1962	1965-1966	1970-1971	1972-1973	1977-1978
Rural						
Bottom 30 per cent	13.1	14.7	15.1	15.4	15.4	
Middle 40 per cent	34.3	33.2	34.3	35.1	33.7	33.1
Top 30 per cent	52.6	52.1	50.6	49.5	50.9	51.9
Urban						
Bottom 30 per cent	13.2	12.9	13.6	13.7	13.8	13.6
Middle 40 per cent	31.7	31.4	31.9	31.8	31.8	32.4
Top 30 per cent	55.1	55.7	54.5	54.5	54.5	54.0

Source: Sixth Five-Year Plan, 1980-85, Planning Commission, p 16.

the aggregate consumption (NSS Report No 201).

These differentials, no doubt, change with changing patterns of inequality in income. It is, however, difficult to quantify the precise changes in the commodity composition of demand induced by the altering income distribution. For example, income inequalities can increase even while all incomes, and hence per capita incomes, are growing, with the poor experiencing lower (than average) rates of growth; per capita income may grow while incomes of the poor are stagnating or falling and inequality is rising; inequalities may increase or decrease with a fall in per capita income; and so on. Even when all incomes rise, the composition of demand may change through differential rates of growth for specific commodities. It is more difficult to speculate on what happens if the incomes of some sections of the people actually decline while the per capita income is increasing. In this case there would be losses and gains in consumption and the aggregate outcome would depend on the precise magnitudes of income changes and the relevant elasticities. Lacking knowledge of distributional patterns at different points of time, we cannot isolate the contribution of changes in inequality to the structure of demand.[4]

For this reason this note gives more attention to the price factor. The price factor is not, however, without relevance to the question of inequality. Food consumption absorbs a major proportion of expenditure not only among the poor but also, presumably, among the middle-income-group households, as Table 1 shows. Further, survey data of the NSS type usually show that foodgrain (and food) consumption keeps rising as incomes rise. Saturation levels of food intake are not reached within the surveyed populations which do not adequately cover the satiated rich. The population segment for which food still appears to be a priority item of consumption has thus certainly a bigger role than that of the 'poor' alone in the determination of the demand structure. More important is the related fact that increasing food prices curtail the purchasing power reckoned in terms of non-food items quite independently of the relative price structure for the simple reason that it is only the residue of money income left after food expenses are covered which will determine how much of 'non-food' can be bought; the importance lies in the fact that such a residual income as a determinant of the demand for manufactures is relevant to all but the rich households.

II

Data on private final consumption expenditure in current and constant prices are available in the *National Accounts Statistics* (*NAS*). The data derived from this source are presented in Tables 3 and 4 in terms of the following broad commodity aggregates:

(A) Cereals and cereal substitutes (item 1.1.1 in *NAS*);

(B) all other food, beverages and tobacco (item 1 excluding 1.1.1 in *NAS*);

(C) clothing, footwear, rent, taxes, fuel, power, furniture, household equipment, etc (covering items 2, 3 and 4 in *NAS*); and

(D) medical expenses, education, transport, etc, covering all other items of consumption (items 5 to 8 in *NAS*).

While (A) and (B) refer to cereal and all other types of food respectively and (D) refers to expenditure on 'services', (C) covers most of the items of a manufactured nature. This last group is the main object of the analysis here.

Table 3 shows that per capita disposable income has increased five-fold in money terms over the two decades from 1960 to 1980, implying a (compound) growth rate of roughly 8.5 per cent per annum. Non-cereal food (group (B)) consumption in real terms has virtually stagnated, while cereal consumption has also tended to stagnate, with somewhat higher levels during years corresponding to good harvests such as 1964-65 and 1970-71. Thus there has been practically no growth in total food consumption (groups (A) and (B) combined)—probably a long-term feature of the economy.[5]

The per capita consumption of services (group (D)) has increased roughly at the rate of 3 per cent per annum while that of items in group (C) grew at the rate of about 2 per cent. However, the growth in group (C) arose mainly from occasional discrete jumps, the series remaining stagnant over certain periods: 1964-68, 1971-75, and 1977-81. What characterises these stagnant periods and how they are related to agricultural performance are questions worth investigating but not pursued here.

The price data in Table 4 show broadly that during the sixties the prices of food articles (both cereal and non-cereal food) rose more rapidly than did the prices of manufactured goods and services. This trend had continued to a lesser extent until 1975, but thereafter the prices of all the three groups of commodities, (B),

(C) and (D), increased at a faster rate than did the prices of cereals. The annual rates of increase in the prices of commodities in the different groups range between 6.5 per cent and 8.2 per cent while, as already noted, per capita disposable income grew at roughly 8.5 per cent. Per capita consumption of *all* commodities (last column of Table 3) in real terms increased at a rate slightly less than 1 per cent.

What follows is a discussion of the impact of rising cereal prices on the demand for other commodities. It may be noted that the time-series on group (B) (representing other food) hardly shows

Table 3: Personal Disposable Income and Private Final Consumption Expenditure, 1960-61 to 1980-81

Year	Disposable Income: Rs Per Capita (Current Prices)	Expenditure by Commodity Group (1970-71 Prices), Rs Per Capita				
		A	B	C	D	Total
1960-61	293	146.7	206.8	76.5	58.5	488.5
1961-62	302	145.3	204.3	76.8	60.0	486.4
1962-63	310	138.1	207.6	78.1	61.6	485.4
1963-64	345	140.8	199.5	82.3	64.5	487.1
1964-65	403	153.4	211.3	86.7	67.0	518.4
1965-66	408	130.6	206.9	84.6	69.4	491.5
1966-67	466	132.2	200.9	88.8	70.5	492.5
1967-68	543	152.0	204.9	89.1	73.1	519.2
1968-69	542	156.1	200.2	91.3	74.7	522.3
1969-70	584	156.4	207.8	89.0	77.6	530.9
1970-71	611	159.0	218.0	94.8	79.7	551.5
1971-72	636	152.5	216.3	101.5	83.9	554.2
1972-73	692	142.7	204.2	100.9	83.5	531.3
1973-74	848	147.7	198.8	100.7	86.1	533.3
1974-75	967	141.0	202.8	100.4	82.8	527.0
1975-76	991	156.0	207.7	103.7	84.8	552.3
1976-77	1035	134.0	201.5	110.9	89.0	535.4
1977-78	1158	159.4	209.5	115.5	92.6	577.1
1978-79	1219	157.7	213.8	120.7	96.8	589.1
1979-80	1305	135.0	203.5	116.8	99.3	554.6
1980-81	1559	158.4	206.8	117.4	103.7	586.4

Note : Commodity groups: (A) cereals and cereal substitutes; (B) all *other* food, beverages and tobacco; (C) clothing, footwear, rent taxes, fuel, furniture, household equipment, etc, and (D) medical expenses, transport, recreation, education, etc.

Source: *National Accounts Statistics.*

any variation. This is possibly due to aggregation of commodities within this group: ranging from essentials like pulses and edible oils to luxury items such as meat and fish. There is no doubt that the structure of relative prices within the food group influences the composition of the food basket. A detailed study of this composition is not attempted here.

For studying the trends in the demand for manufactures and services, time-series demand functions with the following features are employed. (These relationships can at best be regarded as approximations summarising the data. The numerous well known difficulties in specifying such functions are ignored so as to capture the rough orders of magnitudes underlying the data.)

At the household level, the demand functions for groups (C) and (D) are assumed to be linear in two price variables, viz, the

Table 4: *Price Indices by Commodity Group, 1960-61 to 1980-81*
(1970-71 = 100)

Year	Commodity Group			
	A	B	C	D
1960-61	52.7	51.5	71.1	64.1
1961-62	52.9	52.8	75.3	67.5
1962-63	53.2	55.2	76.1	69.6
1963-64	59.8	60.7	79.2	72.9
1964-65	68.5	66.2	84.0	77.8
1965-66	80.2	70.6	89.4	80.1
1966-67	93.6	85.0	94.7	86.5
1967-68	106.6	98.2	98.1	93.0
1968-69	100.0	93.2	102.1	94.5
1969-70	104.6	99.1	105.5	97.3
1970-71	100.0	100.0	100.0	100.0
1971-72	104.4	103.2	107.3	104.9
1972-73	118.1	119.7	113.7	111.4
1973-74	139.1	150.5	129.6	123.6
1974-75	193.9	164.2	149.5	156.5
1975-76	159.8	156.1	156.8	164.1
1976-77	158.6	163.9	162.7	170.8
1977-78	153.4	180.2	176.7	177.3
1978-79	155.8	185.4	191.1	184.6
1979-80	175.7	207.8	217.2	205.2
1980-81	186.7	244.7	233.5	236.6

Notes: These index numbers are derived from the two sets of figures on private final consumption expenditure—in current and constant (1970-71) prices—available in *National Accounts Statistics*.

price of the commodity and the prices of cereals, and quadratic in the income variable. A quadratic function may be expected to capture the tapering-off income effect on demand quite adequately for the two groups of commodities. Linearity is preserved under aggregation. As for the quadratic income relationship, it can be easily shown that aggregation and averaging over households preserve the quadratic, provided the coefficient of variation (cv) of income is constant. It is assumed that the changes in the income distribution have not been significant enough to either increase or decrease the cv drastically. Thus the household specification can be carried over to the aggregates, with all the variables expressed in per capita terms.

It may be noted that a negative sign for the coefficient of the square of the income would indicate the tendency for demand to level off at high levels of incomes in a certain range. Such an income relationship portrays the dampening effect of the inequality in income on per capita consumption and tells us how even a proportionate growth in incomes, with unchanging relative inequality, may bring about a slow-down in the growth of demand. The results of regression analysis based on the specification outlined above are presented in Table 5, and the corresponding estimated elasticities of per capita (real) demand with respect to the price and income variables evaluated at the means of the

Table 5: Estimated Demand Regressions

Commodity/ Group	Coefficient of				
	Cereal Price	Own Price	Income	Square of Income	R^2
(C)	−0.0214	0.0089 +	0.1172	−0.0404	0.974
	(0.0050)	(0.0110)	(0.0176)	(0.0069)	
(D)	−0.0095	−0.0270	0.1142	−0.0193	0.970
	(0.0053)	(0.0128)	(0.0178)	(0.0072)	
Clothing	−0.1180	0.0097 +	0.7527	−0.2383	0.966
	(0.0370)	(0.0710)	(0.1370)	(0.0483)	

Note: The variables (in per capita terms) are scaled suitably and the constants corresponding to the equations are not given here. The results are presented for judging the goodness of approximation and the significance of individual coefficients. All the coefficients except those marked by a + sign are significant at the 5 per cent level. Standard errors are given in parenthesis.

different variables are given in Table 6.

What they suggest can be summarised: (1) The time-series specifications of the demand relationships proposed here provide adequate approximations to the data. (2) For both groups, (C) and (D), there is a significant inverse relationship between the demand and the square of income: this shows how consumption levels off in the upper income ranges and hence, more importantly, why even a proportionate growth of all incomes can dampen the growth in demand. (3) The 'own price' effect is significant in respect of commodity group (C) which includes most of the manufactured consumption goods but negative, as expected, in respect of the demand for services (D). Do prices of manufactures play no role in the determination of the demand for the goods in category (C)? Such an inference cannot be drawn from the analysis mainly because the data are based on a very high order of aggregation which can conceal differential individual commodity demand patterns. For this reason, an attempt is made here to analyse the demand for clothing (2.1 in *NAS*). The regression results for this commodity are also given in Tables 5 and 6. Even in this case, it turns out that clothing prices do not significantly influence the changes in the consumption of clothing. Obviously, aggregation biases are still at work, for certainly the 'clothing' group is composed of very heterogeneous elements characterised by differential demand responses to price.

For the purposes of this analysis, however, the most important result is the inverse relationship between the per capita demand (for items in groups (C) and (D)) and the price of cereals.[6] Other things remaining the same, rising cereal prices depress the demand for manufactures and services, more for the former

Table 6: Estimated Elasticities of Per Capita Demand

Commodity/ Group	With Respect to		
	Cereal Price	Own Price	Income
(C)	−0.255	—	0.330
(D)	−0.138	−0.440	0.727
Clothing	−0.342	—	0.585

Note: The elasticities are estimated at the mean values of the variables and given only for significant coefficients.

than for the latter (Table 6). The specific example of clothing, analysed here as well as in a number of other studies, shows that within
the category of manufactured goods some are more susceptible
than others to the demand constraint imposed by increasing food
prices. (As can be seen from Table 6 the elasticity of demand
with respect to cereal prices is the highest in respect of 'clothing'
among the three commodity groups considered.)

There is no need to set out here a critique of the textbook demand theory according to which the cross-price elasticities (such
as those of (C) and (D) with respect to the price of cereals) are
expected to be positive. The inverse relationship is easily
understandable once we discard the assumption that consumption allocations respond freely to relative prices. If, as seems to
be the case, food consumption levels are either inadequate for
survival (as among the poor) or unsatiated (whether in quantity
or quality, as among some above the 'poverty line'), what determines the allocation process for the majority of the population
is not the total but the 'residual income': that part of income
which is left over after food articles have been bought. The point
is elaborated further later.

III

The analysis in the last section is inconclusive because it is
based on aggregated data. Moreover, there are two different types
of aggregation, both of which can produce misleading inferences:
the first, aggregation over commodities, to which some reference
has already been made and the second, aggregation over income
groups the influence of which has been covered so far only in
part through the assumption of a consistent coefficient of variation in the personal distribution of income.

It is difficult to overcome the difficulties arising out of aggregation, given the nature of published data. Radhakrishna and
Murty have, in their unpublished studies, used the National
Sample Survey (NSS) data for estimating demand relationships
at a more disaggregated level than in this note.[7] To the extent
that their analysis is based on both cross-sections (expenditure
groups) as well as time-series, it is relatively freer of the aggregation biases referred to. They divide the population into quintiles, ranging from the poorest 20 per cent to the richest 20 per
cent, and estimate the quintile-specific elasticities through variants

of a non-linear expenditure system. The data for their analysis are drawn from the NSS 2nd to 25th rounds.

The estimates made by Radhakrishna and Murty of the elasticities of demand with respect to cereal prices of different commodities and by different population groups are given in Table 7. A remarkable feature of these estimates is that the depressing effect of rising cereal prices on demand extends (with a few exceptions) not only to all commodity groups listed in the NSS data but also to all parts of the population including the 'top' 20 per cent. As expected the inverse relationship is the strongest in respect of the bottom expenditure groups.

The persistence of a negative elasticity with respect to cereal prices even in the uppermost quintile requires a word of explanation. Not all households in this group can by any means be characterised as rich. Given the nature of NSS surveys, the rich hardly find a place in the surveyed samples. Indeed NSS data generally show an unabated rise in levels of food consumption as total expenditure levels increase.

IV

The Radhakrishna-Murty calculations confirm the finding of an inverse relationship between the demand for 'non-food' items in household consumption and the price of cereals. The different estimates of the relevant elasticities presented here can be taken as no more than crude first approximations since they are based on far too aggregated data. A finer disaggregation will certainly show much variation in the strength of the inverse relationship.

The relationship itself is easily explicable in terms of a dichotomy of the population into groups consisting of households for which food, especially foodgrain, is a *priority* item of consumption and those for which income levels are sufficiently high to ensure satiation in food consumption. For the former group, it is only the residual income which determines levels of non-food consumption. And if the 'purchasing power' reckoned in terms of food prices alone falls for this group there can be a shrinkage in residual incomes irrespective of the movement of other prices. So, even if for the other group the demand relationships and price responses are 'normal', a negative cereal cross-price elasticity can emerge in the aggregate. This would of course depend on the

Table 7: Estimated Cereal Cross-Price Elasticities

	Rural Classes (Quintiles)					Urban Classes (Quintiles)				
	1	2	3	4	5	1	2	3	4	5
CL	-0.920	-0.784	-0.545	-0.205	-0.327	-0.894	-0.730	-0.357	-0.147	-0.178
MM	0.517	-0.882	-1.068	-0.722	-0.025	-0.113	0.178	-0.632	-0.333	-0.060
EO	-0.523	-0.479	-0.527	-0.379	0.417	-0.265	-0.192	-0.437	-0.107	0.214
ME	-0.761	-0.517	-0.592	-0.409	-0.146	-1.319	-1.680	-0.890	-0.332	-0.415
SG	-0.343	-0.511	-0.674	-0.589	-0.012	0.090	0.604	-0.243	-0.147	-0.293
OF	-0.106	-0.263	-0.279	-0.099	-0.199	-0.052	-0.208	-0.117	-0.205	-0.020
CT	-0.033	-0.047	-0.199	-0.554	-0.232	0.053	-0.210	-0.307	-0.332	0.140
FL	-0.026	-0.033	-0.120	-0.234	-0.119	0.040	-0.142	-0.192	-0.179	-0.071
ON	-0.042	-0.049	-0.209	-0.576	-0.415	0.041	-0.225	-0.347	-0.347	-0.184

Notes: CL: cereals; MM: milk and milk products; EO: edible oil; ME: meat, fish and eggs; SG: sugar and gur; OF: other food; CT: clothing; FL: fuel and light; ON: other non-food.

Source: K N Murty and R Radhakrishna, 'Agricultural Prices, Income Distribution and Demand Patterns in a Low Income Country', mimeo.

relative shares of the two groups in income and the magnitude of relevant elasticities.

The other point is that the depressing effect of cereal prices on the demand for manufactures can continue to operate even without income inequalities getting worsened. Indeed, Radhakrishna and Murty show that a moderate redistribution of income in favour of the poor would promote the demand for food rather than that of manufactured goods. The extreme income inequality, irrespective of its changes over time, and the eroding 'food purchasing power' for the vast majority of the population both contribute significantly to the slow-down in the demand for manufactures. Worsening inequalities would only reinforce this decelerating trend.

NOTES

1 See Ashok Mitra, *Terms of Trade and Class Relations*, London, 1977.

2 Uma Datta Roy Chowdhury, 'Income Distribution and Economic Development in India since 1950-51', *Indian Economic Journal*, 25(2), October-December 1977.

3 See A Vaidyanathan and Gita Sen, 'Growth and Social Justice: India's Experience and Prospects', National Seminar, Institute of Economic Growth, Delhi, April 27-30, 1984. It is shown in this paper that inter-state inequalities have increased with respect to NDP per capita, foodgrain production per capita, proportion of irrigated area, hospital beds per 1,000 population and the ratio of road length to area.

4 For contradictory conclusions on the impact of income inequality, see Ashok V Desai, 'Factors Underlying Slow Growth of Indian Economy', *Economic and Political Weekly*, Annual Number, March 1981, and Nirmal Kumar Chandra, 'Long-Term Stagnation in the Indian Economy, 1900-75', *Economic and Political Weekly*, Annual Number, April 1982.

5 See Nirmal Kumar Chandra, op cit.

6 Such an inverse relationship has been observed before. See, for example, T N Krishnan, 'Demand for Mill Cloth in India—A Study of the Interrelationship between Industry and Agriculture', *Artha Vijnana*, December 1964.

7 R Radhakrishna and K N Murty, 'Models of Complete Expenditure System for India', IIASA, Austria, May 1980, and K N Murty and R Radhakrishna, 'Agricultural Prices, Income Distribution and Demand Patterns in a Low Income Country', mimeo (undated).

6

Agrarian Relations and the Left Movement in Kerala

A Note on Recent Trends

TENANCY was abolished in Kerala through the Kerala Land Reforms Amendment Act (1969). In other states similar acts, concerned more with the regulation of tenancy than its total abolition, passed during recent times, have meant their existence merely on statute books but in reality have led to diverse forms of concealed arrangements between landlords and tenants, usually enforced by the former to protect their own interests which were threatened by the law. In Kerala, however, the abolition of tenancy is widely believed to be an accomplished fact. Effective implementation of the law was possible largely due to the organised strength of the left movement and the related fact that land reforms were implemented by left-oriented governments, unlike in most other states where the reforms were sought to be introduced from 'above' before the peasant masses were politically organised to fight for their rights. An important aspect of the Kerala scene in this context is the conferment of ownership rights on hutment-dwellers, which also was the outcome of intense political struggle and effective legislation. The movement which developed since the abolition of tenancy has three main components: a successful struggle for higher wages (for agricultural labourers); an espousal of the demand for 'fair' prices for farm products which does not require struggle (the peasant interest in this respect being sought to be protected by all political parties); and the struggle for land which has not been very successful.

This note is an attempt to understand these recent trends in the left movement in the light of long-term changes that have taken place in agrarian relations. Section I deals with some aspects of the class structure and Section II with the strategies of the Communist Party of India (Marxist), the strongest representative of the left, on agrarian issues.

I

ASPECTS OF CHANGING CLASS STRUCTURE

The most striking feature of agrarian change in recent times in Kerala, as in other parts of the country, is the continuous growth of rural wage labour in its working population. A significant proportion of the labourers in rural Kerala are engaged, unlike in other regions of India, in sectors other than agriculture, especially in the primary processing of agricultural products such as coir spinning and manufactures. However, even within the agricultural sector, the ratio of cultivators to agricultural labourers has tended to decrease continuously at least from 1921. Trends in the composition of the working population show a fall in the proportion of cultivators and a rise in that of agricultural labourers.[1]

This is no doubt due, in part, to the dispossession of the poor and middle sections of the peasantry at different points of time in the history of the regions comprising Kerala. But to what precise extent it is associated with the development of capitalist agriculture is hard to judge on the basis of available data. In the most recent period, i e, after land reforms (the nature of which will be discussed below) have been implemented, two counter-acting forces have been at work. On the one hand, rights to ownership of land have been conferred not only on the *kudikidappukar* (hutment-dwellers) but also, as a result of tenancy legislation, on poor peasants, who used to cultivate landlords' land under various forms of tenancy arrangements. On the other hand, the poor peasants have not in general been able to raise the productivity of their lands and their living standards for obvious reasons. The question relating to the extent of proletarianisation resulting from the direct alienation of land from the poor peasants cannot thus be easily settled. We have data, however, which show that 'landlessness' among agricultural labourers has decreased during the period 1956 to 1971.[2] To understand the significance of the underlying statistics we need to consider the fact that hutment-dwellers, who are now 'owners' of land, usually put their little bits of land to agricultural use (coconut and tapioca being the common crops) and hence qualify, for statistical purposes, as 'landed' agricultural labourers. This cannot, however, wholly explain the decline in landlessness for there is a distinct possibility of growth in the number of poor peasants, cultivating bits of land but depending on wages, within agriculture and other sectors of the rural economy, for the major part of their subsistence needs. Indeed, there is quite convincing evidence that pauperisation of the peasants has taken place on a wide scale and that the process has been continuous during this century. It is to this process that we now turn.

It is well known that Kerala has the highest man-land ratio among the states of India and that it is one of most densely populated regions in the whole world. But what is perhaps not so well known is the fact that it has been so at least from the beginning of this century. The growth in arable land has not kept pace with the rapid increase in the population; consequently the man-land ratio has increased continuously from 1901 and at a rate more rapid than in other parts of the country.[3]

Data available for the Travancore region show that even as early as 1931 the average size of holding was only 2.6 acres per cultivating household, which declined further to less than 2 acres by 1966-67. With the persistence of gross inequalities in the distribution of land during this entire period, the proportion of households cultivating no more than an acre grew from 38 to 61 per cent.[4] For Kerala as a whole comparable data do not exist for such a long period; estimates available for 1961-62 and 1971-72 show, however, that household operational holdings of less than an acre in size increased from about 60 per cent of the total to 68 per cent during the intervening decade. The proportion of households cultivating less than half an acre in 1971-72 is estimated to be roughly 52 per cent.[5] These data reveal to us a source of growth of agricultural labour as well as an important aspect of its nature: a vast mass of pauperised peasants, not totally dispossessed of land, constitute a significant part of the labouring poor in agriculture.

How is the growth of small farms explained and what are its implications for the changing agrarian relations? To answer this question we need to consider, first, the magnitude of the transfer of land from the poor to the rich (which is relevant also to the question of dispossession); secondly, the impact of land reforms on the transfer of land from the rich to the poor (including the landless) through the distribution of surplus land (above legally stipulated ceilings) as well as conferment of ownership rights on small tenants following the abolition of tenancy; and finally, the partitioning of land among family members, which, even in the absence of vigorous market transactions in land, would result in the growth of small farmers over a long period. All these market and non-market forces are likely to have contributed to the growth of small farms. It is difficult to judge their relative importance to the process for want of the required data. What follows, therefore, is somewhat speculative but based on whatever information is available.

Data on transfer of ownership of land show that during the decade 1957-66 about 146 thousand acres were transferred through direct sale and that about 47 per cent of the area involved in these sales related to those induced by 'monetary needs'.[6] This may uncritically be interpreted to mean that dispossession of the poor and middle sections of the peasantry had taken place to a significant extent. This would indeed be so if it could be established that it was mainly the poor who sold the land to the rich. However, since the peak sales took place in 1960 and 1963, the years of 'critical importance to the agrarian relations in the state' (to be explained later), there is good reason to believe that a great number of these transactions were made by the rich peasants and landlords to evade in advance the proposed ceiling and tenancy laws which were sure to be enacted by 'communist' ministries appearing on the horizon. Viewed in this light, the reason cited in the survey for the sales, viz, monetary needs must be regarded as spurious, at least in the majority of cases.[7]

To assess the overall impact of land reforms on the redistribution of land (and agrarian relations in general) we need to consider three aspects of the reform: provisions relating to (1) hutment-dwellers, (2) tenancy, and (3) land ceilings. Kerala is frequently cited as an example where land reforms have been successfully implemented. The success refers more to the first two of the above-mentioned aspects of the reform than to the third. At any rate, the effectiveness of land reforms in Kerala has been studied by many scholars and we need only to present the consensus in broad outline.[8]

Kerala Land Reforms Act, 1963 (as amended in 1969 and 1972) gave to *kudikidappukar* (hutment-dwellers, who were essentially landless agricultural labourers living in huts on pieces of landlords' land) rights to their dwelling houses and a few cents of adjacent land. Most *kudikidappukar* have obtained *de facto* rights of ownership to such lands although in a number of cases *de jure* rights may still have to be secured. It is the strength of the leftist political forces, rather than the law, which has brought about this change in the status of agricultural labourers in the state. The rights to land, secured and protected by the left movement, in turn, strengthen the latter and give it a special character for a wage labourer with some land is a better fighter than one without any. We may conclude that, although quantitatively the gains to the agricultural labourers in terms of redistribution of land might not have been very impressive, qualitatively the left has emerged as a stronger force in the countryside, especially in the struggle for better working conditions for the labourers.

A series of legislative measures in the state culminated in the total abolition of tenancy in 1969 through an amendment to the Kerala Land Reforms Act of 1963. The resulting gains to the leftist forces are of a mixed nature. To an unknown but possibly limited extent, the law was made ineffective through evasive transfers (of possession) of land resorted to by the landlords. The latter anticipated what was coming and had time to make these transfers, for, in the political environment of the late fifties and sixties, in which the Communist Party was emerging as a strong force, the struggle for land was the most prominent aspect of politics in the state. When the first communist ministry was formed in Kerala in 1957, "big landlords rightly apprehended that their feudal interests in land would be at stake. This fear paved the way for large-scale land transfers in the state even before the Agrarian Relations Act of 1960 was adumbrated." The last mentioned act and the Kerala Land Reforms Act of 1963 prompted some hectic sales and transfers around those years. Over 40 per cent of the disposals of leased-out land during the decade 1957-66 took place in 1963.[9] This need not, however, contradict our tentative assessment that the impact of evasive transfers on the effective abolition of tenancy was limited, for the total land involved in transfers of possession over the whole decade was only about 188 thousand acres (out of a total of roughly 1.9 million acres of leased-in land).[10]

A second aspect of the abolition of tenancy relates to the compensation legally stipulated to be paid by the tenants. While such compensation has been collected in some cases by the government, there do exist former tenants who enjoy rights to land without fear of eviction although they have not yet paid compensation in full. This is a reflection, as in the case of *kudikidap-*

pukars, of the organised strength of the peasants.

However, some former tenants cultivated fairly big holdings and have now acquired ownership rights to these lands. The reforms thus paved the way for the emergence of a new class of capitalist farmers especially in the northern region of the state, i e, Malabar, where not only the incidence of tenancy was high but also tenants cultivating (before the reform) land leased in from *jenmies* in big holdings existed in large numbers. In other regions of Kerala, i e, Travancore and Cochin, where the *jenmi* system disappeared long ago and small tenants were preponderant, the conferment of ownership rights on tenants is unlikely to have contributed to the emergence of capitalist farmers on the same scale as in Malabar. Apart from big tenants, new recruits to the class of capitalist farmers have come also from the ranks of the old landed gentry who now employ wage labour on lands (hitherto given out on lease) which they have 'resumed' for self-cultivation.

A notable aspect of these changes, crucial to the developing agrarian relations, is the unity among landless agricultural workers, poor peasants and big tenants which the communists could bring about in the struggle against 'land-lordism' in the Malabar region. New class divisions—and contradictions depending on them—emerging after the abolition of tenancy have weakened the objective forces for such a unity.[11] We shall deal with this subject later.

Let us now turn to the third aspect of land reforms, viz, ceilings. Unlike the provisions relating to hutment-dwellers and tenancy abolition, those concerned with land ceilings have not yielded substantial gains to the left. Evasion of land ceilings formed an essential part of the bogus transfers which we have already discussed. Moreover, in spite of many legislative exercises to 'plug the loopholes' in the law, sufficient scope was left for evasion through means other than direct transfer of land. The final result was that not much surplus land was available for redistribution. Statistics present a truly revealing picture of this phenomenon. As on March 31, 1978, the area (of surplus land above legally stipulated ceilings) ordered for surrender was only about 133 thousand acres, out of which about 67 thousand acres have been 'taken over' and only 39 thousand acres distributed (to about 62 thousand beneficiaries including 27 thousand belonging to the scheduled castes and tribes).[12] No precise estimates of how much of the 4.5 million acres of cultivated land would be available as surplus, should the ceiling law be implemented effectively, are available.

Before we examine the implications of the changes discussed thus far to agrarian relations let us reconsider the phenomenon of the growth of small farms from a different point of view. Partitioning of land among members of a household creates newly formed households cultivating smaller pieces of lands, and in periods characterised by a high rate of partitioning, a very significant growth in small holdings can result. In Travancore, the decade preceding 1931 is important from this standpoint. During this period, following the passing of regulations for the partition of *tarawad* (i e, joint family) properties of certain communities, over 400 thousand acres of land owned by these communities alone were partitioned. In respect of the Nayar community (which accounted for 83 per cent of the land partitioned), over 70 per cent of the partition deeds created shares of less than an acre each.[13] A sub-division of this magnitude must have contributed significantly to the emergence of small peasants as the most numerous category in the countryside.

As we have seen, the disproportionately large growth of small farms has continued during recent times. Apart from the process of pauperisation, it is likely that the partitioning of land has also contributed to this trend. Moreover, the rates of partitioning appear to be higher in the small holdings than in the bigger holdings: this is partly reflected in data which show that as land size increases not only the family size but also the proportion of joint families tends to increase.[14]

Partitioning of land can thus be seen to have reinforced the trend towards the growth in the number of poor peasants. At any rate the forces altering the shape of the distribution of land have brought about, by the beginning of the seventies, a vast mass of landless agricultural workers and pauperised peasants.

To discuss the nature of relations between them and the other agrarian classes, it is necessary to examine the pattern of utilisation of land and its changes over time.

In other regions of India, commercial crops are grown for sale on the market mainly by the big farmers. But in Kerala, such crops are grown even in the very small holdings. Coconut is the most important of these crops which include rubber and different kinds of spices. The cropping pattern in Kerala is thus distinctly different from that of India as a whole: foodgrains (including tapioca, an inferior cereal substitute) account for roughly 40 per cent of the cultivated area in Kerala but over 75 per cent in the country as a whole.

The cultivation of commercial crops has a long history in Kerala and has grown further in importance in recent times. The main change which has come about in the cropping pattern is the rise in the relative importance of coconut and rubber cultivation. This is partly due to topographical reasons. Paddy (the only cereal grown in Kerala) can be cropped only in the valley land while a variety of commercial crops can be grown on the slopy land. Additional land suitable for paddy cultivation has become unavailable for a long time. Thus extension to the area under cultivation has favoured the growth of commercial farming.[15]

But what is more significant for our purposes here is the high incidence of commercial cropping in very small holdings. Both poor and middle peasants are involved to a great extent in the cultivation of coconut, pepper and other commercial crops. About 55 per cent of the area under coconut and 40 per cent of the area under pepper are in holdings held by households cultivating in all no more than 2.5 acres each.[16] Rubber is generally cultivated on large estates but it is believed that in recent times middle peasants have taken to rubber cultivation on a significant scale. The poor and middle peasants in Kerala are thus involved in the market as sellers of their farm products to a great extent; this is in sharp contrast to the other parts of the country where such involvement is minimal. This poses some problems to the left, as we shall see.

Commercial farming is not, however, conterminous with capitalist farming. In the holdings of the poor and middle peasants work is done largely (but not necessarily wholly) by family members. It is only in the very large holdings, of over 10 acres (roughly four hectares), that employment of wage labour is the predominant mode. However, as we shall see later, capitalist farming exists on a significant scale (though not constituting the predominant mode) even in holdings of five acres (roughly two hectares) and below in size.[17] Thus commercial farming, notwithstanding its long history, has not led to a sharp polarisation of the rural population into the classes of capitalist farmers on the one hand and wage labourers with 'nothing but their labour power to sell' on the other. This is not to deny that a process of differentiation is at work: indeed, the poor and middle peasants do not enjoy the advantages of the richer peasants in the markets either as sellers of farm products or as borrowers of credit. But the point is that the sale of farm products by the middle peasants gives them a greater 'staying power', especially in an era of rising farm prices, and slows down the process of polarisation.

II

STRATEGIES OF THE CPI(M)

To understand the strategy of the Communist Party of India (Marxist) in Kerala it is necessary to begin with the stand of the party on agrarian issues in an all-India context. A very clear statement of the policies of the party, formulated on a countrywide rather than a regional basis, appears in a central committee (CC) resolution adopted at its meeting in March 1973 at Muzaffarpur. This resolution is the result of an assessment of the experience of the party with reference to the programme of work set out in an earlier resolution passed in 1966 and takes into account the differences which have cropped up within the party in the intervening period. There is an explanatory note by P Sundarayya added to the resolution.[18]

The resolution says that the central slogan of the agrarian movement must be: "abolish landlordism, both feudal and capitalist, without compensation and distribution of land of landlords to the agricultural labourers and the poor peasants free".[19] Commenting on the legislative measures of the Congress governments, the resolution says that while the party should extract the "maximum possible concessions from the ruling classes, in the concrete reality of the legislative strength of the democratic opposition as well as the mass movements outside", "no legislation, however limited, under the present ruling classes and corrupt bureaucratic set-ups, gets implemented... unless powerful mass movements are developed."[20]

The concrete programme for struggle, laid down in this context, is based on a five-fold classification of the agrarian population: landless agricultural labourers, poor, middle and rich peasants, and landlords (both capitalist and feudal). The distinction between a rich peasant and capitalist landlord is that the former (or members of his family) participates in agricultural operations through manual labour while the latter relies wholly on wage labour. Landlords in general combine in themselves features of capitalism and feudalism and are defined in terms of an upper ceiling to the size of land, which can vary from region to region depending on fertility and other agroclimatic conditions. Notwithstanding Sundarayya's replies to certain criticisms of this formulation, the definitions and what they imply are debatable from a Marxist perspective. But what is more important is that landlords, so defined, constitute the 'target of attack' for carrying out the struggle for land. The CC resolution accordingly translates the slogan for abolishing landlordism into a programme of action by redefining land ceilings (for purposes of legislation) so as to ensure that all landlords (capitalist and feudal) are caught in the net. Sundarayya explains: "...for fixing up land ceilings, the only point with which we are concerned is what is the demarcating line between a landlord and a rich peasant."[21] Ceilings defined in terms of the resolution may thus adversely affect individual rich peasants (holding land above the limit defining landlords) but not rich peasants as a class. Thus rich peasants are outside the target of attack as far as the struggle for land is concerned.

On the whole there is some equivocation in the stand of the party on rich and middle peasants. In the case of the middle peasantry it is best illustrated by the following sentence in the 1966 resolution: "Working class hegemony over the kisan movement can be ensured only if the proletarian party... places its principal reliance on the rural labourers and poor peasants who constitute 70 per cent of the peasantry, while of course not forgetting for a moment, neglecting or ignoring the middle and rich peasants but drawing them into the struggle for agrarian revolution."[22]

The political task of drawing middle and rich peasants into the struggle, without sabotaging its proletarian character, is, of course, not an easy one; indeed, the party recognises that revisionism within the party springs from the underlying difficulty. The 1966 CC resolution goes on to say: "The struggle against revisionism inside the Indian communist movement will neither be fruitful nor effective unless alien class orientation and work among the peasantry are completely discarded. No doubt this is not an easy task, since it is deep-rooted and long-accumulated and also because *the bulk of our leading kisan activists come from rich and middle peasant origin rather than from agricultural labourers and poor peasants.* Their class origin, social links and the long training given to them give a reformist, ideological, political orientation which is alien to the proletarian class point and prevent them from actively working among agricultural labourers, poor and middle peasants with the zeal and crusading spirit demanded of communists" (emphasis ours).[23]

How such a crusading spirit will emerge and how, in the long run, the composition of activists and leaders is to be changed in favour of those with proletarian origin, are questions relating to the organisation of the party and need not detain us here. The concrete programme in relation to rich and middle peasants, which interests us more, appears to be dictated , however, more by the necessity of not alienating them than by the fear of what compromises with them will entail. The rich peasants were not to be touched by land ceiling and while land "will be distributed to the landless agricultural labour and the poor peasants", at the same time, "for developing the united struggle for land it may be necessary to give a small portion of the land to the middle peasantry".[24]

The struggle for wages and the demand for fair prices likewise entail contradictions which cannot be easily resolved. It is not only 'capitalist landlords' who employ wage labourers. Rich and middle peasants also do so, the former to a significant and the latter to a limited extent. Sundarayya notes that "partial struggles for wages can be successful only if the movement can mobilise the support of the poor and middle peasants and other democratic forces to back them".[25] Here, the underlying unity of classes is obviously to be secured through other means since in wage struggle rich and middle peasants will be on the other side of the fence. As already noted, a factor which offsets this contradiction and works in favour of unity, is the assurance that rich peasants' lands below the ceilings would be left untouched during the course of the struggle for land; the recognition of the necessity to distribute a portion of the surplus land to the middle peasants also works in the same way.

However, a stronger binding force is the struggle for 'fair prices' for the farm produce of the poor and middle peasants. On how fair prices are to be determined, Sundarayya quotes the CC resolution: "fair prices should be fixed... taking [into account] the interest of the mass of the peasantry and they be such as to assure a decent living [for them]...". Sundarayya emphasises the fact that fair prices are thus defined in terms of a 'decent living' for the masses and "not just some reasonable return, or some profit".[26] It is true that the demand for such prices will bring together all sections of the peasantry for united action, but the benefits from 'fair prices' accrue mainly to the capitalist farmers and make them economically and politically stronger. Sundarayya solves the problem in the following way: "When we demand fair prices that would assure decent livelihood for a middle peasant... it does not mean that these minimum prices should be assured even to... landlords. We can certainly raise the demand that the whole of the produce of these landlords be compulsorily procured by the government for meeting the needs of the people...".[27] The story of support prices—and the role they have played in the Indian economy after the advent of the green revolution—is too well known to be retold here. It will suffice to note that in the present political and economic situation of the country there do not exist any means, political or otherwise, for curbing the ability of the big landowners to secure for their produce high prices independently of market forces; nor do means exist for effectively taxing the rich farmers for ensuring that the benefits of fair prices accrue only to the poorer sections of the peasantry. The pursuit of the goal of 'unity' through the demand for fair prices thus works against the interests of the toiling poor.

As already explained, it was the strength and militancy of the left movement which was responsible for the successful implementation of the provisions of land reforms relating to the conferment of ownership rights to land on hutment-dwellers and tenants. In contrast, the movement had not been able to prevent big landowners from successfully evading the ceiling laws. The party is aware of this, and, in accordance with its stand on the issue in the all-India context, has in recent times made these evaders the primary target for attack in the struggle for land. The implicit understanding of the party is that if the ceiling of 10 standard acres (fixed by the 1969 amendment) is successfully implemented, then all landlords—mainly capitalist, since feudal types have practically ceased to exist after tenancy abolition—will be virtually eliminated.

Accordingly, the 'land grab' movement of 1972, which was launched by the CPI(M) in the wake of the fierce hutment-dwellers' struggle in 1970, was concerned more with unearthing surplus land (above the ceiling) and bringing it to the notice of the government than its occupation, although in a number of cases agitators 'entered' such land. The struggle lasted 80 days and about 175 thousand acres 'came to light' in the process. It did not, however, yield any land to the agitators. E M S Namboodiripad (EMS) denies that the movement was a failure. "Not that agitators must get land, but that the government must take it over to distribute it among the deserving, was the slogan of the struggle," he says. EMS regards the unearthing of so much surplus land as no mean achievement. But to him, what was a greater achievement was the fact that "...two lakh volunteers participated in the struggle... People donated lakhs of rupees to cover the expenses of the struggle. Masses of all parties and organisations gave moral support to the struggle." To those who asked how many cents of land were secured through the movement he replies: "...let me remind them of another question, which the loyal adherents of the British asked Gandhi and Congress soon after the salt satyagraha, 'How many tons of salt did you get?' Indian people went ahead ignoring these questions. The British had to leave India."[28]

The gains would of course have been more substantial if there were means for ensuring that surplus land brought to the notice of the government could be established as such and distributed. Many legal obstacles stand in the way, and, as we noted earlier, only a small part of it has been actually distributed. One can only speculate about what would have happened if a CPI(M)-led ministry was formed later. Not much has happened, however, on the land-struggle front after the 1972 movement until very recently (January 1979) when a second 'land grab' movement was launched by the CPI(M). It is too early to assess the results but newspaper reports make it appear to be a satyagraha rather than a militant movement: these reports describe how hundreds of workers 'court' arrest every day in different parts of the state.

The party can thus be seen to have avoided violent confrontations during the course of the struggle for land in recent times. But what stands out more clearly is the failure of the CPI(M) to evolve a satisfactory formula for determining the ceiling in Kerala in conformity with the party line. This failure arises partly from the confusion present in the CC resolution, but partly also, as we shall argue, from political expediency. As already noted, the CC resolution lays down the principle that the party should agitate for a land ceiling which would ensure that all land belonging to the landlords would be confiscated when the ceilings are enforced; it further gives detailed guidelines for fixing such ceilings taking into account regional variations. It is doubtful if a ceiling of 10 standard acres would satisfy this criterion in the case of Kerala. It is well known, in any case, that land size is a poor criterion for judging the class status of the owners. This is especially true in the case of Kerala. There are some data which show that in Kerala even among households operating areas between 1 and 2 hectares (roughly 2.5 to 5 acres) about 39 per cent rely on wage labour. Even more striking are the data for the size class immediately below, which refers to households operating between 0.5 and 1 hectare (1.25 to 2.5 acres): in about 30 per cent of these households work is done largely by wage labour.[29] Any work done by the members of the family of the owner in these cases must be more supervisory than manual in nature. Logically, therefore, the party in Kerala should agitate for lowering the ceiling but it is not easy to determine the ceiling in accordance with the principles laid down by the CC: "if, say, 90 per cent of the holders of a particular size of holding, say ten to twelve and half acres wet [land], or 20-25 acres of dry [land] do not physically cultivate their lands, it can be assumed that holders over ten acres wet [land] or 20 acres dry [land] are broadly, for land ceiling legislations, landlords".[30] The data required for determining the ceiling in the above manner, viz, the distribution of land in standard acres do not exist and hence some arbitrariness is unavoidable. But the point is that the existence of capitalist farmers operating land below the current ceiling size cannot be denied.

It may be argued in this context that the CPI(M) in Kerala is reluctant to attack 'small holders'. The CC defines this attitude in two clauses: (1) "Lands of small holders owning less than half the ceiling, but eking out their livelihood in factories, small shops, schools, small government jobs or as ordinary soldiers and junior army officers, or in *any other profession*, even if they are not cultivating their lands, shall not be taken..." and (2) "landholders, who are owning on the day of legislation less than the proposed ceiling but more than half the ceiling, but who are not cultivating their lands by their physical labour but getting them cultivated by agricultural labour, if they have other professions or means of income, *will be allowed to retain only that amount of land that would be enough to make their total income equal to that derived from the land ceiling*" (emphasis ours).[31] It is not known whether any struggle for land has taken place in accordance with the second clause mentioned above. But what is more relevant to the character of the movement is the first clause which lets out of the net numerous non-cultivating owners of highly remunerative pieces of land below half the ceiling (say, two to three acres of garden land) who derive the major portion of their income from sources other than agriculture. It is interesting to note that the West Bengal Land Reforms Act (Amendment Bill, 1977) brought into being by the CPI(M)-led Left Front government has a clause which ensures that such absentee owners forfeit their rights to land.[32]

In spite of the lack of conclusive data (apart from those referred to earlier which show a high percentage of small farms cultivated wholly by wage labour) it is generally believed that there are numerous 'small holders' who derive a major part of their incomes from not only salaried employment but also trade, transport and other remunerative activities. They are, moreover, organically linked to members of the urban middle classes. It is a two-way link, for, in Kerala, the extent of interest in land which members of the bureaucracy—and salary earners in general— have is probably far greater than what it is anywhere else in the country. The CPI(M) is either unwilling to recognise the existence of this class or not yet prepared to fight it. The attitude of the party in this respect is partly due to its middle class orientation springing from the class origin of the activists and partly arises out of its concern for preserving its electoral base.[33]

It is not our purpose here to analyse the electoral fortunes of the CPI(M) in Kerala but only to attempt to understand how they are related to the character of the emerging left movement. Let us look at the struggle for wages and the demand for fair prices from this point of view. In wage struggle there are no apparent elements of compromise but viewed in combination with the nature of the land struggle, which we have discussed at length, not only do we see such elements clearly but it is also easy to understand why in the CPI(M) view unity of the peasant classes is a necessary condition for successful wage struggle. There is a trade-off here between high wage rates and the assurance of the party that certain classes of the peasantry would be left untouched in the struggle for land. Even so, some observers attribute the recent electoral reverses suffered by the CPI(M) to the alienation of the middle and rich peasants resulting from fights relating to wages. None of this, however, belittles the achievements of the CPI(M) in raising the level of political consciousness of agricultural labourers and poor peasants.

But, as we have argued earlier, the demand for fair prices is a stronger force for securing peasant unity. The CPI(M) treads a cautious course in this respect however. It is other parties—with a clearly dominant 'landlord' interest—which clamour for high prices and the CPI(M), on occasion, accords support. The most recent example of this is in relation to the central government's decision to import rubber. The move, which threatened the interests of rubber growers, was opposed through a resolution passed unanimously in the Kerala assembly. Other examples, concerning coconut prices, of occasions when the CPI(M) stood alongside the other parties for protecting the peasant interest in general can be given. Here the CPI(M) is caught on the horns of a dilemma with little prospect for escape: Coconuts are cropped on a wide scale by poor farmers. It is possible that rubber is also cultivated by some poor and middle peasants. How can the party protect their interests and prevent the 'landlords' from reaping profits? A solution of this problem would require a greater confrontation of class forces than what the CPI(M) is prepared to face today.

The primacy which the party accords to the unity of the peasant classes pays dividends but it also stultifies the movement. The dividends, apart from those already discussed, also lie in the ease with which alliances can be struck and electoral adjustments made between political parties in Kerala. The CPI(M) has a large and fairly stable electoral following in the state. Given the fact that electoral victories in Kerala depend more on who is with whom (among the parties) than on the proportion of total votes that individual parties can poll (this was sharply brought home in the last general election in 1977), the CPI(M) cannot ignore electoral calculations in formulating its strategies. To do so and lift the movement to a higher stage, what is required is a radical reorientation in the overall strategy of the party.

Objective forces for promoting such a re-orientation are present in the changing agrarian structure described earlier, the main feature of which is the continuous process of pauperisation. Wage labourers and poor peasants constitute the vast majority of the rural population and the movement can acquire a more pronounced proletarian character if its focus shifts more sharply in their favour. But the difficulties also arise from the forces which shape the distribution of land and the pattern of its utilisation. How to protect poor peasants without enabling the rich to reap the profits is a question for which no readymade answers can be given. But above all, it is the attitude of the party towards rich peasants and those small landowners who derive a major part of their substantial total incomes from sources other than agriculture, which obstructs the growth of the left movement and if unchanged can make the movement progressively less and less proletarian in character.

NOTES

1 Lack of comparability of data over the long period makes precise estimation of the underlying figures difficult. The conclusion holds broadly, however. For a discussion, see, P G K Panikar, T N Krishnan and N Krishnaji, *Population Growth and Agricultural Development—A Case Study of Kerala,* Food and Agricultural Organisation, Rome, 1978, Chapter IV.
2 The agricultural labour enquiries show that while the total number of agricultural labour households increased from 5,00,000 to 7,10,000 during 1956-57 to 1964-65, those without land decreased from 2,40,000 to 2,10,000; comparable data for 1971-72 show a further decline in the latter category to 1,00,000. See P G K Panikar et al, op cit, p 54.
3 Ibid, Chapter I.
4 The 1931 data are based on *Census of India, 1931, Volume XXVIII, Travancore, Part I—Report,* and those for 1966-67 on *Land Reforms Survey in Kerala, 1966-67,* report, Bureau of Economics and Statistics, Trivandrum, 1968.
5 These are based on the National Sample Survey, Report Nos 144 and 215. For a discussion, see, P G K Panikar et al, op cit, pp 39-41.
6 *Land Reforms Survey,* op cit, Table 10.3, p 98.
7 The *Land Reforms Survey* comes to similar conclusions; see Chapter X of the report.
8 For a recent survey, see, *Poverty, Unemployment and Development Policy: A Case Study of Selected Issues with Reference to Kerala,* United Nations, 1975, Chapter V.
9 The figures are from the *Land Reforms Survey.* For a discussion, see, Chapter X of the report.
10 Ibid, pp 70, 100.
11 The Malabar movement is well documented. Among the recent studies relevant for our purpose here are: Joan P Mencher, 'Agrarian Relations in Two Rice Regions of Kerala', *Economic and Political Weekly,* Annual Number 1978, pp 349-66, and A V Jose, 'Origin of Trade Unionism among Agricultural Labourers in Kerala', *Social Scientist,* July 1977. In this context, see also, E M S Namboodiripad, (a) 'A New Approach Needed on the Agrarian Front', Chinta, September 17, 1971 and (b) *Strengthen the Agricultural Workers Movement through United Struggles,* Kerala Karshaka

Sangham, January 1974 (both in Malayalam). In the last cited reference, EMS says: "...the anti-feudal slogan of the organised peasant movement attracted the agricultural workers also although the movement included rich peasants. The rights of the landlords to evict the tenants, increase the rent and make other exactions and the accompanying social repression disturbed the agricultural workers as well as the peasants. In short, the slogan of 'End feudalism and distribute the land to the peasant', created a common target for agricultural workers as well as the peasantry" (translated from Malayalam). In practice the struggle for land to the tenant was combined with the struggle for hutment land.

12 The data are from the *Report of the Task Force on Land Reforms*, VI Five-Year Plan, Government of Kerala, 1978, p 7.

13 *Census of India, 1931,* op cit.

14 See, P G K Panikar et al, op cit, Chapter IV.

15 Ibid, Chapters II, III and IV.

16 Ibid, p 51.

17 The data are reproduced in Table A.

18 *Central Committee Resolution on Certain Agrarian Issues and an Explanatory Note by P Sundarayya,* Communist Party of India (Marxist). The publication is undated but the resolution refers to that passed in 1973.

19 Ibid, p 3 of the CC resolution.

20 Ibid, p 4.

21 Ibid, p 15, of Sundarayya's note. Replying to the criticism that Lenin did not define landlords in terms of the size of landholding, Sundarayya adds: "Comrade Lenin, in studying the agrarian structure of various countries, analysed the bourgeois statistics and, especially, the landholdings of various sizes as given in the statistics of the bourgeois government and, applying his broad criteria based on production relations, has drawn certain relevant conclusions for practical activities. For a broad understanding and broad

Table A: Percentage Distribution of Holdings within Each Size-Class according to the Nature of Labour Employed—Kerala, 1970-71

Size of Operational Holdings (Hectares)	Work Done by Household Members	Largely by Members of Household but also by Others	Largely by Wage-Labour	Total
0.04-0.25	70.30	15.47	14.23	100.00
0.25-0.50	51.39	26.55	22.06	100.00
0.50-1.00	37.97	32.09	29.94	100.00
1.00-2.00	28.09	33.18	38.73	100.00
2.00-4.00	19.36	33.49	47.15	100.00
4.00 and above	9.01	23.33	67.66	100.00

Source: The Third Decennial World Agricultural Census, 1970-71, Report for the Kerala State, Bureau of Economics and Statistics, Kerala.

propaganda and legislative slogans, we have to follow the same procedure."
22 Ibid, p 2 of Sundarayya's note.
23 Ibid, p 3.
24 Ibid, paragraph 19 of the CC resolution of 1973, p 7.
25 Ibid, Sundarayya's note, p 39.
26 Ibid, pp 43, 44.
27 Ibid.
28 The data and the questions are from E M S Namboodiripad, 'Replies to Questions', *Chinta*, October 13, 1972 (translated from Malayalam).
29 See the data reproduced in Table A.
30 C C resolution, op cit, paragraph 12, p 5.
31 Ibid, paragraphs 20 and 21, p 7.
32 For a discussion, see, N K Chandra, 'Major Move against Semi-Feudal Tenancy', *Economic and Political Weekly*, November 26, 1977.
33 For similar observations, see, JM, 'The Left in Kerala', *Frontier*, September 30, 1978. JM says: "It is the strong impression of this author that one of the major reasons why the Marxists are in trouble in Kerala is that many of the local-level leaders are now landowners. And there is a real contradiction here. Those who are leaders of the labourers are also employers of labour. A few of the former leaders and some former workers have also deserted the party, now that they have their own land... The leaders come from a high social stratum, the agricultural labourers from the lowest stratum. Today there is practically no leadership from the bottom." As we have already noted, the CC resolution of 1973 implicitly recognises these facts.

March 3, 1979

II
Demographic Structure

7

Poverty and Fertility

A Review of Theory and Evidence

I

THE focus of this review is on differences in the levels of fertility between the poor and the rich in rural India. There are two distinct but related aspects of the association between poverty and fertility which have been discussed widely in the literature on development. The first concerns a comparison between countries at various stages of development, while the second relates to differences between poor and rich families within poor countries—for example, those in the contemporary third world. There is some confusion in the literature on fertility in relation to levels of living and development, which can be traced to a mixing up of these two—macro and micro— aspects of the relationship.

Following economic and social development, countries in western Europe experienced a passage from high rates of mortality and fertility to low ones. This has led to the 'theory of demographic transition' which is no more than a crude summary of some events in the 19th century. Death rates fell rapidly as levels of living rose; fertility also began to fall but only much later. However, the timing of the sequence of events as well as the factors associated with it varied from country to country: in France fertility decline started much earlier than in other countries; and the reasons are thus far not quite well understood despite much speculation.[1] Reviewing the process of demographic transition, Cassen [1978] writes:

The reasons for this pattern of population change are... uncertain. There is no simple and continuous relationship between the rise in living standards and the decline in mortality and fertility. There were periods in each country while incomes rose when mortality did not fall significantly, others when it did, with or without significant increases in incomes. And all the influences working to reduce fertility were in operation for some time without much effect. The present state of knowledge is that factors which account for changes in mortality and fertility can be listed but it is not possible to demonstrate quantitative relationships between these factors and their results.

Despite—or because of—the unevenness of this process there is no escape from the question: why do birth rates in poor countries tend to be high? This is a social (or macro) question, but, since children are born within families, the answers are sought for in family behaviour. It is not surprising therefore that theories of fertility are micro theories based on family attitudes, etc.

Theorising is necessary because an association between poverty and high fertility is paradoxical: the poor would be better off with small families. The search for rationality in behaviour for explaining high fertility has given rise to many theories. Some of these are formally elegant while others are stated in simple terms with great appeal to common sense: there are neo-classical economic as well as radical versions of the theory of high fertility. The substance of these apparently different theories is the same: children can contribute to family income either directly by doing paid work or indirectly by attending to unpaid domestic duties and thereby releasing adults for more gainful employment; the rationality for high fertility lies in the economic value of children, calculated on a long-term basis.[2]

One factor considered very important in this context is the high rate of infant mortality in poor societies: the poor produce a large number of children simply to ensure enough survivors and continuation of families, given their experience of frequent deaths. The rationality is then regarded as 'unconscious' in character, a reflex response to social experience of child deaths. The motive may look non-economic but models can—and do—convert it into an economic one by considering expected benefits derivable from surviving children. The models are so flexible that they can encompass even such non-economic variables as the frequency of coitus without altering the conclusions.[3]

Models, as well as the theories they suggest, are thus fairly general in scope, and cite easily understood reasons for high social fertility. Hence their relevance to poor countries at the macro-level cannot be questioned. But their uniform applicability to all families and social classes is doubtful, for a little reflection leaves too many questions open. Consider first the question of high infant mortality. Surely, it is consistent with lower rates for some classes—say, the rich. Or take the so-called pension (or in-surance) motive: couples produce a lot of children so as to en-sure at least one survivor (preferably a son) who would, in the absence of social security, take care of the parents when they grow old. This motive, again, should not for obvious reasons apply to all rural classes with the same degree of importance. It follows that the theories can make some sense—as they are specifically stated, i e, in relation to decision-making by individual couples—if at least it can be demonstrated that class differences in fertility are in the expected direction, the poor characterised by higher levels than the rich to whom conditions laid down in theory do not apply. On the other hand, historical evidence indicates, as we shall see, that in pre-industrial Europe, well-to-do classes had in fact higher levels of fertility than poorer classes.

To put it in slightly different terms, these theories will acquire meaning only if control on fertility can be demonstrated to exist for those classes of people to whom the pronatal poverty condi-tions described by theory are irrelevant. If no such control can be discerned explicitly in data, it would follow that the theories merely capture general conditions underlying uncontrolled fer-tility which can be high or low for the population as a whole. For this reason, it is necessary to assess the pronatal conditions arising from poverty as they operate differentially for classes remote from each other, such as, for example, labourers and landlords.

A second difficulty with respect to theorising about family behaviour arises from chance variation in demographic events, which produces a considerable variability in family size. Even if we restrict ourselves to the poorer classes and grant that there is a desired number of children calculable from theory, not all families succeed in attaining this size: only a small fraction would. Some would in the end have either too few or too many surviv-ing children. The rational strategy, adopted whether through con-scious economic calculation or unconsciously, is defeated in most cases. Once again we can easily see why theory can have a macro validity but still be very incomplete in relation to families. It is true that those who fail to produce a surviving son, as well as those who produce too many, live somehow and die ultimately. Unless theory describes also the social adjustment mechanisms which attend upon such chance variation in family size and further how the underlying processes vary as between different social classes, it is not of much use. To give examples: widow remarriage tends to be class-specific in its frequency and so does the practice of adoption of children to pass on family property; children do take care of parents when the latter become old, but among the poorer classes parents rarely survive—given low levels of expected life—to an age at which they cannot work any more and need to be taken care of by surviving progeny; children in some families may work and contribute to family income, but whether they do so and how much they earn would depend on the economic and social status of the family. The difficulty lies in absorbing this wide range of social and economic phenomena into a simple theoretical scheme through a single calculable device such as per capita income.

Even if we leave aside these theoretical issues as esoteric, a question persists: Do the poor produce more children per couple than do the rich? The question which theory investigates—why do the poor produce more children?—arises only if the answer to the previous question is in the affirmative. There are masses of data which help us to give an answer. But perhaps due to their abundance, the data are full of ambiguity and seem to have been misinterpreted.

It is not for satisfying idle curiosity that the question is raised here. The belief that the poor breed faster—through what Malthus called improvidence[4]—is widespread but lacking in factual basis. It is taken as almost axiomatic that all family planning effort to control fertility should be directed towards the poor, howsoever vaguely defined. Whether axioms are true or not is of no concern to rulers. This was brought home to us sharply during the political emergency inaugurated in June 1975. The populist economic programme which followed had family planning for limiting family size as one of its important goals. When, in the sequel, the policy of compulsory sterilisation was imposed during 1976, the so-called target groups were constituted largely by poor and working people or destitutes. The policy was implemented with violence and it led to deaths.[5]

II

Who are the poor? Unless we answer this much-discussed question satisfactorily, we cannot say much about fertility levels among the poor. Historical writing relating to pre-industrial Europe relies on what to us would appear as crude classification schemes. The categorisation of population groups and classes ranged from destitutes, vagabonds and labourers to serfs and freemen, and further to clergymen, lords et al. Social and economic hierarchies were well understood and could be easily discerned from these categories.

Economics relies exclusively on income irrespective of how it is generated. Differences between households earning income from wages and those from cultivation or rent or trade do not matter to a ranking of families according to a vaguely conceptualised standard of living. Per capita income is all that counts now in economic statistics; data-gathering methods ensure that it can be measured in some way or other and so displayed that all other features which distinguish families go under the carpet.

Historical data show that in European as well as other countries, family size and wealth were directly associated. Wealth, especially in terms of landholdings, was the principal characteristic determining the socio-economic hierarchy. Wealthy families had large numbers of children and the labouring classes had small families.[6] The family size-wealth correlation holds besides for poor agrarian communities of contemporary times. Differences in average family size need not, of course, accurately reflect differences in fertility, for family size variations are influenced also by possibly differential age-compositions of women in the reproductive period and rates of mortality. However, the scanty European data available on direct measures of fertility do show that fertility increases with landed wealth (and other similar measures).[7]

Contemporary data which relate fertility to levels of living present, on the other hand, a confusing picture. We shall discuss the data later. But let us refer to just one aspect of the data on rural India. They exhibit a high degree of inverse relationship between fertility levels and per capita expenditure. This appears to be consistent with the popular belief that the poor are prolific. We have argued elsewhere why such an inference cannot be drawn from these data.[8]

The trouble is that per capita expenditure is not always suitable for demographic analysis: it can be shown to lead, when employed in correlation analysis with cross-sectional data, to demonstrably invalid inferences. Demographic profiles of families are determined only in the long period over which per capita income and expenditure are highly unstable. Per capita incomes of families can change not only from year to year but even within a year as a result of births, deaths, migration and marriage— demographic events, for which precisely an explanation is being sought. These changes produce very serious biases, especially when demographic parameters are estimated on the basis of a year's data. A birth reduces the per capita income of a family (by a very significant proportion if the family income is small) and this alone can introduce a spurious correlation between low incomes and high fertilities derived from short-period data. Long-period fertility measures such as the number of children produced by a woman over her entire reproductive period cannot, on the other hand, be related to per capita income, for it is difficult to define and measure a long-term per capita income for a given family.

In contrast, the class status of a family remains fairly, even if not wholly, stable. This is especially true in the case of poor families. Most agricultural labour households remain so through generations and their economic and social status, viewed in the most general sense, hardly changes irrespective of short-period fluctuations in per capita income. For this reason, property and wealth holdings which to a good extent determine class divisions may be regarded as measures of levels of living much better suited for analysing demographic differentials than per capita expenditure.

There are other reasons as well. The manner in which property, especially land, is held and transmitted from generation to generation influences family structure in agrarian populations.[9] Such structures have a considerable impact on fertility. This can best be illustrated through the example of the so-called 'European pattern of marriage' described by Hajnal [1965], and characterised by high rates of celibacy and late marriage among both males and females. Even with a fairly high order of fertility within marriage, this pattern tended to keep the overall fertility—measured in terms of number of children per woman— at a somewhat low level. It is quite legitimate to regard the European pattern of marriage as a basic condition for the fertility decline that took place in the late 19th century [Tilly 1978]. Fertility levels in the post-colonial poor countries are estimated at five children or less to every married woman and are somewhat lower than those in pre-modern western Europe; the reason why in contemporary poor societies fertility looks much higher than it was in 'poor' Europe is that marriage is nearly universal and tends to be early.[10] The explanation for the European pattern has been quite convincingly traced to lie in primogeniture (or unigeniture, more generally) through which a given property holding was transmitted intact to (say) the eldest son. Others—apart from the inheritor—had maintenance allowances (sons) or dowries (daughters). This system—its economic rationale in a historical sense is well understood—promoted celibacy and late marriage.[11]

A close parallel exists in Kerala in recent times, where population density was quite high even during the first half of this century, both in absolute terms as well as in relation to other parts of the country [Panikar et al 1978]. Kerala has—and probably always had—the highest rate of celibacy and of average age at marriage, among the regions of India. A study of the recent fertility decline in Kerala—the most pronounced among Indian states—argues that one important factor behind this decline is the further lengthening of the average age at marriage [Krishnan 1976]. It is possible to suggest on the basis of the fragmentary available evidence that changes in the structure of property holdings brought about by recent land reform are at least in part responsible for the changing patterns of marriage in Kerala.

These are specific examples. General theories of the family in relation to property are as old as Engels [1884]. Some social anthropologists investigating kinship structures, marriage patterns, etc, begin with who has command over land and, how it is used and transferred from one generation to the next [e g, Goody 1976]. Such an approach gives us some insights into fertility variation. Analytical frameworks set out wholly in unidimensional economic terms do not reveal much.

Looking at modes of property transfer pays further dividends in that it throws some light on chance-induced phenomena as well. Goody [1976] has shown how under high mortality regimes a certain significant proportion (of about 23 per cent) of couples remain without a heir to pass on property; this would happen even under conditions of uncontrolled fertility and absence of 'rational' strategies for attaining desired family size. The practice of adoption of children, for which an answer can be sought in this promising direction, may not apply to all agrarian classes uniformly but there is no doubt that the key to understanding family structures is in the pattern of property holdings.[12]

III

There are many historical surveys of differential fertility and
fertility decline in Europe. In one of these, Clark [1970, p 183]
raises the question about the poor and rich. He writes:

'The rich get richer and the poor get children' was the Victorian
epigram; and it was believed (on fairly good evidence) that larger
families were associated with poverty, unskilled occupation, lack of
education and rurality...
This group of generalisation was first challenged in 1930 by Arvin and
Edin in Sweden, one of the countries where restriction of fertility had
already proceeded furthest. Birth restrictions, in Sweden as everywhere
else, first appeared among the wealthier, more educated urban families,
with the fathers in more skilled occupations. But, in time, this movement had run its course. Family restriction spread to the less wealthy,
less educated and rural families, in some cases to an even greater extent than among those who had first practised it, *turning differential
reproductivities in favour of the more educated...*
Since the original Swedish study, more and more evidence... has been
accumulating which points in the same direction. Perhaps it will appear to our successors that the period of declining fertility, which began
about 1780 in France, spread over all western Europe, and north
America in the 19th century, and was reversed about the 1940s, was
no more than a temporary period, during which the normal differential reproductivities were reversed, while both before and after this
period *it was normal for wealthier and better educated families to be more, not
less, reproductive than their neighbours*[13] (emphasis ours).

Clark's conclusions are based on the experience of several countries. Poor-rich differences are captured in his data through landholdings and similar measures of wealth and status.[14] What they
broadly suggest is that, in the absence of controlled fertility,
biological and other factors tend to depress the levels of fertility
among the poor.

Control, to which theory mainly refers, may reverse the implied differences. If this interpretation of the demographic transition is valid, it raises several questions: Are high fertilities in
poor countries the result of generally high and uncontrolled natality among all classes with possibly lower levels among the poor?
What then is the use of theories, particularly those purely
economic in content? What are the lessons of the European
experience to the third world? Would the rich, perceiving the
economic advantage of small families as Malthus assumed,

reduce their fertility and then the 'improvident' poor follow suit ultimately?

Turning now to biological factors, it is best to begin by considering the reproductive period: from menarche to menopause. Historical data show that the age at menarche tends to fall as standards of living rise; and cross-sectional data demonstrate that menarche is delayed among the undernourished poor.[15] It is believed also that the age at menopause is positively associated with good nutrition, sound health and general well-being. More importantly—and this is a factor which is often ignored by demographers studying differential fertility—higher rates of mortality (among the poor, for example) reduce the average reproductive period per woman through a higher proportion of deaths before menopause.[16]

Given the reproductive period, fertility (i e, number of live births) can be expressed equivalently in terms of the time interval between successive births. These intervals are longer— and, hence, births fewer—among the poorer classes; one common reason cited is that breast-feeding lengthens post-partum amenorrhoea, the infertile period between births; the poor feed infants at the breast for longer periods than the rich do. The evidence on these aspects of poor-rich differentials is quite overwhelming.[17] Another factor which could account for lower fertility among the poor is the possibility of higher rates of pregnancy wastage including still births. On the whole, the biological balance favours the rich in reproductive capacity, and most of the underlying factors seem to be related directly or indirectly to nutritional status—in quantitative as well as qualitative terms—which in both the short and the long period is bound to be inferior among poor families.

One reviewer says that the question whether 'persistent malnutrition excites sexual instinct' has been raised in the literature [Jain 1975, p 115]. As we have suggested, this idea is quite explicit in Malthusian analysis (see note 3). However remote its origin, there is hardly any evidence to support the view. Some evidence from Bangladesh shows in fact that the poor 'do it' less frequently. Besides, experimental findings suggest that starvation is associated with "a loss of all interest in sex"[18] In reproductive biology there is reference to the 'comfort factor' which regulates the frequency of sexual intercourse.[19] Half-empty stomachs and comfort presumably do not go together. The frequency of sexual intercourse depends also on social practice: taboos and prohibitions of different kinds limit sexual activity. Whether it is the rich or the poor who are more diligent in such practice cannot, however, be easily ascertained from any worthwhile data. [20]

In any case, following our understanding about biologically-induced fertility differentials, the presence or absence of controls—individually chosen or socially imposed by custom—becomes crucially relevant to theory as well as evidence. If the evidence indicates significantly lower levels of fertility among the rich, there would be much scope for theorising, for it would clearly imply controlled reproduction.

The contemporary evidence is somewhat conflicting. Indian data referring to different regions and periods of time have been reviewed before [Hussain 1970; Jain 1975]. What they show is that when families are ranked according to criteria such as family income or wealth, fertility differences tend to be either narrow or positively associated with economic status, as they should in the absence of significant controls. [21] The ambiguity arises from National Sample Survey data—the only set of data referring to the country as a whole at several points of time—which exhibit higher fertilities among households with low levels of per capita expenditure. [22] As already suggested, these data are misleading and do not reflect the true pattern of fertility differences between the rich and the poor. The argument that the observed correlation can arise purely out of statistical artefacts is presented separately [Krishnaji 1984].

Following such a reasoning, if we agree to define poverty and riches by wealth rather than current per capita incomes, the evidence on direct measures of fertility (such as the number of children ever born per woman) shows unambiguously that the differences are either narrow or in the expected direction: lower levels among the poorer classes. That fertility differences are narrow is also indicated by indirect measures such as the proportion of children in different landholding classes.

It appears reasonable to conclude from the data on fertility and family size differentials that a low average size of family among agricultural labourers and poor peasants arises mainly from high rates of mortality and family formation; and a high average size of family among big landowners from low rates of mortality and a tendency for families to remain undivided.

Joint families are large simply because they are undivided. But are they pronatal? Extrapolation of economic and social theories of fertility leads to two equations: between high fertility and 'tradition'; and 'traditional backwardness' and joint family [Lorimer 1954; Davis 1957]. Evidence does not support these theories [Nag 1965]; joint families appear, on the contrary, to be somewhat antinatal.[23] If we treat property holdings as a crucial determinant of family structure, joint families can be seen as those corresponding to unpartitioned property, mainly in land. The strategy for keeping landholdings intact is consistent with late marriage (as historical data also indicate) and would be antinatal to some extent. Narrowness in differential fertility does indicate the existence of controlled fertility among the rich; but it seems that controls are more social than individual in character, influenced, as they appear to be, by variables such as family structure.[24]

IV

Purely economic theories are unrealistic and the economics of babies vs refrigerators is unaesthetic: children are not "instrumentalities that can be bought and sold" [Blake 1968]. Reviewing such theories, Hawthorn [1978] says:

The conventional neo-classical models of growth have... at least ignored a set of factors which may be intrinsic rather than incidental to growth and a relatively low level of fertility. And to the extent they have taken the English case as typical, they may have sacrificed some not only desirable but also arguably crucial realism.

...the argument about the 'rationality' of high fertility in poor households has developed from a set of arguments about the economic advantage of relatively low fertility in rich ones. For rich households and for poor, these arguments make the standard suppositions of neo-classical micro-economics... each of these suppositions is in doubt. Nevertheless the argument persists...

...the rough and ready approximations of the neo-classical models have shown themselves to be so rough and ready, so approximate, as to make one wonder whether they do not actually constitute a systematic distortion of the facts and the mechanisms which connect them...

...in specifying the conditions under which the standard neo-classical assumptions might reasonably hold one had at least to remember that 'exchange' may differ in different societies ...to an extent to which many of them may not be able to be accommodated in even the most ambitious of models.

The relevance of theory can however be questioned on grounds other than those of aesthetics and generality. The most important component of the economic theory of high fertility is the one based on the 'economic value' of children; others such as the 'pension motive' or son-preference can ultimately be converted into economic terms.

The question about the economic value of children has been discussed threadbare in demographic and development literature.[25] No conclusive answers are available however. We, as economists and demographers, can calculate these values making assumptions about when and under what conditions children work; whether they can find work and how much they can earn, etc. But we do not know whether and how parents make these calculations. In any case, the results would depend on the specific assumptions underlying the calculation. It is not surprising that different researchers arrive at different conclusions.[26] Quite apart from the ambiguity arising from the use of questionable specific numerical magnitudes, these calculations often ignore the differentiated nature of peasant classes (which is relevant for both costs and benefits in a fundamental sense) and are usually derived from 'peasant rationality', a supra-rationality applicable to all peasants. If one takes into account differentials in motives as well as in costs and benefits, these calculations may indeed be more useful but they are unlikely to associate high fertility uniformly with all peasant classes.[27]

It is possible to look at theories from a different angle. Since poverty conditions are assumed to promote high fertility through specific mechanisms, the evidence can be evaluated, whenever possible, directly in terms of such conditions and mechanisms. For instance, if the son-preference theory is valid one should find higher subsequent fertility among families with daughters only; if the 'replacement hypothesis', which says that a large number of children are produced so as to ensure enough survivors, is valid, higher subsequent fertilities among those who experience child loss should be demonstrable; if children are 'poor man's capital', it must be shown that poor families receive higher net benefits than do other classes.

There are numerous studies relating to these specific aspects of the poverty-fertility relationship. The weight of evidence thrown up by these studies does not seem to favour the general validity of the mentioned hypotheses.[28] One difficulty in assessing 'subsequent fertility' in case of child loss arises from the fact that a part of the variation is conditioned by purely biological factors: an infant death reduces the following infertile period and can promote a quicker next birth.[29] Moreover, under conditions of generally high levels of infant mortality, a family with a larger number of children faces a higher risk of an infant or child death, and thus there is also reverse causation which associates high infant mortality with high fertility.[30] Hence, the validity of this association across countries and over time notwithstanding, it is difficult to capture poor-rich differences unambiguously in this respect. Another difficulty—and this applies to son-preference as well—in interpreting data lies in the fact that the effects of uncontrolled fertility and chance variation cannot be easily separated from those of conscious control. Even if couples 'desire' another child on grounds of son-preference or child-loss there is no guarantee that they will succeed.[31] Family-level data cannot be satisfactorily organised so as to remove the influence of such confounding factors and set out the pure motivational relationship clearly.

Let us now turn to economic factors. To the extent that different micro studies relate to villages widely separated over space and refer to different points of time, at least one important reason why generalisations fail to hold is that conditions of child labour are extremely variable, possibly more so than conditions of adult employment.[32] The conflicting results of the studies of Mamdani [1972] on the one hand, and of Dasgupta [1978] and Vlasoff [1979] on the other, should serve as a good warning in this respect.[33] A child may be an asset in one village but a burden in the next. It may be recalled that Mamdani's characterisation of peasant rationality is derived from conditions in one Indian village.[34] The theory that the poor produce a lot of children because they are poor—Malthus turned upside down—cannot be easily validated in terms of class behaviour, for data would generally show lower levels of fertility among the poor and (or) absence of controlled fertility within the richer peasant classes, irrespective of social conditions favouring high fertility.

Recent years have seen the beginnings of a fertility decline in India, as well as in some other countries of the third world. Clearly, the discussion in this paper does not apply to this period.

Evidence for earlier times does not unambiguously show a higher level of fertility among the poorer rural classes as compared to the rich. To the extent that such a higher level is a logical corollary of theories based explicitly (as in the case of purely economic theories) or implicitly (as in the case of theories set out in terms of peasant rationality) on the economic value of children, theories are either redundant or require a drastic revision. Observed differences are not inconsistent with features of uncontrolled fertility. This is not to deny that fertility variations are modified to a limited extent by socially-imposed controls. To understand these controls and the demographic structures they have evolved, it is necessary to take into account class differences among the peasantry. It is equally important to study the influence of chance factors which produce a considerable variation in individual family size: these factors can swamp systematic, i e, theoretically postulated, causation and lead to gross misinterpretation of data, and hence cannot be ignored in useful theory.

NOTES

1 See, for example Clark [1970], Berkner and Mendels [1978], van der Walle [1978] and Cassen [1978].

2 Becker [1960] presents a standard version of the economic theory of fertility. The theory has since been honed to perfection by him and others—too many in number to be listed. Radical theories are set out by Mamdani [1972 and 1976] and Macfarlane [1978], among others. Writing about Mamdani's work, Hawthorn [1978] says, "...despite its unconventional method and its moral and intellectual distance from the University of Chicago and the micro-economic models of fertility developed there and elsewhere in the United States, it did lend some weight to the arguments behind such models...". This assessment is correct, for, economic value of children plays the central role in Mamdani's theory.

3 See, for example, Easterlin [1978]. He says that economic analysis of fertility is "a notably sexless subject" and adds: "Without reference to sexual intercourse one is hard put to explain why households would engage in the 'production' of children once the desired number is reached and consequently why excess fertility would ever occur" (p 59).

We must point out that Malthus' approach was not sexless. In fact, 'the passion between the sexes' looms large in his theory. The two postulates from which Malthusian theory was built up are: "First, that food is necessary to the existence of man", and "Secondly, that the passion between the sexes is necessary, and will remain nearly in its present state" These he describes as "fixed laws of nature", Malthus [1798].

4 Malthus restricted the wisdom to limit family size to the 'educated classes', "who had both the wit to perceive the limits to their ability to keep large

families and the self-discipline to control sexual desire. The poor were improvident— the more they prospered, the more they would add to their numbers" [Cassen 1978, p 10]. Malthus opposed the 'poor laws' on these grounds. Perhaps he thought that doles cannot help the poor in getting educated and learning to control sexual desire.

5 News about family planning and compulsory sterilisation was censored during the emergency. We can get some idea of what happened from *Economic and Political Weekly*: 'Drastic Solutions', editorial note, March 27 1976; 'Dangers of Compulsions' by a Special Correspondent, May 22, 1976; 'Clippings' (from published news), March 5, 1977. The *Economic and Political Weekly* featured several articles on the subject: see for example, Banerji [1979], Kamat [1980,] and Visaria [1976].

A large number of books about the emergency describe the violence against the poor; a few examples: Selbourne [1977], Mankekar and Mankekar [1977,] and Lewis [1978].

6 For a number of studies relating to pre-industrial France and England, see, Laslett and Wall [1972]. Russian data are presented and analysed in Shanin [1972]. A discussion of this universal correlation is given in Krishnaji [1980].

7 Clark [1970].

8 The data refer to the National Sample Survey. For discussion see Krishnaji [1984].

9 For studies on western Europe, 1200-1800, as well as theoretical generalisations, see, Goody et al [1976]. Some further discussion on western Europe is in Berkner and Mendels [1978]. 'Family formation' in transitional societies is discussed in Levine [1977].

10 Historical data of total fertilities for different countries are given in Clark [1970, p 180]. See, also, Kumar [1971] for a comparison of current Indian fertility with that of Sweden and Finland in the late 19th century. These data, despite possible inaccuracies in older estimates, prompt the question why Indian fertilities are low (and not high). Clark says (p 28), "In comparison with Europeans not restricting conception, Asians definitely show lower fertilities. They appear to have a higher proportion of infecundable women at any given age, and also a lower rate of fecundability in marriage. The figures for India are brought lower still by the Hindu religious prohibition on the re-marriage of widows" and continues, "Total fertilities are at their lowest in Africa. We have already seen some information which gives some idea of the cause. There appear to be quite high proportions of total infecundability... and probably many more couples whose fecundability is reduced by disease.'

11 See the references cited in note 9 above. Two further points need to be noted in this context. There were possible differences between lord and serf with respect to inheritance customs; but ultimately manorial law prevailed, with the serfs lacking real freedom to decide how rights could be passed on. Secondly, during at least the initial phase of transition (industrialisation) the marriage patterns did not change much; those who moved to towns and became apprentices and so on had in theory the freedom to marry without inheriting land rights but in reality could not marry until they became independent craftsmen.

12 This idea has been extended to urban family structures in a more general setting [Singer 1968].

13 Clark's reference to the post-1940 period is full of meaning. During the immediate post-second world war years many European countries as well as the US experienced a 'baby-boom'. Friedan [1963] argues that it was connected to the 'women-back-to-the-home' movement designed to support expanding markets of consumer appliances, etc. What it suggests quite convincingly is that even in the presence of controlled (social) fertility the middle and richer classes can deliberately choose to have a large number of children.

14 Among the data sets there is one on Poland, in which the positive association between landholding and total fertility is clearly established. The data cover mothers born between 1855 and 1929, arranged in three groups which, to some extent, show the reversal of poor-rich differences during 1915-29.

15 Parkes [1976] says, "It is well known that the age at puberty in Europe and United States has decreased substantially in modern times. A figure of 1 year every 10 years is sometimes quoted, but this alarming estimate is much exaggerated. More likely, the age at menarche has decreased by about 4 years in the last century." We must add that most of the decline is likely to have taken place during the early part of this century. Studies in Bangladesh show that menarche tends to be delayed among the malnourished [Chowdhury et al 1977].

16 In studying demographic differentials, demographers often talk about total fertility or completed family size related to the hypothetically completed reproductive period. One index which takes into account mortality differences is the net reproductive rate, but this is employed more in the context of rates of population growth than of fertility differences.

17 "The average period (amenorrhoea) is quite long (in India), about 12 months or more, due to widespread practice of breast feeding... this factor alone may account for a substantial part of fertility differentials by regions and socio-economic groups in India. It is one of the factors responsible for longer birth interval among Indian women when compared with western women," says Jain [1975, p 117], reviewing the literature. And further (p 185), "Average birth interval is over 30 months, which is large compared to that found in other societies, in the absence of contraception. It is considered that this is mainly due to the widespread practice of prolonged breast feeding." For data on other developing countries, see, Mosley et al [1977]; a useful review of old French studies on the subject is included in the work of Mondot-Barnard [1977] which refers to African data. For Bangladesh studies, see Huffman et al [1978; 1980].

18 Jain [1975] writes, "The view has been advanced that persistent malnutrition excites sexual instinct, which according to Nag is contradicted by a thorough study conducted at the University of Minnesota during World War II of the effects of starvation on men. This study revealed that the first effects of starvation on the volunteering men was a loss of all interest in sex. Nag cites the findings of a Bombay study showing that women with higher levels of nutrition had a higher average frequency of coitus and also higher fertility." The reference is to Nag [1972].

Some recent data collected in Bangladesh reveal that frequency of sexual intercourse is the lowest among the poorer classes [Maloney et al, 1981, p 143]: "The highest frequency is among those in 'service', 3.4 times a week, those in modern occupations 3.2 times, teachers 3.2 times, and businessmen 3.0 times. However, day labourers, servants, fishers and artisans do it 2.8 to 3.0 times. Cultivators have middling rank, 2.4 times. Those in traditionally low occupations do it only 2 times: they are poorer...". Further (p 144), "the poorest people (in terms of income) seem to have less coitus," but this is shown "more clearly for women than for men".

19 Parkes [1976] discusses the 'comfort factor' mainly in relation to climate and weather.

20 An interesting descriptive account of social beliefs and norms on sex practice in Bangladesh is given in Maloney et al [1981].

21 We shall refrain from listing in detail the findings of these different studies since the reviews (referred to) are fairly exhaustive in this respect. The conclusions of the reviewers are: "In general, it appears that fertility differentials due to income are small" [Jain 1975, p 143]; and, "In rural areas it is found that the number of children ever born to married women increased with increase in economic status but the differences were not large" [Hussain 1970, pp 144-45].

22 See for example Report No 186, National Sample Survey, for the 19th round (1964-65) data.

23 The argument (stated by Davis and others) that joint families promote high fertility is quite appealing: child-rearing in such families is shared (releasing mothers for more productive work); couples need not wholly support themselves and hence marriage tends to be early; brides are strangers until they produce a baby; stigma against barrenness promotes demand for children; and so on.

Nag reviewing the Indian data concludes that fertility in nuclear families tends to be higher than that in joint families, for the majority of age groups and all groups combined. He further gives numerical data which show that coital frequency for simple families is consistently higher, for each of the six age groups he considers, when compared with that of joint families. One of the reasons he cites is the lack of privacy in joint households.

Another reviewer, Jain [1975, p 151], says, "Most of the empirical studies show that the average number of children born, when standardised for the mother's age or duration of marriage, is lower for a joint family."

24 The hypothesis that nuclearisation of families is associated with proletarianisation is discussed in Krishnaji [1980]. For survey data relating to some Mysore (Karnataka) villages, see Scarlett Epstein [1973]. "Landless families and those with insignificant holdings have for the most part remained elementary units," she says after revisiting the villages, "...By contrast all of the ...magnates, who were already the wealthiest in 1955 (when the villages were first surveyed) live now in joint families... it is clear that magnates fully realise the economies of scale to be derived by living in joint families."

25 Among the latest reviews are those by Cassen [1978] and Chaudhury [1982].

26 Mueller [1976], among others, argues that the net 'returns' from children in peasant societies are negative.

27 Rao [1976] considers class differences, recognising explicitly that they in-

fluence fertility behaviour. His conclusion is that fertility motives can be expected to be the highest among 'peasants and petit bourgeoisie'. Both 'workers' and 'capitalist farmers' are categorised separately in his theoretical framework.

28 The literature is reviewed exhaustively in Chaudhury [1982]. However, to illustrate the opposite point, let us refer to a couple of examples. Repetto [1972] shows that families lacking sons or with a high proportion of daughters tend, other things being equal, to have fewer children, while those with a high proportion of sons tend to have more children. His data refer to Lucknow (urban), Delhi (rural), Bangladesh (rural and urban) and Morocco (rural and urban).

Balakrishnan [1978] referring to some rural and semi-urban areas of Costa Rica, Colombia and Mexico, concludes from data that they do not support the replacement hypothesis. He says, "Women at any parity seem to exhibit higher subsequent fertility when they have experienced child loss. However, this is largely a function of exposure time. These women had their early births at a younger age and were older at the time of the survey than women who experienced no child mortality. Controls for these factors largely eliminate the differences".

29 Chaudhury [1982], chapter 6.

30 Ibid.

31 Indeed, some couples (among the poor as well as the rich) will remain childless, while others will see all their children die and yet others, despite poverty, experience no child loss and have to cope with large numbers of surviving children.

32 The difficulties in analysing fertility variations in relation to levels of unemployment are explained by Reddy [1979]. Some of these difficulties arise from the confusion in theory between familial and social conditions. An example: "In the Indian context, with its high level of unemployment, there is... a 'paradox of family size': the smaller the chances of employment for young men, the greater the incentive for individual parents to produce more sons, so as to increase their own chance of ensuring that at least one of their sons earns a regular income. The cumulative effect of individual parents each wanting to increase their own chances of finding employment for at least one of their offspring, inevitably results in reducing the overall chance even further. This may account for the vicious circle of large families suffering extreme poverty, which in turn encourages them to have many children which keeps them poor" [Epstein 1975].

We must add, in accordance with Reddy's analysis, that if 'rational' strategies are defeated by external, social conditions, families must learn from social experience. Probably they do. What is perhaps wrong is the ascribed 'rationality'.

33 Dasgupta, surveying Rampur, a village near Delhi, says, "Mamdani's conclusions that high fertility is economically rational... do not apply in the context of Rampur." The landless in Rampur are faced with very limited possibilities of productive work. Vlasoff says, "economic opportunities in the village were so limited that few older sons became fully productive unless they were fortunate enough to find urban employment..."; "...Contrary to recent theories, families with greater demand for labour including poor

households received no more and in some comparisons fewer benefits from the children than did other classes," and further, "the common sense view of young children as 'poor man's capital' is not accurate. The crucial limiting factors...appear to be employment opportunities and unemployment."

34 See, in this context, Mamdani [1976] wherein he examines the role of the family in the underdeveloped third world: relations remain rigid and hierarchical and the head of the family exercises absolute control and parents enjoy the fruits of their children's labour (shades of Caldwell's [1968] theory), in contrast to developed capitalism where family is no longer the unit of production (but only of consumption and procreation).

For credibility, Mamdani's theory requires a much bigger data base than he has so far provided. What is probably true in Khanna, Punjab, may, if generalised, be no more than a homily.

REFERENCES

Balakrishnan, T R [1978], 'Effects of Child Mortality on Subsequent Fertility of Women in Some Rural and Semi-Urban Areas of Certain Latin American Countries', *Population Studies*, 32, pp 135-45.

Banerji, D [1979], 'What Next in Family Welfare?' *Economic and Political Weekly*, March 19, pp 876-77.

Becker, G S [1960], 'An Economic Analysis of Fertility' in *Demographic and Economic Change in Developed Countries*. NBER, Princeton, pp 209-13.

Berkner, Lutz K and Mendels, Franklin F [1978], 'Inheritance Systems, Family Structure, and Demographic Patterns in Western Europe, 1700-1900' in Charles Tilly (ed), *'Historical Studies of Changing Fertility'*, Princeton University Press, pp 209-23.

Blake, Judith [1968], 'Are Babies Consumer Durables? A Critique of the Economic Theory of Reproductive Motivation', *Population Studies*, 22, pp 5-25.

Caldwell, John C [1968], *Population Growth and Family Change in Africa*, New York Humanities Press.

Cassen, R H [1978], *India, Population Economy and Society*, Macmillan.

Chaudhury, Rafiqul Huda [1982], *Social Aspects of Fertility*, Vikas, New Delhi.

Chowdhury, A K M Allauddin et al [1977], 'Malnutrition, Menarche, and Marriage in Rural Bangladesh', *Social Biology*, 24, pp 316-25.

Clark, Colin [1970], *Population Growth and Land Use*, Macmillan.

Dasgupta, Monica [1978], 'Production Relations and Population: Rampur', *Journal of Development Studies*, Vol XIV, pp 177-85.

Davis, K [1957], 'Institutional Patterns Favouring High Fertility in Underdeveloped Areas' in Lyle W Shannon (ed), *Underdeveloped Areas*, Harper and Brothers, New York.

Easterlin, Richard A [1978], 'The Economics and Sociology of Fertility: A Synthesis' in Charles Tilly (ed), *Historical Studies of Changing Fertility*, Princeton University Press, pp 57-133.

Engels, F [1884], *The Origin of Family, Private Property and the State*, Progress Publishers, Moscow (seventh printing: 1968).

Epstein, T Scarlett [1973], *South India: Yesterday, Today and Tomorrow*, Macmillan, London.

–[1975], 'Population Growth and Its Social Dimensions' in T Scarlett Epstein and Darrel Jackson (eds), *The Paradox of Poverty,*, Macmillan.

Economic and Political Weekly, issues dated March 27, 1976; May 22, 1976; and March 5, 1977.

Friedan, Betty [1963], *The Feminine Mystique*, 11th printing (1967), Dell, New York.

Goody, Jack [1976], *Production and Reproduction: A Comparative Study of the Domestic Domain*, Cambridge University Press.

Goody, Jack et al (eds) [1976], *Family and Inheritance: Rural Society in Western Europe, 1200-1800*, Cambridge University Press.

Hajnal, John [1965], 'European Marriage Patterns in Perspective' in David V Glass and D E C Eversley (eds), *Population in History*, Aldine, Chicago, pp 101-46.

Hawthorn, Geoffrey [1978], 'Introduction' to the Special Issue on Population and Development, *Journal of Development Studies*, 14, pp 1-21.

Huffman, Sandra L et al [1978], 'Nutrition and Post-Partum Amenorrhoea in Rural Bangladesh', *Population Studies*, 32, pp 251-59.

—[1980], 'Breastfeeding Practices in Rural Bangladesh', *The American Journal of Clinical Nutrition*, 33, pp 144-54.

Hussain, I Z [1970], *State and Status of Demographic Research in the Country*, Lucknow University.

Jain, S P [1975], *Demography: A Status Study on Population Research*, Vol II, Tata McGraw Hill.

Kamat, A R [1980], 'Quality and Control of India's Population', *Economic and Political Weekly*, March 29, pp 635-37.

Krishnaji, N [1980], 'Agrarian Structure and Family Formation: A Tentative Hypothesis', *Economic and Political Weekly*, Review of Agriculture, March 29, pp A38-A43.

—[1984], 'Family Size, Levels of Living and Differential Mortality in Rural India—Some Paradoxes', *Economic and Political Weekly*, pp 248-58.

Krishnan, T N [1976], 'Demographic Transition in Kerala: Facts and Factors', *Economic and Political Weekly*, pp 1203-24.

Kumar, Joginder [1971], 'A Comparison between Current Indian Fertility and Late 19th Century Swedish and Finnish Fertility', *Population Studies*, 25, pp 269-80.

Laslett, Peter and Wall, Richard (eds) [1972], *Household and Family in Past Time*, Cambridge University Press.

Levine, David [1977], *Family Formation in an Age of Nascent Capitalism*, Academic Press, New York.

Lewis, Primila [1978], *Reason Wounded*, Vikas, New Delhi.

Lorimer, Frank [1954], *Culture and Human Fertility*, UNESCO, Paris.

Macfarlane, Alan [1978], 'Modes of Reproduction', *Journal of Development Studies*, pp 100-19.

Maloney, Clarence et al [1981], *Beliefs and Fertility in Bangladesh*, International Centre for Diarrhoeal Disease Research, Dacca.

Malthus, Thomas Robert [1798], *First Essay on Population*, Macmillan, New York, 1966 edition.

Mamdani, Mahmood [1972], *The Myth of Population Control,* Monthly Review Press, New York and London.

—[1976], 'The Ideology of Population Control', *Economic and Political Weekly,* Special Number, pp 1141-48.

Mankekar, D R and Mankekar, Kamla [1977], *Decline and Fall of Indira Gandhi,* Vision Books.

Mondot-Barnard, Jacqueline M [1977,] *Relationship between Fertility, Child Mortality and Nutrition,* Development Centre of OECD, Paris.

Mosley, W H et al [1977], 'Interactions of Contraception and Breast-feeding in Developing Countries', *J Biosoc-Sci, Suppl,* 4, pp 93-111.

Mueller, Eva [1976], 'The Economic Value of Children in Peasant Agriculture' in Ronald G Ridker (ed), *Population and Development: The Search for Selective Interventions,* Johns Hopkins University Press, Baltimore.

Nag, Moni [1965], 'Family Type and Fertility' in *Papers Contributed by Indian Authors to the World Population Conference, Belgrade, Yugoslavia,* Office of the Registrar General, pp 131-38.

—[1972], 'Sex, Culture and Human Fertility', *Current Anthropology,* 13, pp 231-20.

National Sample Survey, Report No 186.

Panikar, P G K et al [1978], *Population Growth and Agricultural Development—A Case Study of Kerala,* FAO, Rome.

Parkes, Alan S [1976], *Patterns of Sexuality and Reproduction,* Oxford University Press.

Rao, S K [1976], 'Population Growth and Economic Development—A Counter Argument', *Economic Political Weekly,* Special Number, pp 1149-58.

Reddy, C Rammanohar [1979], 'Household Size and Unemployment in Rural India: A Cross-Sectional Analysis', unpublished MPhil thesis, CDS, Trivandrum.

Repetto, Robert [1972], 'Son Preference and Fertility Behaviour in Developing Countries', *Studies in Family Planning,* 3, p 70 ff.

Selbourne, David [1977], *An Eye to India,* Penguin.

Shanin, Teodor [1972], *The Awkward Class,* Cambridge University Press.

Singer, M B [1968], 'The Indian Joint Family in Modern Industry' in M Singer and B S Cohn (eds), *Structure and Change in Indian Society,* Aldine, Chicago, pp 423-54.

Tilly, Charles [1978], *Historical Studies of Changing Fertility,* Princeton University Press.

Visaria, Pravin [1976], 'Recent Trends in Population Policy', *Economic and Political Weekly,* Special Number, pp 1187-02.

Vlasoff, M [1979], 'Labour Demand and Economic Utility of Children: A Case Study in Rural India', *Population Studies,* 33, pp 415-28.

van Der Walle, Etienne [1978], 'Alone in France: The French Fertility Decline until 1850' in Charles Tilly (ed), *Historical Studies of Changing Fertility,* Princeton.

8

Agrarian Structure and Family Formation

A Tentative Hypothesis

THIS paper is an attempt to formulate hypotheses which relate characteristics of family formation to the agrarian structure under transition. The focus of current research on the subject is mainly on family size and one of its determinants, viz, fertility. Hypotheses usually investigated in this context refer to fertility differences among different socio-economic groups and are cast in terms of the economic rationale of large or small families. The aim of such research is to discover why some couples adopt family planning practices while others do not. This kind of research is of course useful to the policy-maker who is concerned with measures for reducing overall fertility; but it is insufficient for understanding family size dynamics for, apart from fertility, two other factors, viz, mortality and partitioning (which gives rise to new families), also play a crucial role in determining the size of the family. Large families could be large simply because they have remained undivided. For understanding family size variations it is necessary thus to study the phenomenon of partitioning. This paper is restricted in scope to differentials in rates of partitioning among households belonging to different agrarian classes. The hypotheses are concerned with the economic rationale of partitioning or resistance to it and hence with the advantages and disadvantages springing from market forces, specific to different classes, which can arrest or promote partitioning. Since no hypotheses are advanced here on rates of fertility and mortality the paper must be regarded as merely a first step—but a necessary one—towards a theory of the determination of family size.

The agrarian structure we are concerned with here is one which is associated with developing capitalist relations and has agricultural labourers and poor peasants at one extreme and rich peasants and capitalist farmers at the other. Let us consider first agricultural labourers and poor peasants. They are usually involved in the markets mainly as sellers of labour power and buyers of wage goods, and only to a limited extent as sellers of agricultural produce. The labour market, characterised by a high degree of unemployment, does not confer any special advantage to a joint family (loosely defined); on the other hand, uncertainty of finding work, especially in the lean seasons, may make intra-family income sharing difficult for joint families. With regard to buying of commodities and the limited selling of agricultural produce no gains accrue to undivided households. There are thus no economic forces which tend to arrest partitioning among such households. Moreover, low levels of expectation of life among them induce a faster-than-average time-rate of reproduction (of households) which is realised partly through early marriage. The latter reinforces the tendency towards partitioning. For 'attached' labour households, however, because of lack of freedom to partition or of security of employment that such attachment entails, forces working against partitioning may operate to a limited extent.

On the other hand, in rich peasant and capitalist farmer households, wherein economic activity is diversified, work—both on-farm and off-farm—is mainly supervisory in nature and is associated with not only cultivation but also the processing and marketing of produce. There are thus distinct economic advantages which a joint family with a large number of adults enjoys compared to a nuclear family (with more or less children). Besides, the involvement of such households in trade and transport confers economic advantages in buying (of inputs) and selling (of output) and hence constitutes a disincentive to partitioning. Apart from all this, the difficulties of liquidation of indivisible assets (which may be necessary for partitioning the household) also tend to slow down the process of partitioning. What is important in this context is not merely the relationship between 'cumulation of economic advantage' based on land ownership and accumulation which is external to the household but also the diversification of economic activity within the household itself. Salary earnings can play an important role in bringing about such diversification.

We may thus hypothesise that rates of partitioning will be high among agricultural labourer and poor peasant households and low among rich peasant and capitalist farmer households. Apart from these two categories of households we need to consider middle peasants. The middle peasantry is not a homogeneous category, especially with respect to the nature and extent of their market involvement. The category thus contains some who resemble poor peasants and some who resemble rich peasants in relation to the markets. We may therefore expect rates of partitioning among middle peasants to lie between those of the rich and the poor peasants.

To explain observed variations in the average size of the household among different agrarian classes in any specific region of the country much more than the above hypotheses is needed; apart from hypotheses concerning fertility and mortality, a consideration of family size dynamics under pre-capitalist relations, which is essential for the purpose, is outside the scope of this note. If any 'explanation' is sought after (or can be suggested by the hypotheses) it is for the universally observed fact that agricultural labour households have the smallest average size among all agrarian households. While morbidity and mortality rates among them (and poor households in general) are expected to be high and these can partly explain the smallness in family size, it is generally believed that levels of fertility among the poor are also high. This belief underlies the contemporary politics of family planning which does not directly concern us here. What we are interested in is the possibility of the tendency towards 'nucleation' being more prominent among labouring households than among households owning large landholdings; such a tendency will reinforce the effects of high mortality and counteract the possibly high fertility levels to keep average family size low.

This bring us to an important qualification to our hypotheses which makes them rather specific to the contemporary Indian context. The association between industrialisation and 'nucleation' of families was a feature of the development of capitalism, especially in its later stages, in the west. The pattern of capitalist development in India, especially in rural areas, differs from the western experience in many respects. Among these the most important for us here is the fact that land is still the principal asset in rural areas. Investment finds its way either directly into activities related to land improvement and productivity or into areas related to the marketing of commercial produce such as trade and transport. Since land thus plays a central role in the process of investment, other things remaining the same, its indivisibility in family holdings gets strengthened. The obvious implication is that joint families need not disappear automatically with the rise of capitalism. Ramakrishna Mukherjee's study, *West Bengal Family Structures, 1946-66,* which goes into this question, is quite appropriately subtitled *An Example of Viability of Joint Family.* We shall refer to this study again later.

Let us now comment briefly on the relationship between rural-urban migration and the tendency towards nucleation of families. Although a satisfactory analysis of this relationship cannot be attempted here, we may note at once that ownership of land is one of its crucial governing factors. The seasonal migration of agricultural workers and peasants during periods when work is not available in rural areas is well known. Apart from this, while migration may often mean a final break with rural parent families in the case of landless households, such may not be the case for families owning land. This can be expected to be true especially in the case of families owning large landholdings. In such cases while the family is sub-divided in a physical sense, its different branches may continue to invest jointly in activities allied to agriculture and centred on the family holding. This may sound speculative in the absence of the relevant data but we mention it here so as to highlight the need to consider the role of families as units of investment and not merely as units of production and consumption.

In sum, we may hypothesise that nucleation of families, while being associated with capitalist development in general, need not affect all agrarian classes uniformly. The processes of dispossession and pauperisation of the peasantry can promote nucleation at one end of the peasant spectrum while consolidating the joint family system (or rather, retarding its decay) at the other, especially when ownership of land remains the principal means of acquiring wealth.

II

Available data throw some light on the hypotheses. Before discussing the implications, in this respect, of some well known empirical observations it is necessary first to sort out some methodological issues.

What we generally have are survey data relating to average household size among different population groups. In sample surveys a household is usually defined as a group of people living under the same roof and sharing their meals from the same kitchen. Household data based on surveys are thus not quite suitable for investigating our hypotheses since we are interested in families as landowning units.[1] A more serious problem is the lack of data on rates of partitioning, fertility and mortality of households classified by size of landholdings. For this reason we shall be satisfied with seeing whether anything can at all be indirectly inferred on rates of partitioning from household size statistics and not attempt to obtain conclusive results on patterns of partitioning.

For a closed population, the average size of household is determined in the long run, by the birth, death and partitioning rates. Household size increases with the birth rate and decreases as the death rate increases. Partitioning reduces the average household size since a partitioned household gives rise to two or more households of smaller size. More precisely, the rate of increase in the average household size can be shown to be $(b-d-p)/(1+p)$ where b, d and p are the birth, death and partitioning rates respectively.[2] Accordingly, when we look at empirical correlations involving household size we can indirectly infer something about the rates of partitioning provided we have some knowledge about the rate of natural increase $(b-d)$. This is possible, however, only if there are reasons to believe that the correlations are the result of long-run tendencies (since in the long run it is the rates of increase and not the initial levels which determine the variations in the average size). A second issue relates to the relationship between rates of birth and mortality and the age distribution of the population. It is well known in demographic theory that age distributions are more sensitive (by a factor of 10 to 1 or more) to birth rates than to mortality rates. If one population has a significantly higher proportion of children than in another, it is a reasonable inference that the first population has higher rates of birth and natural increase.[3] Let us now turn to the empirical observations.

(1) Among agricultural labour households those with land have higher average size than those without land. This holds among both the 'casual' and 'attached' labour households. Among agricultural labour households without land, attached households have higher average size than casual labour households.

These relationships (readily verifiable on the basis of various agricultural labour enquiries) appear to have a universal validity over space and time and hence we must look for an explanation in the rate structure, i e, b, d and p. The age distributions among the above different categories look practically alike. One can thus infer that while the birth and death rates do not differ radically among these classes (there are no a priori reasons for believing that they may differ), rates of partitioning are lower among those with land; further that among households without land casual labourers partition their households at a rate faster than do the attached labour households. It is quite significant, in this context, that among labour households with land the relationship (with respect to average size) between attached and casual labour households is not unambiguous: in some states one category has the higher average size and in some the other has. Two factors may be at work here: attachment and size of landholding. We may infer that even among agricultural labour households ownership of land influences family formation behaviour.

(2) We now turn to the universally observed positive correlation between the size of landholding (or asset holding or wealth in general) and the size of the household. This can be verified from practically any source of data giving the distribution of land (or assets) among rural households. Because of the universality of the correlation, we must look for an explanation in differentials in birth, death and partitioning rates. The explanation need not, however, be universal, for different configurations of these rates can bring about the correlation. We shall indeed argue that in at least two cases, viz, the Russian data analysed by Shanin[4] and others and the Kerala (and possibly other Indian) data, the rate structures are strikingly dissimilar.

Before we do that it is necessary, however, to clear up a methodological point. Land distribution data do not refer to closed population groups. In particular, newly partitioned households are smaller in size than parent households and constantly move into a lower size-class of landholdings. It can be shown through a simple mathematical model that if the rates of natural increase of population are not widely different among the different size-classes, then even uniform rates of partitioning can, in the long run, produce a positive correlation between size of holding and size of household (since partitioning reduces the size of the household as well as that of landholding at the same time); however, such a possibility would depend on the extent of skewness in the distribution of land as well as the precise magnitudes characterising the rate structure.

But, roughly speaking, if the rates of natural increase decline significantly as the size of holding increases, and the distribution is highly skewed, uniform rates of partitioning cannot systematically lower the average size of household (which has a tendency to be high because of a high rate of natural increase) in the small holdings so as to bring about the positive correlation. At any rate the correlation cannot be unambiguously interpreted without a knowledge of the variations in the birth and death rates.

Bearing the above remarks in mind let us consider the data in Table 1. The changing age distribution indicates that rates of natural increase are higher in the smaller holdings; however, the differences could be narrow. If we are willing to assume that death rates are higher in the small holdings (this appears to be a reasonable assumption) it would follow that birth rates must also be higher. The data would then be consistent with the hypothesis of higher rates of partitioning associated with smaller landholdings. However, the possibility of uniform rates of partitioning bringing about the positive correlation between size of land and household size cannot be wholly ruled out on the basis of these data.

A factor which could make the data more favourable to our

Table 1: Age Composition of Population by Size of Landholdings— Kerala, 1970-71

Size of Operational Holding (Hectares)	Average Size of House- hold	Age-Group (Years)				
		0-15	15-55	55-65	Above 65	Total
		(Per Cent of Population in Size-Group)				
0.04-0.25	5.97	40.42	50.04	8.02	1.52	100.00
0.25-0.50	6.38	40.42	50.13	8.20	1.65	100.00
0.5-1	6.73	40.23	50.70	7.45	1.62	100.00
1-2	7.24	39.22	51.08	8.07	1.62	100.00
2-3	7.39	38.38	52.12	8.29	1.21	100.00
3-4	7.59	36.56	52.96	8.33	2.15	100.00
Above 4	8.38	36.03	52.56	9.19	2.22	100.00

Source: 'The Third Decennial World Agricultural Census, 1970-71', Report for the **Kerala State, Bureau of Economics and Statistics, Kerala.**

hypotheses is the nature and magnitude of land transfer through sale. If we identify the latter with the process of dispossession of poor peasants, mobility in terms of the size of land induced by such sale will be associated, in the short run, with the movement of higher sized households into smaller holdings (in case a poor peasant household is dispossessed of a part of its land; if it is wholly dispossessed it would move into the landless class, in which the average size of household is the least among all agrarian classes) and vice versa. Thus the differentiation process (inducing sale of land) works against the positive correlation in the short run and the persistence of positive correlation can result, especially in periods of considerable land transfer from the poor to the rich, only from higher rates of partitioning in the smaller holdings. However, data relating to land transfer through sale, especially by poor peasants, are lacking. Hence, no firm conclusions emerge from the data we have been discussing. The data are not, however, in conflict with the hypothesis.

The Russian data of the late 19th century present a different pattern: the rates of partitioning rise with the size of landholdings, but surprisingly, so do the rates of birth and natural increase (see Table 2). The data in Table 2 would imply that the proportion of children must have been higher in the larger holdings (in Kerala it is the other way round). Shanin combines these figures with (available) data showing higher rates of partitioning in larger holdings, to buttress Chayanov's life-cycle theory of mobility. However, a critique of Shanin's study by Mark Harrison shows that partitioned households were better off than undivided households (in terms of productive assets) and constituted the base for the emergent rural bourgeoisie.[5]

The differences between the Kerala and Russian cases are of

Table 2: Rates of Natural Increase in Veronezh Gub by Land Held Per Household (Per 1000), 1897

Land Held (Des)	Birth Rate	Death Rate	Natural Increase
Less than 5	51.8	35.0	16.8
5-15	53.8	33.2	20.6
15-25	53.0	28.6	24.4
More than 25	55.8	26.2	29.5

Source: Teodor Shanin, op cit.

great significance to our treatment of the economic rationale of family formation. Since partitioning of households—or rather the ensuing sub-division of landholdings—implies a reduction in the scale of operation, it may appear to go against the economic logic of capitalist development. Higher rates of partitioning among large landholders would then render meaningless any association between family size dynamics and the development of capitalism. Harrison has shown however that this is a superficial interpretation of the Russian data: he has examined in detail and uncovered the capitalist logic underlying the sub-division of large landholdings. The important point is that the same logic, viz, that of profitable investment, can lead to different results in different historical situations. Apart from Harrison's observations we need to note in this context another factor, related to the degree and nature of capitalist development, which accounts for differences such as those between contemporary Kerala and Russia at the turn of the century. In Kerala (and large parts of India in general) land ownership continues to be the principal means of accumulation in the countryside. The corresponding lack of significant industrialisation is associated with low levels of consumption of commodities other than food by labourers and poor peasants on the one hand and the almost exclusive nature of the involvement of the emerging rural bourgeoisie in land-related activities (including trade and transport) on the other. Lenin's data for Russia of the same period bear adequate testimony, in contrast, to both much higher levels of consumption of non-agricultural commodities by the poor and a far higher degree of involvement of the emergent bourgeoisie in rural industries.[6]

For us the differences are important from another point of view however. The positive correlation between family size and wealth can arise out of different demographic configurations. Death rates can be expected to be higher among the poor than among the rich everywhere under all historical situations. The universality need not hold however in respect of the behaviour of rates of birth and partitioning. In Russia the largeness of the family size among the upper sections of the peasantry was maintained in spite of a high degree of partitioning by high birth rates whereas in Kerala (and India in general) it is maintained in spite of possibly low birth rates (as implied by the age distributions which generally show higher proportions of older people and lower

proportions of children among the rich than among the poor)
by low rates of partitioning.

III

Let us now consider some direct evidence on joint families.
Table 3 summarises data relating to a stratified random sample
of 133 households chosen from a village in south Kerala. These
data show that agricultural labour households have the smallest
proportion of joint families (defined as those in which more than
one related couple live); and that this proportion rises with the
size of landholding. The average age of the head of the household
also increases with the size of land (Table 3).

Table 4 gives data relating to 521 households chosen from four
districts of Kerala. They constitute a sub-sample of a larger sample of households surveyed by the Bureau of Economics and
Statistics. These data show that there are no joint families (of
the B or B' type wherein there is more than one related couple
living) in households with holdings below one acre in size. The
proportion of joint families increases with size of holding. The
data also show the existence of joint families in both agricultural
labour and plantation labour households (giving them a higher
average size than among all but the large cultivators). However,
all but four agricultural labour households had land; and among
the plantation labour households the differences between those
with land and those without land are as expected. The existence

*Table 3: Household Size and Related Characteristics—
A Kuttanad Village, 1976*

Category of Household and Size of Land (Acres)	Average Household Size	Average Age of Head (Years)	Proportion of Joint Families (Per Cent)	Total Number of House- holds
Agricultural labour				
Less than 0.10 acre	5.21	45.6	12.12	33
More than 0.10 acre	5.06	47.8	12.50	16
Cultivator households				
Less than 1 acre	5.77	48.4	31.80	22
1-5 acres	5.78	51.6	36.11	36
More than 5 acres	6.00	58.4	38.50	26

Source: Data collected by Joan Mencher and P G K Panikar.

of joint families among agricultural labour households may be partly due to the fact that recent legislation has conferred on them rights to ownership on huts and hutment land. Among plantation labourers it may be due to the type of labour contracts which ensure continuity of employment to the members of the labourer's family. We do not, however, have any direct factual evidence on these issues.

The 1961 Census data on household composition, although not suitable for classification by family types as in Table 4, are in general consistent with the hypothesis that the proportion of joint families rises with the size of landholding. Table 5 gives these data in respect of Kerala. The data for other states exhibit similar patterns and thus whatever can be inferred from these data would hold good for all parts of rural India.

Variations in the household composition across the different landholding groups have the following features:

(1) Heads of households and their spouses constitute as much as 30 per cent of the total population in the lowest size group but only 21 per cent in the highest; this percentage has a pronounced tendency to fall as the size of landholding increases.

(2) The proportion of 'married relations' rises with the size of landholding; this is true in respect of both sons and other relations (presumably brothers). This indicates the association between large holdings and undivided families.

(3) The proportion of 'never married, widowed, divorced or separated' has a mild tendency to decline as the size of landholding increases. This category consists not only of children but also adults who are either unmarried or widowed. As we have seen from Table 1, the proportion of children has a mildly declining tendency as the size of landholding rises; this may imply a rough constancy in the proportion of unmarried adults and widowed, divorced or separated persons.

Let us now briefly consider possible alternative explanations for the empirical observations. The latter—especially, the correlation between the size of the family and wealth—are often interpreted as evidence in support of Chayanov's life-cycle theory. However, a crucial requirement of this theory is the ability of peasant households to acquire additional land, as family size increases, either through communal repartition of land as in Russia or through an emerging land market.[7] Further, since

Table 4: Household Characteristics in a Sample of 521 Households—Kerala, 1977-78

Size of Land-holding (Acres)	Number of Households	Average Size of Land-holding (Acres)	Average Size of House-hold	Percentage Distribution of Households by Types				
				0	A	A'	B	B'
Cultivators								
0-1	43	0.66	4.46	37	54	9	0	0
1-2	83	1.89	5.44	14	51	23	10	2
3 or more	74	5.83	6.32	7	39	32	20	1
Agricultural labour with land	196	0.32	5.45	16	51	19	8	6
Plantation labour without land	89	0.00	5.85	6	66	18	8	2
„ with land	36	1.12	6.41	0	69	8	19	3

Note: Household types are defined with respect to the number of married persons with spouse living in the household (M) and number of persons widowed, divorced or separated (W).

0: M=0 (i e, the household is headed by an unmarried person or one who is widowed, etc).

A: M=2, W=0; A': M=2, W≥1; B: M≥4, W=0; B': M≥4, W≥1.

Table 5: *Composition of Sample Households by Relationship to Head of Family Classified by Size of Land Cultivated—Kerala, 1961*

Size of Holding (Acres)	Average Size of Households	Composition of Population (Per Cent)				
		Heads of Household and Spouses	Married Relations		Never Married, Widowed, Divorced or Separated Persons	Unrelated Persons
			Sons	Others		
Less than 1	5.70	30.7	2.2	6.7	59.9	0.3
1-2.4	6.42	27.9	3.1	7.9	60.2	0.9
2.5-4.9	7.16	25.3	3.7	9.2	59.6	2.2
5-7.4	7.48	24.0	4.1	9.9	58.4	3.6
7.5-9.9	8.00	23.9	3.8	10.9	58.2	4.9
10 or more	8.18	21.9	4.2	10.3	57.5	6.1

Source: *Census of India 1961*, Vol VII, Kerala, Part II-C.

Chayanov considers the peasantry as a homogeneous category, all peasant households at a particular stage of the demographic development of the family must behave alike. Notwithstanding data which show some upward mobility of peasant households in terms of landholding in some parts of India,[8] it is difficult to accept such mobility as the exclusive explanation for the cor-relation between family size and wealth. All historical evidence on land relations in India points unmistakably to a continuous process of pauperisation of the peasantry; the ability of poor peasants surviving on tiny bits of land to acquire additional land (or other assets) remains no more than an unrealistic theoretical possibility. Moreover, the emergence of large landholdings and concentration of land is a complex historical process in which the demographic experience of individual families could not have played a decisive role.

A second, more plausible, explanation for the empirical obser-vations is simply that the rates of mortality are higher among the poor than among the rich: poor people do not in general live long enough to form large joint-family units. This alone may suffice as an explanation but, as we have already noted, differen-tial rates of partitioning (with high rates among the poor) rein-force the effects of differential mortality. In any case, since nuclear units are formed out of large families both among the rich and the poor there is a need to hypothesise on possible differentials in rates of family formation.

IV

Published data based on the agricultural labour enquiries, the National Sample Survey and the Census of India show that the empirical observations we have made in respect of Kerala hold good for other states also. But there are strong a priori grounds for expecting the hypothesis of a relationship between family for-mation and land ownership to be specially valid for Kerala. Among different states Kerala has the highest degree of com-mercial crop production, with food crops (mainly paddy) being allocated roughly only 40 per cent of the total cropped area. However, the degree of industrial development is poor; existing industries mainly relate to the primary processing of the com-mercial produce of agriculture. Besides, the high level of pro-ductivity of land (in value terms) and the scope for its further

increase through investment create an 'urban interest' in land
and a consequent rural-urban nexus in land relations which are
perhaps unparalleled anywhere else in the country.[9] All these
factors contribute to the association between large landholdings
and large family units.

But the 'viability' of the joint family has been noticed even
in West Bengal, an industrially advanced region. Ramakrishna
Mukherjee[10] concludes on the basis of data collected through a
carefully designed survey that the extended family organisation
is the most marked among certain sections of the 'landed gentry' and is least marked among other groups which include 'those
who depend on others in the society for their survival'. Mukherjee
does not, however, consider land ownership, specially in rural
areas, as a possible explanatory variable for the observed
differentials.

This points to the general validity of a process of nucleation
being more pronounced among the poor peasants than among
the rich. It is in this context that the characteristic of land being
the principal means for augmenting wealth assumes importance.
Thus, while it is possible to formulate a fairly general hypothesis
which relates family formation to capitalist development, the
specific features of this development have to be taken into account for understanding family size dynamics. One implication
of this is that it is not possible to generalise the hypotheses we
have discussed in this paper even to all pre-industrial societies
in spite of data which show correlation between family size and
wealth in some of these societies.[11] Indeed, an interesting study
by David Levine shows that in pre-industrial England, in certain rural communities the rise in demand for labour, following
limited mechanisation in the developing industries and the consequent induction of women and children into the labour force,
led not only to increase in fertility but also to unrelated working
class families living together to form joint households as a
response to the disorganisation of domestic work brought about
by the specific nature of industrialisation under way.[12]

NOTES

1 The corresponding data on landholdings usually refer to land owned or
  operated by households defined by the criterion discussed in the text. Thus
  a branch of the family living away (say, in an urban area) but retaining

rights to ownership of land is not regarded as a part of the household in survey statistics.

2 If N and H are the initial population and number of households respectively, they increase to N (1+b−d) and H(1+p). Hence the average household size increases from N/H to N(1+b−d)/H(1+p). The rate of increase is easily derived from this.

3 See Ansley J Coale, *The Growth and Structure of Human Populations: A Mathematical Investigation*, Princeton University Press, 1972 and Nathan Keyfitz, *Applied Mathematical Demography*, John Wiley, 1977.

4 Teodor Shanin, *The Awkward Class*, Cambridge University Press, 1972.

5 See Mark Harrison, 'Resource Allocation and Agrarian Class Formation', *Journal of Peasant Studies*, Vol 4, January 1977.

6 V I Lenin, *Collected Works*, Vol 3, Progress Publishers, Moscow, 1964. Lenin's data on peasant budgets show that in respect of the bottom-most group, i e, the horseless peasantry, food accounts for only about 56 per cent of the total expenditure (p 151). In contrast, for example, even in Punjab where subsistence has in recent years reached higher levels than in other parts of the country, it is estimated (for the year 1970-71) that small cultivators, as a group, spend about 80 per cent of the total on food: among the poorer of the group as well as agricultural labourers the percentage is even higher (National Sample Survey, 25th Round, July 1970-June 1971, 'Tables on Consumer Expenditure, Indebtedness, and Other Economic Aspects in Rural Areas, State: Punjab', mimeographed).

7 In his introduction to Chayanov's work, Daniel Thorner remarks, "where the peasants could not readily buy or take in more land, his theory would have to be seriously modified", see, Daniel Thorner et al (eds), *A V Chayanov on the Theory of Peasant Economy*, Richard D Irwin, 1966.

8 See, for example, D W Attwood, 'Why Some of the Poor Get Richer: Economic Change and Mobility in Rural Western India', *Current Anthropology*, Vol 20, September 1979. For a comment on Attwood, see, N Krishnaji, op cit.

9 For a fuller discussion, see, N Krishnaji, 'Agrarian Relations and the Left Movement in Kerala: A Note on Recent Trends', *Economic and Political Weekly*, March 3, 1979.

10 Ramakrishna Mukherjee, *West Bengal Family Structures, 1946-66*, Macmillan, 1977.

11 For a number of studies relating to pre-industrial France and England, see, Peter Laslett and Richard Wall (eds), *Household and Family in Past Time*, Cambridge University Press, 1972. A study in this volume by Michael Anderson, 'Household Structure and the Industrial Revolution, Mid-Nineteenth Century Preston in Comparative Perspective' gives data from which the proportion of families with married children are derived for different agrarian groups as follows: farmers with 100 acres or more—10 per cent; 20 to 99 acres—7.8 per cent; up to 19 acres—4 per cent; and agricultural labourers—2.3 per cent.

12 David Levine, *Family Formation in an Age of Nascent Capitalism*, New York, Academic Press, 1977.

March 29, 1980.

9

Family Size, Levels of Living and Differential Mortality in Rural India

Some Paradoxes

I
INTRODUCTION

AT a given level of family income the size of the family determines how much is available for spending per head. This simple arithmetic describes the apparent economic rationale of small families. Data show, however, that family size varies considerably from small to big not only as between income classes but also within homogeneous groups such as the class of agricultural labourers.[1]

The relationship between family size and income is two-sided. On the one hand, family size and its composition with respect to children, men and women, determine income. This is especially true in respect of rural areas, the sole concern of this paper, where children and women generally contribute to family income. However, family size cannot be the decisive determinant of income for much depends on landholding and other resources which a household has at its command. This side of the relationship between family size and income is easy enough to understand, and can be analysed, for given distributions of resources, family size and its composition, in terms of differentials in wage rates as between men, women and children and productivity variations across holdings of different size and so on.

On the other hand, the reverse side of the relationship, viz, the dependence of family size on income (or, more generally, on level of living) is less straightforward, and more difficult to analyse. The major difficulty appears to lie in defining an appropriate measure of level of living once we admit that the latter influences demographic variation. That this problem is nontrivial will be seen from the contradictory correlations one obtains by using different indices of levels of living. Per capita income is the index most favoured by economists and demographers. We shall argue in this paper that while it is not without merit as a measure of level of living (for assessing food consumption levels, for example), per capita income is not an appropriate index for analysing demographic differences between groups of households.

The reasons are not far to seek. The demographic destiny of a family is decided only in the long period, whereas, per capita income is subject to much short-run fluctuations: a death or a birth in the family can change per capita income quite drastically. A more suitable index appears to be landholding, or more generally holding of all income-earning assets, for such asset holdings remain fairly stable over long periods and may reflect better the 'economic status' of the family most suitable for demographic analysis.

Here are some paradoxical correlations which lead to the problem of choice just described. Average household size is found to systematically decline as per capita expenditure increases. This correlation appears to hold uniformly across time and space: it is valid not only for the different states of India as well as the country as a whole at different points of time, but essentially also, as Simon Kuznets and Pravin Visaria have shown, for some other countries in Asia and even countries such as the US.[2] The relationship is not wholly arithmetical in content, for one may legitimately ask why on the average a large family cannot earn or spend more (or at least the same) in per capita terms as a small family does.

We shall pay adequate attention to the last question. But what interests us more is the picture painted by other sets of correlations: when households are classified not by per capita expenditure but by total household expenditure or the size of landholding, the correlation is reversed. As total household expenditure or landholding increases, so does the average household size.

One paradox immediately appears if we talk in terms of the 'poor' as differentiated from the 'rich': If we define the poor by a level of per capita expenditure it would follow that the poor have large families on the average; on the other hand, if we define the poor in terms of total family income or expenditure or landholdings, it would follow that the poor have small families. Of special significance in this context is the fact that in rural India agricultural labour households have the smallest average size among all agrarian classes.[3] For this reason a definition of poverty or level of living based on property holdings cannot be dismissed lightly; agricultural labourers and poor peasants, lacking in resources, are always at the bottom end of the economic scale interpreted in a very general sense.

At first sight, it may appear that the paradox constituted by the two correlations discussed above can be easily resolved: as family size increases income derivable from given resources (and, hence, expenditure) does not rise in proportion, for increases in family size generally arise from addition of children whose income-earning and spending propensities are lower than those of adults. The explanation is basically correct but inadequate when applied to heterogeneous data in which both adult-dominant and child-dominant large families are present. Moreover, the explanation is valid only *within* groups of households corresponding roughly to the same resource base: it breaks down when we analyse the differences *between* such groups. For example, when households with large landholdings are compared to agricultural labour households, both the average size of household and per capita expenditure are far higher in the former than in the latter.

The paradox is thus fully articulated when variations in landholdings are specifically brought into the discussion. When households are classified by landholdings, not only the average size of household but also per capita expenditure is found to increase as the size of land rises. This is an important characteristic of all survey data.[4] Here then is a version of what we shall call the family size paradox: household size and per capita expenditure are both positively correlated with the size of land but they are themselves inversely correlated.

Other paradoxes, involving variables such as child-adult ratio, can be stated but they are essentially a part of the family size paradox. A résolution of these paradoxes requires a careful analysis of both sides of the two-sided relationship between family size and income.

If, in this context, we refer to survey data for understanding the nature of the dependence of family size on the level of living, we run into another set of paradoxes, the most important of which is the death rate paradox. In rural areas, death rates—infant mortality rates (IMR) in particular—are found to be positively correlated with per capita expenditure: death rates increase as per capita expenditure rises. This correlation is nonsensical at first sight and requires an explanation if for no other reason than that it is an enduring feature of National Sample Survey (NSS),[5] a decisive source of empirical information. Let us note, however, that this correlation is based on observed variations between averages corresponding to different per capita expenditure groups. A per capita expenditure group conceals much variation within: large families with large landholdings and landless agricultural labour households of small size may belong to the same group.

We shall argue in this paper that the explanation of these two different sets of paradoxes lies in a 'selection bias' resulting from the use of per capita expenditure as a classificatory variable. The bias arises from two-way dependence between pairs of variables such as family size and income and can be readily imagined in respect of households governed by the same set of economic and demographic factors. Within such a group of households corresponding roughly to the same level of family income, all households are, for example, exposed to more or less similar mortality risks, but deaths during fixed periods such as one year (or more), occur in some households but not all. Leaving aside some necessary qualifications for highlighting an important issue, we can see that, within such groups, deaths reduce family size and increase the arithmetically determined per capita expenditure; as a consequence, high death rates may be associated with relatively high levels of per capita expenditure and low levels of family size. The family size and death rate paradoxes are thus easily explained in very simple terms for 'homogeneous' population groups. The analytical conditions under which the correlations emerge need, however, to be laid down with care.

But the explanation is inadequate in respect of a heterogeneous population characterised by wide differentials among sub-groups in both income and demographic rates. For extending the argument to a general population it is necessary to consider also the variations (and correlations) as *between* homogeneous sub-groups into which a whole population can be partitioned. Correlations (or, covariances) between groups need not necessarily be of the same sign as those within groups. The overall correlations depend on relative weights.[6]

This paper is an attempt to resolve the paradoxes concerning family size and related variables taking into account the complexity resulting from inter-group differences. We shall, in the process discuss the adequacy of per capita income as a measure of poverty. Here is a description of what follows: In Section II are presented the data which lead to the different paradoxes. In the next section we attempt at a verbal explanation derived from simple algebraic and statistical models not elaborated here. We revert to data in Section IV and make some concluding remarks in the final section.

II

HOUSEHOLD SIZE AND RELATED STATISTICS

In this section we shall present the data which lead to the paradoxes involving household size. All the correlations we shall discuss in the sequel hold good uniformly across time and space over the rural areas of India. For this reason we shall refer only to one data set in each case as illustrative of the 'general' underlying relationship. The choice of particular data sets is determined by their availability in a form suited for our purposes here.

Tables 1 and 2 present the regressions (i e, the conditional averages) of household size on per capita expenditure (PCE) and total household expenditure (THE) respectively. Table 1 shows that average household size declines as PCE increases, while Table 2 shows that it increases as THE rises. In both the tables households are classified by a level-of-living index and hence the data tell us how family size responds to variations in levels of living.

Interchanging the variables we see in Table 3 that as the size of the household increases, total household expenditure rises but per capita expenditure falls. These are the regressions of levels of living of household size, which are complementary to the regressions in Tables 1 and 2. A simple inference which can be drawn from these data is that the elasticity of total household expenditure (and possibly income) with respect to household size is less than unity.

The complexity introduced by two-way causation can be overcome by bringing into the analysis one or more exogenous variables. This leads us to a search for other factors which influence both family size and family income. Let us consider land-holding as an important variable in this context. Table 4 shows that as the size of land possessed increases so do averages of household size, total household expenditure and *also* per capita expenditure.

We have already seen from Table 3 that as household size increases total household expenditure also increases but not proportionately, so that per capita expenditure decreases. We now see from Table 4, however, that when households are classified by the size of landholding not only family size but also per capita expenditure increases as the size of land rises. *Thus, as between households belonging to different landholding groups, it is no longer true that an increase in family size is associated with a decrease in per capita expenditure.*

Table 1: Average Size (S) of Households Classified by Monthly Per Capita Expenditure (PCE)—Rural India, 1961-62 and 1964-65

PCE (Rs)	S 1961-62	1964-65
0-8	5.54	5.86
8-11	5.76	5.95
11-13	5.61	5.85
13-15	5.53	5.89
15-18	5.57	5.69
18-21	5.19	5.45
21-24	5.02	5.25
24-28	4.91	5.24
28-34	4.72	4.93
34-43	4.31	4.52
43-55	3.97	4.28
55-75	3.49	3.59
Over 75	3.32	3.48
All classes	5.12	5.22

Source: Reports No 135 (1961-62) and 189 (1964-65), National Sample Survey.

Table 2: Average Size (S) of Households Classified by Monthly Total Household Expenditure (THE)—Rural India, 1961-62

THE (Rs)	S	THE (Rs)	S
0-25	1.85	100-150	5.82
25-50	3.08	150-300	7.25
50-100	4.63	Over 300	10.10

Source: Report No 135, National Sample Survey.

Table 3: Average Per Capita Expenditure (PCE) and Total Household Expenditure (THE) of Households Classified by Size of Household—Rural India, 1961-62

Household Size	THE (Rs)	PCE (Rs)
1	45.56	45.56
2	68.76	34.38
3	86.58	28.86
4	101.28	25.32
5	119.30	23.86
6	133.92	22.32
7	159.74	22.82
8	174.32	21.79
9 and above	—	—
All sizes	129.61	24.83

Note : Figures for THE are derived from PCE and household size. PCE for 9 and above is given in the report as 57.61 which appears to be a printing error.

Source: Report No 189, National Sample Survey.

Table 4: Average Household Size (S), Total Household Expenditure (THE) and Per Capita Expenditure (PCE) of Households Possessing Cultivated Land—Rural India, 1955-56

Land Possessed (Acres)	S	THE (Rs)	PCE (Rs)
0	2.60	21.00	16.05
0.01-0.49	4.31	41.37	9.98
0.50-0.99	4.74	46.98	10.76
1.00-1.49	4.71	48.87	10.58
1.50-2.49	4.78	50.82	11.19
2.50-3.49	5.10	57.59	11.64
3.50-4.99	5.56	67.95	12.89
5.00-7.49	5.68	69.96	12.74
7.50-9.99	5.82	72.68	13.40
10.00-14.99	6.48	85.16	13.30
15.00-19.99	6.42	88.12	13.87
20.00-29.99	6.90	95.09	14.62
30.00-49.99	6.93	104.55	15.71
50.00-99.99	7.51	145.08	20.68
100 and above	6.40	125.21	20.98

Note : Figures for the 'landless' class are out of line with the rest of the data. This may be due to the presence in majority in this category of non-agricultural households with high per capita incomes.

Source: Report No 140, National Sample Survey.

Within a given landholding size-group we may, however, expect household (income and) expenditure variation to be narrow: this expectation will be borne out if, for example, landholding contributes more to family income variation than does family size. The outcome will be an inverse relationship between family size and per capita expenditure *within* land size classes. Table 5 gives the results of regression analysis of PCE on landholdings and family size. They show that while the coefficients of landholding are positive, those of family size are negative. The latter imply that when landholding is held constant family size and per capita expenditure are inversely related as expected.

These correlations lead to a variant of the family size paradox stated in the introduction: family size and per capita expenditure are inversely correlated in general but *not so* when reckoned in average terms as between households belonging to different landholding groups.

A consideration of variations in landholding thus brings into focus an important analytical characteristic of the correlation between family size and per capita expenditure: intra-group correlations are negative but inter-group correlations are positive. Landholdings are no doubt important from this point of view but other kinds of grouping can produce the same result. For example, *within* each state of India the correlation is inverse but if we consider state averages as a cross-section, household size and per capita expenditure are positively correlated.

Table 6 gives the NSS estimates of average per capita expenditure and household size for the 27th round for rural areas of

Table 5: Regression of Per Capita Expenditure on Landholding and Household Size—India, 1958-59

Occupation Group	Coefficient of	
	Landholding	Family Size
Farmers	0.422	−1.204
Farm workers	0.355	−1.377
Professional and administrative workers	0.782	−1.523
Others	1.110	−2.338

Note : The analysis is based on the NSS'data for the 14th round (1958-59).
Source: A Vaidyanathan, 'Some Aspects of Living Standards in Rural India' in T N Srinivasan and P K Bardhan (eds), *Poverty and Income Distribution in India*, Statistical Publishing Society, 1974, p 228.

different states. The table presents also the ranks of states in descending order of these two variables. The assertion made at the end of the last paragraph can be verified from these data. At the top of the table are states where averages of both household size and PCE are high while at the bottom are states where both these magnitudes are low;[7] the correlation coefficient between the two variables calculated on the basis of these state-wise averages is 0.61 while the rank correlation is 0.68.

We can readily see the relevance of child-adult ratios to the differences in sign between inter- and intra-group correlations. When increases in family size are associated with increases in the number of children and hence in child-adult ratios we may expect household expenditure to rise less than proportionately since children earn and spend less than adults do. This can be an explanation for the inverse correlation within groups. But as *between* groups (such as those corresponding to classes of land-holdings or to different states in India) increases in average household size may not be similarly associated with increases in child-adult ratios; thus a positive inter-group correlation may

Table 6: Average Household Size (S) and Per Capita Expenditure (PCE)— Rural Areas of States, 1972-73

State	S	PCE (Rs)	S-Rank	PCE-Rank
Haryana	6.33	70.07	1	3
Punjab	5.79	74.62	2	1
Gujarat	5.79	51.70	3	5
Kerala	5.72	42.19	4	8
Karnataka	5.69	44.53	5	7
Rajasthan	5.62	51.98	6	4
Assam	5.58	41.67	7	10
Bihar	5.42	41.20	8	12
West Bengal	5.42	38.45	9	15
Himachal Pradesh	5.39	70.14	10	2
Maharashtra	5.39	41.55	11	11
Jammu and Kashmir	5.34	48.14	12	6
Madhya Pradesh	5.20	40.72	13	13
Uttar Pradesh	5.08	42.12	14	9
Orissa	4.86	34.96	15	17
Andhra Pradesh	4.73	39.79	16	16
Tamil Nadu	4.29	37.70	17	15

Note : The data are based on NSS.
Source: *Sarvekshana*, Vol II, No 3, January 1979.

well arise from differences in household composition with respect to children, men and women.

A more important contributing factor, however, is the difference in the resource base (and hence income-earning capabilities) of households belonging to different groups. Thus even if the 'pure' family size effect on income-earning propensity is roughly the same across landholdings of different size, higher per capita income and expenditure may tend to be associated with larger landholdings since incremental income per person derivable from a larger landholding may outweigh the dampening effect of family size. It is therefore necessary to separate the effects of landholdings and child-adult ratios.

Let us take a brief look at child-adult ratios. NSS data show without exceptions over time and space that the proportion of children in the population of each group declines generally as per capita expenditure rises. The 27th round (1972-73) data for rural India are given in Table 7. These data are usually taken to imply higher rates of fertility among the poor—characterised by low levels of per capita expenditure.

Data classified by total household expenditure are unfortunate-

Table 7: *Children Aged 0-14 Years as Per Cent of Total Population in Each Expenditure Group—Rural India, 1972-73*

Monthly PCE (Rs)	Average Number of Children	Average Household Size	Proportion of Children (Per Cent)
0-13	3.04	5.64	53.90
13-15	3.02	5.79	52.16
15-18	3.03	5.85	51.79
18-21	2.89	5.78	50.00
21-24	2.79	5.74	48.61
24-28	2.61	5.59	46.69
28-34	2.44	5.44	44.85
34-43	2.25	5.31	42.37
43-55	2.06	5.12	40.23
55-75	1.77	4.78	37.03
75-100	1.59	4.51	35.25
100-150	1.42	4.29	33.10
150-200	0.85	3.23	26.32
Above 200	1.14	3.94	28.93
All classes	2.23	5.22	42.72

Source: Same as for Table 6.

ly not available in such abundance. In Table 8 are given the data
for two states, Gujarat and Maharashtra, tabulated by Visaria.

Table 8 shows that when households are grouped according
to levels of total household expenditure the proportion of children
in the group population does not exhibit much variation except
at the extreme ends (especially in the bottom two deciles) where
it is lower than in other groups. Visaria makes the generalisation that the proportion bears an inverted U-shaped relationship with total family expenditure.

We may note incidentally that differentials in the proportion
of children broadly indicate differentials in rates of birth. A crude
inference which can be drawn from these data, therefore, is that
rates of birth of rural population groups classified by levels of
total household expenditure may be roughly constant except in
the extreme end groups.

Since, however, expenditure classifications give rise to the selection bias referred to already, it is analytically more useful to look
at classifications based on landholdings. The data in Table 9 show
that the proportion of children hardly varies across holdings of
different size. This, we may note here, is true only in respect

*Table 8: Children Aged 0-14 Years as Per Cent of Total Population—Rural
Gujarat and Maharashtra, 1972-73*

	Households Ranked by PCE			Households Ranked by THE	
Decile	Gujarat	Maharashtra	Decile	Gujarat	Maharashtra
1	50.5	50.7	1	29.1	28.7
2	48.2	48.9	2	29.8	36.5
3	48.7	46.6	3	43.9	42.0
4	43.0	44.0	4	44.7	42.2
5	42.0	42.8	5	44.7	43.6
6	43.1	41.6	6	45.3	45.3
7	41.1	40.5	7	44.6	45.2
8	38.2	37.5	8	43.5	45.7
9	34.8	36.9	9	43.2	44.1
10	32.1	36.0	10	41.3	44.6

Note : PCE stands for per capita expenditure and THE for total household
expenditure.

Source: Pravin Visaria [October 1980], *Poverty and Living Standards in Asia:
An Overview of the Main Results and Lessons of Selected Household
Surveys*, Living Standards Measurement Study, Working Paper
No 2, World Bank.

of all-India data. Other data sets relating to individual states show that in general, as in the case of data classified by total household expenditure, the proportion of children has a tendency to be somewhat lower at the extreme ends while varying within very narrow limits on the whole. These data strongly suggest lower fertility levels at the extreme ends; but this must remain speculative in the absence of relevant direct data.

Thus far we have considered the data, explicitly or implicitly, in terms of how family size determines the level of living. Let us now look at the reverse side of the relationship. Let us take it as axiomatic that levels of living determine the size of a family at a given point of time. We have discussed the plausibility of certain hypotheses relevant to this determination elsewhere.[8] For our purposes here it suffices, however, to remember that mortality (especially of infants and children), incontestably depends on 'levels of living'.

Definitions of levels of living and poverty have been under debate for a long time, shedding a little light but generating much heat. Definitions can never be wrong but they can be inappropriate for a given purpose or inconsistent in a given context.

Table 9: *Estimated Average Number of Children and Household Size by Size of Household Operational Holdings—All India, 1961-62*

Size of Holding (Acres)	Average Number of Children	Average House-hold Size	Proportion of Children (Per Cent)
0	1.85	4.52	40.9
0-0.49	1.09	2.71	40.2
0.5-0.99	1.91	4.59	41.6
1.0-2.49	1.97	4.77	41.3
2.5-4.99	2.14	5.27	40.6
5.0-7.49	2.41	5.85	41.2
7.5-9.99	2.52	6.13	41.1
10.0-12.49	2.72	6.54	41.6
12.5-14.99	2.78	6.70	41.5
15.0-19.99	2.86	6.91	41.4
20.0-24.99	3.14	7.40	42.4
25.0-29.99	3.04	7.24	42.0
30.0-49.99	3.35	7.84	42.7
50 and above	3.48	8.73	39.7

Source: Report No 144, National Sample Survey, 17th Round, 1961-62.

Table 10 shows that per capita expenditure is not an appropriate measure of level of living for analysing demographic differentials: when households are classified according to levels of this variable, mortality rates (in rural areas) are found to increase *consistently* as PCE increases. Any measure of level of living suitable for demographic analysis must associate low levels of mortality with high levels of living.

NSS reports attribute this 'unexpected' result to under-reporting of deaths among poor, i e, low PCE-households, and possibly high sampling errors in upper PCE groups associated with small sample size. This explanation is false and misleading, as we have suggested elsewhere.[9] For example, if we assume that IMR in the lowest expenditure class is 150 instead of 33 as reported, it would imply that roughly only one out of five actual deaths is reported. This is absurd for these infant deaths refer to traumatic family experience occurring less than a year before the survey.

The correlation can, however, be given the status of a paradox for birth rates do decline as per capita expenditure rises—an 'expected' result if one accepts the latter as an appropriate measure of level of living. The question is whether it is so. These demographic differentials can be looked at also in conjunction with variations in family size. Since family size declines as per capita expenditure increases it follows that a large average family size in low PCE groups is the result of a high birth rate combined

Table 10: Differential Fertility and Mortality Rates in Rural India, 1964-65

Monthly Per Capita Expenditure (Rs)	Birth Rate	Death Rate	Infant Mortality Rate
0-11	44.28	10.03	32.94
11-15	41.25	10.58	71.71
15-21	38.01	13.38	122.29
21-28	36.01	16.06	152.37
28-43	33.16	17.88	153.13
43 and above	32.30	21.81	293.27
All groups	37.32	14.75	127.29

Note : All figures refer to annual rates. The birth and death rates are per 1,000 persons. Infant mortality rates refer to number of infants dying within a year of birth per 1,000 births.

Source: Report No 186, National Sample Survey.

with a low death rate (as data paradoxically show) while a small family size in the upper PCE groups is the product of a low birth rate and an 'unexpected' high death rate.

Put this way the selection bias introduced by reverse causation becomes quite transparent although it certainly merits further analysis. Large families result from high family-specific birth rates and (or) low death rates; when families are reclassified by levels of per capita expenditure large families dominate the bottom PCE groups which then yield low death rates and high birth rates among these groups. All this goes to support our arguments against the use of per capita expenditure for studying certain types of demographic variations.

III

AN EXPLANATION

The paradoxes involve per capita expenditure on the one hand and variables such as family size and death rates on the other. Since we are dealing with data in which levels of per capita expenditure are fixed, let us approach the paradoxes from the angle of dependence of household size and death rates on PCE and levels of living in general.

Given the 'age' of a family at a point of time, its size is determined to a large extent by the number of births and deaths taking place within it. The size of the household is altered also by marriages and migration. The last two factors are no doubt important but let us ignore them for the sake of simplicity in argument. New families spring from old families and therefore the process of partitioning—by means of which 'new' households are created—is relevant to 'age' and hence to the size of household. In the works of Chayanov, Kuznets and a number of others, the age of a family corresponds to the stage in the life-cycle of the family and is sometimes identified by the age of the head of the household.[10]

In demographic work, family size variations are analysed in terms of a slightly different set of components: fertility, mortality, age and marital status of women, etc. In any case, the average size of a given group of households is determined by not only the relevant birth and death rates but also by the distribution of households according to 'age', such a distribution being determined by the rate of new family formation. Demographic rates vary widely between sub-groups of population and hence, for understanding the paradoxes, it is necessary, as suggested in Section I, to classify the population into homogeneous sub-groups within which the demographic determinants can be assumed to be roughly constant.

With such a classification in mind we can set out a simple method for analysing correlations between demographic and economic variables. Variations *between* homogeneous sub-groups arise out of differences in demographic parameters while those *within* sub-groups must be attributed to other (indeterminate) factors since each sub-group is defined by homogeneity with respect to demographic rates. In general, when a population is broken up thus into sub-groups the inter- and intra-group correlations between any given pair of variables need not be of the same sign. Intra-group correlations are based on data relating to households within a sub-group, while inter-group correlations are based on sub-group averages. When inter- and intra-group correlations are of different signs, the sign of the overall correlation is determined both by the absolute magnitudes of the contradictory correlations and the relative 'weights' of the inter and intra components.

How does one partition the population into homogeneous groups? We need for this purpose hypotheses concerning what determines birth, death and family formation rates. Levels of living can be assumed to determine these rates but again the question is: what is the level-of-living index best suited for the purpose? Per capita expenditure must be ruled out in this context for, as we have seen, mortality rates exhibit a nonsensical behaviour when households are classified according to levels of this variable; total household income and expenditure are certainly better candidates but even in the case of these two variables, their dependence on family size—less direct than in the case of per capita expenditure but nevertheless obvious—introduces analytical complications.

In contrast, the size of landholding (and other income earning assets) appears to us as the most appropriate variable from this point of view, given the nature of data at our command. We have argued in an earlier contribution to the subject that at least two demographic determinants, viz, rates of mortality and family formation, depend more on the resource base or property held by families than on per capita incomes in fixed periods such as a year. To recapitulate briefly: In the event of serious illness in a family, its ability to meet medical and other expenses for preventing death can be reasonably assumed to be independent of family size; such an ability would depend more on total income and resources of the household. In the case of family formation it is argued that it is inextricably linked to partitioning of property; there are economic advantages in keeping large property holding intact.

The specific hypothesis suggested in this context is that rates of mortality and partitioning decline as the size of land increases. Given data restrictions, no direct evidence is available to establish the hypothesis conclusively. However, the evidence is unambiguous and overwhelming in favour of strong positive relationships between landholdings on the one hand and (a) family size and (b) proportion of joint families on the other.[11] If we assume that a low average size of family in small holdings is the outcome of high rates of mortality and partitioning and that a high average size of household in large holdings results from both low rates of mortality and a strong propensity for families to remain joint (and hence large), there appears to be no conflict between hypothesis and data.

The property base of fertility variations will be examined from a theoretical standpoint in a separate contribution. The question is whether in reality the poor have higher levels of fertility than the rich have. Even if fertility levels are high among the poor (identified by small holdings), high rates of mortality and family formation appear to offset fertility and keep the average family size in small holdings at a low level. However, a more plausible hypothesis, suggested by the rough constancy (at 40 per cent) in the proportion of children across landholdings of different sizes, is that fertility differences are likely to be narrow howsoever they may be specifically related to landholdings: the possibility is that fertility is somewhat lower at the extreme ends.[12]

In what follows we shall discuss inter- and intra-group correlations with landholdings—a good proxy for asset holdings—as the classificatory variable defining the groups which we shall designate as L-groups. The covariance (or correlation) between any pair of variables can be decomposed into inter- and intra-L-group components. Since each L-group consists of households of different 'age' we can further decompose the intra component into parts representing variations between 'generations' and those within.

The importance of intra-generational variations is obvious but often overlooked or confounded with inter-generational variations.[13] Families of the same generation, governed by similar demographic rates, still vary with respect to family size. A given death (or birth) rate applicable to a group of households distributes actual deaths (births) in such a way that only some but not all households experience deaths (births) in a given year. Since we are not bringing into the discussion non-economic factors which may possibly influence death rates, we shall, of necessity, attribute this differential experience of similarly placed households to indeterminate factors.

Let us now examine the observed correlations with respect to inter- and intra-L-group components.

Family size and per capita expenditure are inversely correlated in general but positively correlated *between* L-groups for not only the total expenditure and household size but also PCE increases as landholding rises.

The interpretation of the positive inter-group correlation is straightforward: with an increase in L both improvement in survival rates and the tendency against partitioning give rise to an increase in the average size of family, the former contributing directly to the increase and the latter through keeping large joint families intact over long periods at the upper end of the landholding scale.

Increases in household (income and) expenditure must be attributed to increases in the average household size as well as those in resource holdings. One implication of the positive inter-group correlation between family size and PCE is thus obvious: of the two variables, family size and landholding, both positively associated with total household expenditure, the latter is in some sense more important. We can express this more precisely in terms of the relevant elasticities—of demographic rates and family income with respect to landholding and of family income with respect to family size—but what interests us more at the moment is the implication that the inverse correlation between family size and PCE must be wholly attributed to the intra-L-group component.

Further, decomposing the latter, we can readily see that the inter-generational component within a given L-group can indeed be positive. This possibility arises from the fact that both very young and very old families can be expected to have, in general, lower child-adult ratios than those among families in the middle-age generations, for, with increasing age of a family, the child-adult ratio keeps rising with the addition of surviving children only to fall ultimately as the children grow into adulthood.[14] With the advantage of low child-adult ratios, families at the extreme ends of the 'age' spectrum may thus have higher per capita incomes. But whether such is actually the case and whether such inter-generational differences can lead to a positive relationship between family size and per capita expenditure would depend not only on how strongly the restriction imposed by the resource holding operates but also on the relative weight of older generations in the household-age composition: it is only the older generations, characterised by both large family size and large family income, which can contribute to a positive correlation; the very young families which also have low child-adult ratios can in any case be expected to be small in size and cannot hence, despite possibly large per capita incomes, contribute to a positive association between household size and PCE.

Since, however, the relative weight of 'old' generations within all but the very large landholdings is unlikely to be very high we may expect a priori the inter-generational component to be negative rather than positive. Questions relating to both the weight of old generations and the actual magnitudes of inter-generational differences in per capita income (within L-groups) are empirical in character, which cannot be settled without reference to data of the right type.

Turning now to the intra-generational component, let us note that family size variations result mainly from births and deaths (of infants, children and adults). A birth always (irrespective of the 'age' of the family) raises both the family size and the child-adult ratio simultaneously while death of an infant or child reduces both these magnitudes. Thus, barring adult deaths, vital events in a family contribute to a positive relationship between family size and child-adult ratio, and hence to an inverse relationship between family size and PCE.

Adult deaths, no doubt, reduce the family size and raise the child-adult ratio and thus contribute to a negative relationship between the two variables; but births as well as infant and child deaths are more frequent than adult deaths in any population and consequently, the net effect of all these vital events is the emergence of a positive association between family size and child-adult ratio (which underlies the inverse relationship between family size and PCE). We may note in passing, moreover, that while an adult death raises the child-adult ratio, it need not simultaneously raise per capita income (corresponding to the reduced family size) for family income itself can be expected to decrease with the loss of an adult. Indeed, given our wholly realistic assumption that income-earning propensities of children are lower, the decrease in family income will be proportionately larger than the reduction in family size.

We thus see that the intra-generational negative association between household size and PCE is brought about wholly by indeterminate factors which distribute vital events unevenly even among families governed by similar demographic rates. This correlation, in turn, gives rise to the inverse association between family size and PCE in the population as a whole by dominating over the positive inter-L-group component. Neat analytical descriptions of underlying conditions can be given but they can be summarised by simply stating that the 'burden' of family size operates only when the landholding is fixed: with a sufficiently large holding, large families can and do enjoy high levels of per capita income.

Let us now turn to the paradoxical positive association between death rates and PCE. As landholding increases so does per capita expenditure but mortality rates fall by our assumption. Hence it follows that the paradox arises solely from the intra-L-group component.

A death reduces the family size and hence in a group of households belonging to the same generation, and subject to similar mortality risks, death rates and 'observed' family size (net of deaths) will tend to be inversely correlated. To put it differently: the posterior probability of observing a death in a large family will be smaller than what it is in a small family, although the prior chances are alike, since observed family size is already influenced by the family-specific event of death or its absence.[15] And since family size and PCE are negatively associated within each generation of an L-group, it follows that the death rate paradox is a direct descendant of the family size paradox.

One can argue along similar lines that, since a birth increases the family size, birth rates and family size will be positively correlated; and this implies an inverse correlation between birth rate and PCE. Hence at least a part of the observed decrease in birth rates (associated with rising PCE) is spurious. Many research workers attribute a differentially high fertility of the poor on the basis of this dubious correlation.

These arguments become quite transparent if intra-generational family size variations are seen from a long-term point of view—within any generation, relatively large families have to be those in which many births and (or) few deaths take place: this statistical artefact underlies the inverse correlation between death rate and family size and the direct relationship between birth rate and family size.

However, we need to modify the argument taking two factors into account: (1) mixture of generations leading to a household-age composition within each L-group and (2) the reference period of reporting vital events, viz, one year (and not the whole span of family life). We shall show that, subject to a condition to be satisfied by the family size distribution, a reclassification of households takes place in such a way that a paradoxical correlation appears between family size (and hence PCE) and death rates.

The underlying logic is simple: reported deaths (births)— even during one year—at a given level of per capita expenditure actually occur in households with a lower (higher) PCE before the death (birth). A death reduces family size and moves the households into a higher PCE group while a birth does exactly the opposite. What proportion these births and deaths form in the reporting group and whether the reclassification would lead to paradoxes, can be shown to depend on the relevant distribution of households by family size.

Before we present the argument it is necessary to point out that the unit of analysis—person or household—plays a significant role in interpreting observed data. Death rates are usually computed on a per-person basis. Now, if death rates per household are constant (for reasons which can be justified) within a group it would follow that larger families would necessarily have a lower death rate per person. Thus constancy of death rates per household is alone adequate as a hypothesis for explaining the death rate paradox. We shall show, however, that 'reclassification' produces the paradox even if we assume that it is death rate per person which has a tendency to be same among families within a L-group—implying a larger number of expected deaths in large families.

In what follows we shall assume for the sake of simplicity in argument that only one vital event, birth or death, can take place in a given year within a family. This implies that at the end of the year the family size remains the same if neither birth nor death takes place and increases (decreases) by unity if there is a birth (death). Let us restrict ourselves to a given L-group in which the per-person birth and death rates are b and d respectively.

Thus if N_r is the number of households of size r at the beginning of the year, rN_r is the population size in the family size group; the expected number of births is rbN_r and those of deaths is rdN_r. Since only one birth can occur per household it follows that the rbN_r households move into the next higher family size group: size(r+1). Similarly rdN_r households move into the next lower family size group: (r−1).

By the same logic the number of deaths reported in family size r group would be $(r+1)dN_{r+1}$; and those of births would be $(r-1) bN_{r-1}$. Likewise, the population in family size class r gets readjusted by the end of the year by the movement of households: it can be shown to be $P_r = rN_r (1-rb-rd) + rbN_{r-1} + rdN_{r+1}$. The reported birth rate which is $b_{(r-1)} N_{r-1}/P_r$ can be shown to increase and the reported death rate which is $d_{(r+1)} N_{r+1}/P_r$ to decrease, as family size r increases, provided N_{r+1}/N_r is a decreasing function of r.

We shall call the latter as the condition for 'paradoxical re classification'. A crude interpretation of the condition can be easily given. N_{r+1}/N_r represents the ratio of number of households in a given family size class to the number in the preceding class and hence measures, in a rough sense, the long-term net rate of growth of family size at the given size.[16] The condition then requires the 'marginal growing propensity' of the family to decline as family size increases. This appears to be a plausible condition, given our understanding about the behaviour of age-specific fertility rates.

In the case of infant mortality rate, the algebra requires some modifications: First, we have to make allowance for the occurrence of more than one event—a birth and a death—for infant deaths refer to deaths before the completion of the first year of life; second, IMR is usually measured as a ratio of deaths to births (and not population); and third, we have to make a distinction between infant and other deaths. A discussion of these complications in algebraic detail is out of place here: it suffices, however, to note that under the same reclassification condition, reported IMR rates can be shown to be inversely correlated with family size.[17]

We thus see that even when birth and death rates per person are the same for all families within a homogeneous group the reported rates depend on the family size observed at the end of the year. When per capita expenditure (inversely related to family size) is used as a classificatory variable, the resulting reclassification produces the paradoxes.

One important lesson is that the observed high levels of fertility in low PCE groups are also spurious and arise in part from the presence of large 'reclassified' families in these groups. The negative association between birth rates and PCE appears to confirm the widespread belief that poverty and high fertility go together. In the light of our discussion it is clear, however, that for testing this belief we cannot rely on PCE classifications.

As in the case of birth rates, high proportions of children in the low PCE groups arise from the predominant presence therein of large families with large numbers of surviving children. Here again the intra-generational component is the most important determinant: this component associates large families with high child-adult ratios over a wide range of family-age. The behaviour of the proportion of children in other kinds of grouping merits further comment however. The evidence indicates that in cases of both total family expenditure and landholdings the proportion exhibits a narrow variation with somewhat lower values at the extreme ends of the classificatory variable. At first sight it may seem that this behaviour can be explained by the 'family life cycle' which associates lower child-adult ratios with the extreme ends of family age. This, indeed, is a possibility but instead of analysing the role of the family cycle in mixed data (relating to different generations) let us speculate on the direct effects of demographic differences in such classifications.

At the upper end of the landholding scale IMR is expected to be low and hence a low child-adult ratio indicates the distinct possibility of low fertility which can be attributed to a set of interrelated variables: age at marriage, proportion of married women (nuptiality) and their age composition. Low rates of family formation, a characteristic of families with large holdings, are realised partly through postponement of marriage which results in an age composition that favours a lower-than-average fertility.

In contrast, child-adult ratios at the bottom end of the land-holding scale can be expected to be influenced to some extent by high rates of infant mortality. A low rate of fertility can also contribute to low child-adult ratios in these groups, as some data indicate. We shall refer to these data in the next section: they show that the proportions of (a) female-headed households and (b) widowed, divorced or separated persons both tend to be high in the bottom groups.

Thus, if we admit an inverted U-shaped fertility curve with respect to levels of living as a possibility, the reasons for lower fertility at the two extreme ends can be seen to be quite different although they can be traced to a common causal variable, viz, property holdings, which accounts for differences in mortality as well as the tendency for families to remain intact.

IV

SOME MORE DATA

In this section we shall attempt to fill some of the gaps in the reasoning outlined thus far by appealing to some suggestive data.

Let us begin by examining inter-generational variations in per capita income which, we admitted, *could* produce a positive association between per capita expenditure and family size even within L-groups. Data classified by age of head of household or some other suitable variable for identifying the family age are not available. For some insights into inter-generational variations we shall use a part of recent survey data relating to Kerala, wherein the age compositions of individual households, with respect to children, adults and old persons, are available. We have divided the families into two groups: households with three adults (above 14 years of age) or less; and with four adults or more. The latter group has generally low child-adult ratios and hence this division into two groups gives us some idea about the influence of generationally-induced child-adult ratios on PCE.

The data in Table 11 show, as all survey data do, that both family size and PCE rise with landholdings. However, within each landholding group adult-dominated large families with far lower proportions of children have in fact lower levels of PCE than those in families with fewer adults. This confirms our inference, drawn from inter-L-group variations, that landholdings constitute by far the most important source of variation in family income. It also follows, at least insofar as these data reflect, that even between generations family size and PCE tend to be inversely associated within L-groups in spite of the advantage of lower child-adult ratios among the older generations.

The data we discussed refer to cultivator households wherein the major source of income is cultivation. However, in respect of agricultural labour households deriving a major part of income from wages, we may expect a priori adult-dominated families to have relatively higher levels of PCE in accordance with the advantage of low child-adult ratios. Even this expectation is not borne out by the data for Kerala, which refer to 200 agricultural labour households (see Table 12).

As in the case of cultivator households higher levels of per capita income among labour households seems to be associated (directly) with the size of minuscule landholding rather than a favourable age composition with lower proportions of children. This certainly is a contra-intuitionistic finding which requires further analysis. We may incidentally point out that there is some

Table 11: Monthly Per Capita Expenditure of Households Classified into Broad Groups by Number of Adults—Sample of Cultivator Households, Kerala, 1977-78

Size of Landholding (Acres)	Family Type		No of Households	Average Household Size	Proportion of Children in Group (Per Cent)	Per Capita Expenditure (Rs)
Less than 1	3 Adults or less	(X)	21	3.76	41.77	63.81
	4 Adults or more	(Y)	16	6.00	20.23	39.83
1 - 2		X	36	4.33	42.95	70.51
		Y	21	6.00	20.63	70.40
2 - 3		X	19	5.24	42.69	85.94
		Y	15	7.58	29.67	69.08
3 and above		X	40	4.80	37.50	111.10
		Y	32	7.97	25.49	83.00

Note: These data relate to a sub-sample of a larger sample of households surveyed by the Bureau of Economics and Statistics, Kerala.

192   *Pauperising Agriculture*

evidence which shows that in Kerala, wnere unemployment is
high, available work is 'rationed' among the labourers.[18] It
would seem, from the data just cited, that such a rationing is
in some way tied to households rather than individuals, for otherwise adult-dominated large families should certainly earn a higher
wage income in per capita terms than those with few adults.

Let us now turn to low child-adult ratios (possibly implying
low levels of fertility) at the extreme ends of the landholding and
family expenditure scales.

We first present the NSS data tabulated by Visaria with respect
to households headed by females (Table 13). The data show that
in the bottom deciles, defined by family expenditure, a high
proportion of households are female-headed—in rural
Maharashtra this proportion is 46 per cent in the lowest decile.
However, female-headed households are fairly evenly distributed
among deciles defined by PCE levels.

To digress a little, Visaria discusses these data in relation to
the question: Are women over-represented among the poor? In
other words: Are households handicapped if they are headed by
women? Visaria's conclusion is: "On the whole, our data provide rather limited confirmation of the hypothesis that women
are over-represented among the poor." He also says that, "In
terms of their living standards measured in per capita terms,
however, they do not seem to be heavily over-represented among
the poor"—shades of another paradox, involving female-headed

*Table 12: Monthly Per Capita Expenditure of Agricultural Labour
Households Classified into Broad Groups by Number of Adults—
Kerala, 1977-78*

Size of Landholding	Family Type	No of Households	Average Household Size	Proportion of Children in Group (Per Cent)	Per Capita Expenditure (Rs)
Less than 15 cents	3 Adults or less	77	4.22	43.1	40.17
	4 Adults or more	23	7.27	25.6	37.99
15 cents or more	3 Adults or less	58	4.76	43.1	44.62
	4 Adults or more	42	7.07	24.2	42.72

Note: See Note to Table 11.

families: evenly distributed in per capita expenditure groups but concentrated among the low family-income groups.[19]

We must point out that such families contribute to possibly low levels of fertility (and low proportions of children) in the bottom family expenditure and landholding groups. Visaria's findings are consistent with such an interpretation of the data: he notes that the average size of households with female heads is generally lower and says that, "between 60 and 80 per cent of females who were reported as heads of households were widowed, divorced or separated"[20]

Let us now look at the Kerala data. We could separate households in which all the adults were reported as widowed, divorced or separated, i e, households in which there is no married person with a living spouse. The distribution of such households according to various criteria are presented in Tables 14 and 15 (along with distributions of joint families—which are defined as those in which at least two married couples are present).

Among cultivator households joint families tend to be concentrated in the upper landholding and family expenditure groups

Table 13: Percentage of Females among Household Heads in Different Deciles with Alternative Ranking Criteria—Rural Gujarat and Maharashtra, 1972-73

Deciles by Per Capita Expenditure	Gujarat	Maha-rashtra	Deciles by Total Household Expenditure	Gujarat	Maha-rashtra
1	4.8	10.2	1	27.3	46.3
2	4.5	13.6	2	8.2	17.2
3	3.5	10.5	3	5.0	10.9
4	4.7	9.0	4	4.8	8.4
5	6.0	9.0	5	5.3	6.2
6	5.3	11.5	6	1.7	4.1
7	5.5	9.2	7	1.4	3.8
8	5.9	11.6	8	1.5	3.2
9	6.7	10.3	9	0.6	2.6
10	9.5	9.1	10	0.6	1.5
All	5.6	10.4	All	5.6	10.4

Note : These are based on NSS data.
Source: Same as for Table 8.

Table 14: Number of Joint Families and Households without Married Couples—200 Cultivator Households, Kerala, 1977-78

Ranking Criterion	Quintile	No of Households	Average Household Size	No of Joint Families	No of Households without Married Couples
(A) Per capita	1	40	6.75	7	5
expenditure	2	40	6.25	7	7
	3	40	5.67	4	5
	4	40	5.02	3	4
	5	40	4.28	5	6
(B) Total household	1	40	4.05	0	12
expenditure	2	40	4.85	3	8
	3	40	5.95	8	0
	4	40	6.45	6	5
	5	40	6.67	9	2
(C) Size of land	1	40	4.22	0	15
owned	2	40	5.05	4	6
	3	40	5.87	6	2
	4	40	6.68	9	2
	5	40	6.15	7	2

Source: Same as for Table 11.

Table 15: Number of Joint Families and Households without Married Couples—200 Agricultural Labour Households, Kerala, 1977-78

Ranking Criterion	Quintile	No of Households	Average Household Size	No of Joint Families	No of Households without Married Couples
(A) Per capita	1	40	6.75	11	3
expenditure	2	40	6.42	9	5
	3	40	4.90	2	7
	4	40	4.78	1	9
	5	40	3.72	3	10
(B) Total household	1	40	3.07	1	17
expenditure	2	40	4.52	0	9
	3	40	5.42	6	5
	4	40	6.72	6	3
	5	40	6.92	13	0

Source: Same as for Table 11.

while households in which all adults are widowed, divorced or separated tend to concentrate in the lower groups. The latter, 'abnormal', non-reproductive households are evenly distributed among the per capita expenditure quintiles.

These findings are similar to Visaria's and the inferences are: low proportions of children and possibly low levels of fertility in the bottom landholding (and family expenditure) groups must be attributed at least in part to high proportions of 'demographically destitute' families headed by widowed, divorced or separated adults, and constituted by them and their child-dependents.

A possibly low level of fertility in the upper landholding and family expenditure groups must, in contrast, be attributed in part to the high proportion of joint families, for jointness in family is associated with low rates of nuptiality and late marriage. This must remain a conjecture which, however, is supported by evidence which shows that the proportion of children is significantly lower in joint families than in other families: in respect of the data on 200 cultivator households in Kerala which we have discussed, this proportion is about 27 per cent in joint families and 34 per cent in other families—the differences being somewhat larger in the upper landholding groups. Nevertheless, we must treat this as suggestive rather than conclusive evidence. A fuller review of the available evidence on differential fertility will be set out in a forthcoming essay.

V

CONCLUDING REMARKS

Family size and death rate paradoxes which we have discussed in this paper arise wholly out of the inappropriate use of per capita expenditure for analysing demographic differentials. On the logical plane, the paradoxes disappear once we bring in an appropriate variable such as property holdings into the analysis. The underlying reasoning must remain in part conjectural until data-gathering agencies become alert to the issues raised here. And the issues have far-reaching implications, not only for our understanding of demographic differentials but also for measurement of poverty.

If our arguments are valid, it would follow that theories of fertility which seek to explain supposedly high levels of fertility among the poor are wholly redundant.[21] The supposition derives from a misinterpretation of data.

Poverty measurement places an undue emphasis on per capita expenditure and food consumption. The 'reclassification' phenomenon, which we have discussed at length in this paper, can transfer even agricultural labour households into upper per capita expenditure groups for in such households an infant death raises the 'level of living' quite significantly. Apart from this, there is the question of 'demographically destitute' families (including those headed by women) concentrated in low family income groups.

Not only per capita income but also family income and property holdings are thus relevant to any discussion on poverty. To move from estimates based on food consumption in per capita expenditure groups to a better understanding of dimensions of poverty would, however, require the explicit recognition of the importance of infant and adult mortality to the measurement of poverty.

NOTES

1 In this paper we shall use the words family and household interchangeably; the conclusions are unaffected by the substitution.
2 Simon Kuznets, 'Demographic Aspects of the Size Distribution of Income: An Exploratory Essay', *Economic Development and Cultural Change*, Vol 25, 1976, pp 1-91; Pravin Visaria, 'Poverty and Living Standards in Asia: An Overview of the Main Results and Lessons of Selected Household Surveys', Living Standards Measurement Study, Working Paper No 2, The World Bank, October 1980; and also by Visaria, 'Poverty and Living Standards in Asia', *Population and Development Review*, Vol 6, June 1980, pp 189-223.
3 This observation is based on the results of the first agricultural labour enquiry wherein rural households were classified into: agricultural labourers, tenants, landowners and non-agricultural households. The 1951 Census, which classified rural households into owner-cultivators, tenants, labourers and landlords, also showed that labour households had in general the smallest average size among classes. See *Rural Manpower and Occupational Structure*, Agricultural Labour Enquiry, Ministry of Labour 1954 and *Census of India*, 1951, Vol 1, India, Part IIC, Economic Tables.

   Moreover, agricultural labour households are expected to be concentrated in the bottom-most classes defined according to land ownership. All land distribution surveys show that the average size of household increases systematically with the size of land.
4 See, for example, Table 4 in the text.
5 The correlation persists from the seventh round (1953-54) to the 22nd round (1967-68)—the latest for which such data are available. We may note,

however, that the data for urban areas do not throw up the nonsensical association in a clearly visible fashion; the underlying reasons require further investigation.

6 The condition for one component to dominate the other can be expressed in terms of 'between' and 'within' elasticities.

7 Does this imply that per capita income and fertility are positively correlated as between states? It is interesting to note in this context that cross-country correlations sometimes exhibit unexpected behaviour. See, for example, Steven E Beaver, *Demographic Transition Theory Reinterpreted*, Lexington Books, 1975, for the observation, "It is quite easy to obtain high correlations between development measures and birth rates if one includes all nations of the world with appropriate data in the sample...In one striking demonstration...It was found that the association between development and natality virtually disappeared when the sample was partitioned into more and less developed societies—within these groups correlations were close to zero." Beaver refers to a number of cross-country studies in which paradoxical correlations involving per capita incomes are reported.

This paper demonstrates the unsuitability of per capita income for analysing demographic differences within spatial units: the studies mentioned above demonstrate the same for cross-country analysis.

8 N Krishnaji, 'Agrarian Structure and Family Formation: A Tentative Hypothesis', *Economic and Political Weekly*, March 29, 1980, and 'Poverty and Family Size', *Social Scientist*, No 100, November 1980.

9 'Poverty and Family Size', op cit.

10 Simon Kuznets, op cit, A V Chayanov, *The Theory of Peasant Economy*, edited by Daniel Thorner et al, Richard D Irwin Inc, 1966.

11 The evidence is discussed in the papers cited in footnote 8.

12 Even NSS data recast according to alternative indices of levels of living show that the inverted U-shaped fertility curve is a possibility. See, for example, P B Gupta and C R Malaker, 'Fertility Differentials with Levels of Living and Adjustments of Fertility, Birth and Death Rates', *Sankhya*, Series B, Vol 24, 1963, pp 23-47. We may note that Gupta and Malaker were the first to notice the death rate paradox thrown up by NSS data but their effort seems to have made no impression on demographers and data gatherers.

Direct evidence indicating lower fertility levels among labour households is found in *The Mysore Population Study*, United Nations, 1961.

13 In analysing levels of income in relation to 'consumer-worker ratio' Chayanov does not separate the inter- and intra-generational components: we shall discuss the implications of this for Chayanov's analysis in a separate paper.

14 This behaviour typifies Chayanov's analysis of the life cycle.

15 If S and S_1 stand respectively for the family size at the beginning and end of a period, $S_1 = S + B - D$, where B and D denote respectively the number of births and deaths during the period. Given that B and D are independent of S, one can show that they are not independent of S_1.

16 If the observed distribution of households is regarded as a stationary distribution corresponding to the birth and death process described, such an interpretation is justified.

We may note in passing that the reclassification condition is satisfied by, for example, the negative binomial distribution which can be shown to fit the observed family-size distributions quite well. Models leading to such a distribution can be readily suggested: If births are distributed binomially given the generation and deaths are also so distributed given births, the resulting compound distribution can be shown to be binomial within generations. A generational distribution is governed through the process of family formation: if it is assumed to be a typical waiting-time distribution, the negative binomial can reasonably be suggested for the family-age distribution. This latter mixing of generations can be shown to yield an overall negative binomial for the family size distribution. .

The model, however, requires considerable modification to make it realistic taking into account at least differential mortality as between, say, infants and adults.

17 This argument is based on a simple algebraic model which is omitted.
18 This is a theme discussed in a number of studies done at the Centre for Development Studies, Trivandrum. It has not been conclusively demonstrated however.
19 Visaria, October 1980, op cit, p 53.
20 Ibid, p 58.
21 For a discussion, see, 'Poverty and Family Size', op cit.

February 11, 1984

10

Poverty and Sex Ratio

Some Data and Speculations

THE Indian population has an excess of males over females and the gap has tended to widen during this century.[1] In a pioneering study, Visaria [1961] has shown that higher female mortalities in both the child and reproductive age groups are mainly responsible for the deficit of females in India.[2] Data on mortality differentials between the sexes available from recent surveys and censuses confirm this finding.[3] It seems reasonable to infer that while death rates in general have fallen throughout the century, rapidly after independence, 'the rate of decline has been larger for males than for females, at least in some age groups.

The 'often overt but occasionally subtle discrimination against female children and the neglect of females even at adult ages' as factors underlying differential mortality to which Visaria[4] makes a brief reference constitute the subject matter of much recent research work. This work is mainly concerned with the discrimination against and neglect of females in respect of two crucial determinants of mortality: nutrition and health (or, more precisely, access to food and medical care). Agarwal [1986] presents a succinct review of this literature. The review shows that the available evidence, while suggesting discrimination against females, is inadequate in coverage and somewhat inconclusive. The difficulty arises from the fact that direct observation and measurement of food intakes by members within families is not at all easy[5] and the alternative, usually resorted to, of looking at anthropometric measurements such as body weights and heights in relation to certain standards or norms, leads in turn to numerous problems of interpreting data unambiguously. These difficulties are discussed in an influential study of some data from Bangladesh [Chen et al 1981]. On the other hand, it seems a priori that observation of health care practices and underlying sex biases may be easier but so far there have

200   *Pauperising Agriculture*

not been many studies based on such observation.

This note is not, however, concerned with the factors behind the level and the declining trend in the female-to-male ratio (FMR) in India but with a related question: How are the mortality differentials and the imbalance between the sexes related to poverty? In other words, are the differences wider in poor families than in rich families? The question has both theoretical and empirical contexts, and interesting in itself. The regional distribution of the sex ratio within India which has remained fairly stable over time, as Visaria has shown, with very pronounced deficits of females occurring in the north-west and distinctly balanced sex ratios in the south, has led to the speculation that the ratio is governed by and hence related to women's role in agricultural work, more prominent in the poorer regions and mediated to some extent through the cropping patterns.[6] While neat correlations across regions between agricultural prosperity and crop-mix on the one hand and the sex ratio on the other are lacking, it is nevertheless true that the agriculturally rich wheat-based states of Punjab and Haryana have very low female ratios and low rates of participation of women in work whereas the poorest states in India, viz, Orissa, Bihar and Madhya Pradesh are more balanced with respect to numbers of females and males, and the paddy-based south has the highest sex ratio. The deficit of females in the north-west has been repeatedly noted in the early British-Indian censuses, and indeed so were Rajput villages without female children or with only a few.[7] The census authorities discuss female infanticide in this context and attribute practices linked to what is now mildly described as discrimination mainly to landowning families of certain castes and their strong preference for male progeny ascribed to both economic and cultural factors.[8] Moreover, it has been suggested that for easily understandable reasons, apart from the role of women in work, property and asset transfers following marriage also play an important part in the determination of sex preferences Miller [1981] argues, for example, that there is greater reciprocity between families of partners in marriage in such transfers in the south than in the north-west where it tends to be almost unilateral in favour of the bridegrooms' family.[9] All this has obvious implications for the question raised here for two reasons: first, in poor families women have to work for survival and second, the property transfer mechanism can act only in a relatively weak

manner in their case because there is not much to be transferred from one poor family to another. If the suggested arguments
are valid, these factors can be expected to promote higher female
proportions among the poor.[10]

The question about the relationship between poverty and sex
ratio is prompted also by famine mortality studies. Some studies
of the recent famines in Bangladesh have, for example, shown
that severe food shortages lead to a greater 'excess', i e, famine
induced, deaths among females, especially children.[11] Likewise,
the data for the 1943 Bengal famine exhibit a higher excess female
mortality among children.[12] The implication for this note could
be that when food is in short supply, as it normally is in poor
families, the males get a disproportionately bigger share. To
digress a little for good reason, it may be pointed out that the
British-Indian census compilers looking at famine mortality have
observed higher male mortalities till about the first decade of
this century; they say that earlier, under famine conditions, men
had to go out in search of food and were subject to higher mortality risks but later, with famine administration becoming effective, could stay at home for the arrival of relief.[13] The insights provided by the famine studies are of limited value,
however, to the question of differences between the poor and the
rich families for the simple reason that famine is a rare occurrence (affecting also sections of the non-poor) in contrast to the
chronic deprivation among the poor.

Against this hazy background, two relationships are analysed
here. The first refers to sex ratio variations across families with
landholdings of different size and an embedded contrast between
agricultural labour and other rural households in India with
respect to the balance between the sexes. The second is concerned
with poverty, defined as it usually is by per capita consumption
of families, and its relationship with the sex ratio. Needless to
say, this is a speculative exercise, for, in a field wherein direct
observation can provide no more than useful insights, secondary
information cannot be more illuminating.

Demographic data, especially on mortality rates by sex, relevant to the discussion here, are not available separately for
agricultural labour and other poor households, so that for comparing the latter with the non-poor rural households one has to
rely on indirect information on variables such as household size
and sex ratio.

In rural India as a whole there were, in 1971, only 950 females for every 1,000 males (Table 1). For agricultural labour households covered by the rural labour enquiries the ratio was 986 in 1964-65 and 976 in 1974-75. If one takes 980 as a plausible estimate for 1971 for the labour households, since they constitute about a quarter of the rural families, it implies that the non-labour households had a sex ratio of about 940 in 1971. So it can be seen that agricultural labour households are characterised by a better balance between the sexes than other rural families consisting mainly of middle and big landowners. Significantly, labour households without land have higher proportions of females than those with some land, the sex ratio being respectively 990 and 976 in 1964-65, and 982 and 969 in 1974-75 (Table 1). This suggests that if land-related variables influence the sex ratio, they perhaps do so even at the lowest end of the landholding scale, among the labour families.

The sex ratio varies from one age group to another and hence the overall ratio depends also on the age distribution of the males; the aggregate ratio is a weighted average of the values within the age groups, the weights being the proportion of males. It can be seen from Table 2 that the female ratio in the prime adult age group (15-49) is significantly higher among labour households than in the rural population as a whole (1,000 as against 971);

Table 1: Average Household Size and Sex Ratio—Agricultural Labour and All Rural Households, All India

Variable	Year	Labourers with Land	Labourers without Land	All Labour House-holds	All Rural House-holds
Average household size	1964-65	5.00	4.16	4.53	—
	1974-75	5.15	4.38	4.76	—
	1971 Census	—	—	—	5.52
Female per 1000 males	1964-65	976	990	986	—
	1974-75	969	982	976	—
	1961 Census	—	—	—	963
	1971 Census	—	—	—	949
	1981 Census	—	—	—	952

Sources: Rural Labour Enquiry, 1963-65 and 1974-75, and Census of India various issues.

the difference between the two categories of households is even more marked in respect of the 50+ age group. But the age distributions of males are not radically different, despite a higher proportion of males in the 50+ group in the population as a whole (arising possibly from lower levels of life expectation among labourers). Thus the differences in the FMR mainly arise from higher sex ratios among adults in the labour families. Indeed, if the age distribution of males for the whole rural population in 1971 is taken as 'standard', the standardised FMR for the agricultural labour households turns out to be 988 in 1964-65 and 973 in 1974-75, as against the actual values of 986 and 976 respectively, showing that age distributions do not contribute significantly to the differences being discussed here. Sex ratios in the aggregate—and among adults in particular—are influenced by sex-selective out-migration, apart from differential mortalities. Leaving aside migration for the moment, one can discern another correlation from the data presented so far: an inverse correlation between the average household size and the FMR; the highest female proportion is observed among the landless labour households who have also the smallest average size (Table 1). They have an average size of slightly over four with sex ratios close to 990 in contrast to all rural families with a size of about 5.5 and a sex ratio of 950.

These correlations hold in a more general sense with respect to the variations according to landholding size (Table 3). First, the average household size increases steadily with the size of the landholding, rising from 2.71 in households with less than half an acre to 8.73 among families with over 50 acres; and second, in contrast, the female-male ratio among the adults declines as the landholding increases, with females outnumbering males in

Table 2: Sex Ratio and Male Population by Age Groups— Agricultural Labour and All Rural Households, All India

Category of Household	Year	FMR by Age Group (Per 1000)			Males by Age Group (Per Cent)		
		0–14	15–49	50 +	0–14	15–49	50 +
Agricultural labour	1964-65	935	1000	1125	41.9	47.3	10.8
	1974-75	925	1000	1038	43.9	45.4	10.7
All rural	1971	938	971	904	43.0	44.3	12.7

Source: Same as for Table 1.

households with small landholdings, and big deficits of females occurring exclusively in the middle and the big land size classes. As a consequence, household size is inversely associated with the sex ratio: big landholdings and big families go with a big imbalance between the sexes; small families and high female proportions are characteristics associated with tiny landholdings.

However, the observations are based on the sex ratios in the adult populations. Fortunately, data covering persons of all ages classified by land size are available for the different states from the 1961 Census (Table 4). Once again the FMR can be seen to be over 1,000 in the smallest land size class of less than an acre in the different states of India, with only a few exceptions. It is noteworthy that even in Punjab (including Haryana) and Uttar Pradesh, where the female deficits are among the largest

Table 3: Sex Ratio and Related Statistics by Landholdings—
Rural India, 1961-62

Household Operational Holding (Acres)	Average Household Size	Sex Ratio (Adults)	Proportion of Children (Per Cent)
0.0-0.5	2.71	1077	40.2
0.5-1.0	4.59	1061	41.6
1.0-2.5	4.77	1014	41.3
2.5-5.0	5.27	969	40.6
5.0-7.5	5.85	923	41.2
7.5-10.0	6.13	941	41.0
10.0-12.5	6.54	910	41.6
12.5-15.0	6.70	922	41.5
15.0-20.0	6.91	947	41.4
20.0-25.0	7.40	963	42.4
25.0-30.0	7.24	990	42.0
30.0-50.0	7.84	952	42.7
Above 50.0	8.73	959	39.9

Notes: (1) The sex ratio (female to male) refers to the value among adults (15+) and the percentage of children refers to the ratio of the (0-14) age population in the total. The data are derived from the National Sample Survey, Report No 144.

(2) The lowest class (i e, 0 to 0.5 acres) excludes 'non-operating' households—presumably comprising non-agricultural and pure landlord households. The average size of household for this excluded category is 4.52.

(3) Here the classification is by operational holdings but variations are similar when ownership holdings are considered instead.

Table 4: *Sex Ratio (Female: Male) among Cultivating Households by Landholdings, 1961*

(Per 1000)

State	Landholding (Size in Acres)									
	1	1–2.5	2.5–5	5–7.5	7.5–10	10–12.5	12.5–15	15–30	30–50	50 +
Andhra Pradesh	1025	991	974	960	957	949	944	942	952	974
Assam	921	942	927	912	901	897	878	873	862	867
Bihar	1085	1041	1004	987	977	982	982	955	912	880
Gujarat	1005	969	955	951	953	947	951	949	935	934
Karnataka	1074	1027	987	959	953	939	931	930	951	915
Kerala	1026	989	962	934	934	941	946	933	897	951
Madhya Pradesh	1013	1005	984	973	968	966	966	964	978	1003
Maharashtra	1162	1070	1026	999	988	987	972	970	966	957
Orissa	1052	1033	1015	1005	994	995	986	999	1024	1027
Punjab	1005	960	936	892	875	863	847	843	847	859
Rajasthan	967	942	927	919	912	908	913	906	899	887
Tamil Nadu	1023	1000	977	965	961	961	959	955	955	937
Uttar Pradesh	1003	972	931	904	893	890	889	896	905	899
West Bengal	978	975	957	938	923	916	902	897	896	888

Source: Census of India, 1961 (Table C1, Part II C—'Social and Cultural Tables', different issues).

in the country, females outnumber males in the smallest land-holding class. Equally noteworthy are the sex ratios below 900 corresponding to huge female deficits observed only in the middle and big landholding groups. Even in the south, where the FMR is generally high, it is low at the upper end of the land-holding scale.

Migration: What do these mutual associations between no land or small landholdings—associated with poverty of an undeniable sort—on the one hand and small families and a balanced sex ratio on the other convey to our understanding of mortality differentials and the underlying discrimination against females? As hinted earlier, these variations in the sex ratio are influenced to some extent by the rural-to-urban migration, demonstrably more prominent among males seeking work. Such a sex-selective migration tilts the balance in favour of females in the rural areas, especially among population groups with high migration propensities.

Some arithmetic will show that while this kind of migration accounts for a part of the high female ratio observed among agricultural labour and land-poor households, it can by no means be the whole explanation for it. The calculation can be done in a crude but quick fashion on the basis of the 1971 Census migration data [Mehrotra 1974]. Remember that for 1971 the FMR was roughly 980 and 940 for the agricultural labour and non-labour populations respectively. The 1971 Census counted, among the 438.8 mn rural people, about 23.7 mn birth-place rural-to-urban migrants, i e, persons enumerated in urban areas but born in rural areas, with a FMR of 919. Assume that all these migrants were from labour households (a wholly unrealistic thing to do as will be presently seen, and least favourable to the hypothesis being developed here). Migrants (23.7 mn) then constitute about 5 per cent (23.7 mn out of (438.8+23.7) mn) of the redefined rural population, but 20 per cent of the labour population (labour households constituting roughly a quarter of all households). If all these migrants are thus added to the observed labour population in rural areas, the sex ratio for labour will come down from 980 to 965, but the last figure is still far higher than the FMR for the non-labour rural population (940).

A similar arithmetic can be done with respect to the land-holding data. All we need to remember is that more than a half of the rural households in India have holdings below 2.5 acres, so that even under the implausible assumption that all rural-urban migration arises from these households, the differences in the sex ratio between them and the big landowners will remain substantial.

But, more conclusive at least in a qualitative sense are the fragmentary data thrown up by small-scale studies of migration. Thus, for example, a study of four villages in east UP [Saxena 1977] notes that out of 300 villagers migrating to Gorakhpur, only 129 (i e, 43 per cent) came from households with less than 5 acres of land back at home. It is said that even well-to-do farmers with over 50 acres migrate to towns aspiring for higher standards of living. In Saxena's sample only 39 migrants out of 300 had an agricultural labour background. Similarly, a comprehensive study of the Ludhiana district [Oberai and Singh 1983] shows that despite the landless constituting the bulk of the out-migrants the 'propensity' to migrate is no less high among those who have large landholdings.

In this study of the agriculturally most prosperous district in India, viz, Ludhiana, the authors find that in the surveyed villages only about a half of the migrants to urban areas were landless or land-poor; about 9.5 per cent of the households with out-migrants had over 15 acres of land in the village (Table 5). While the average migration propensity for all households (defined as the ratio of households with outmigrants to the total in the village in each landholding class) was 23.72 per cent, households with over 15 acres (the biggest landholding category) had a

Table 5: Outmigrants from Ludhiana Villages by Landholding Size

Landholding (Acres)	Households with Outmigrants Per Cent N(=504)	All Households Per Cent N(=2124)	Relative Migration Propensity
Landless	45.8	47.6	96
Below 1	3.0	2.4	121
1–2.5	2.0	3.3	65
2.5–5	10.3	13.7	74
5–7.5	8.9	7.4	120
7.5–10	13.1	9.5	136
10–15	7.3	7.9	93
Above 15	9.5	8.2	114

Note: N refers to the total number.
Source: A S Oberai and H K Manmohan Singh [1983].

corresponding propensity of 27.5 per cent. Some of the rural poor migrate, but so, it appears, do some of the non-poor; the migration propensities may not be very different.

The reasons for migration differ, of course, as between the landless and those who can, remaining in villages, earn high incomes from agriculture. The point, however, is that there is a marked sex-selectivity in out-migration, with males outnumbering females, and this can and probably does influence the balance between the sexes in not only the poor but also the non-poor rural families.

The explanation for the observed, more balanced, sex ratios among the labour and land-poor families does not, therefore, lie wholly in male emigration but possibly in relatively narrower mortality differentials between males and females. No doubt, the magnitude of the influence of migration on sex ratios in rural areas has to be worked out in a more satisfactory manner than has been possible in this note to make this more conclusive: studies of migrant backgrounds are needed for states such as Orissa and Bihar having high rates of labour migration. And, to conclude this section, it must be emphasised that mortality differentials between the sexes among the poor as among others need not exclusively depend on 'discrimination' (more on this later).

Poverty calculations are usually based on a classification of households by levels of per capita income or expenditure. It has been argued elsewhere that while the latter are good indicators of how much food and other basic necessities families can consume to determine whether or not they are poor, they are not suited for the analysis of relationships between demographic and economic variables. The main reason is that such relationships are expected to depend on the long-run, i e, durable, characteristics of families whereas per capita incomes are subject to wide fluctuations even in the short period, caused by vital events such as births, deaths, and migration of members within families [Krishnaji 1984]. Another reason is that per capita classifications create inhomogeneous groups in which agricultural labour families of small size may appear alongside landowning households of large size. The resulting pictures can and do cause much confusion.

But, for what they are worth, sex ratio variations according to levels of per capita expenditure are presented in Table 6. These again refer to female ratios among adults only. They show that, with a few exceptions, the FMR tends to be the highest in the lowest per capita expenditure group and vice versa. The sex ratio is close to or over 1,000 in many states of India at the bottom end of per capita expenditure, while very low ratios of 800 and below (an unimaginably low 555 in Assam) are observed at the other extreme, i e, among families which can be described as the richest according to the criterion of per capita consumption.

It is tempting to conclude that these data are consistent with the observation of balanced sex ratios among the agricultural labour and land-poor households. The conclusion may be valid but there is the nuisance of two-way determination: the direction of causation runs both ways between low per capita incomes and high female proportions.

To elaborate a little: the purpose here is to see whether and how economic status determines sex proportions. However, given landholding and other resources, the size and composition of families (with respect to age and sex of members) in turn

Table 6: Sex Ratio (FMR) among Adults (15+) by Per Capita Expenditure—Rural India, 1973-74

State	Per Capita Expenditure Per Month (Rs)			
	0 – 34	34-55	55-100	Above 100
Andhra Pradesh	1031	943	939	802
Assam	994	952	861	555
Bihar	1072	1126	1041	844
Gujarat	936	955	883	813
Haryana	834	939	942	847
Jammu and Kashmir	865	902	845	812
Kerala	1204	1048	1030	1036
Madhya Pradesh	996	981	931	841
Maharashtra	1045	1026	985	850
Karnataka	1021	964	918	920
Orissa	1080	1010	958	800
Punjab	1022	979	927	913
Rajasthan	986	992	953	988
Tamil Nadu	1080	1021	1002	854
Uttar Pradesh	997	956	942	748
West Bengal	962	975	828	788

Note: The larger number of expenditure groups available in the NSS have been collapsed into the four given above to avoid the problems created by small sample sizes in some groups.

Source: National Sample Survey, Report No 240.

influence the family income and give rise to a two-way causation of the relationships between per capita income and demographic variables. Generally, family income increases with family size but not proportionately, so that per capita income tends to be inversely related to family size within each landholding class as it does even among agricultural labour households. As a result, in sample surveys, large families get classified into the lower per capita expenditure groups. For illustrative purposes some out-dated NSS data (1955-56) are given in Table 7, which show that about 15.5 per cent of big landowners with over 100 acres appear with per capita expenditures of less than Rs 12 along with 33 per cent of landless households, and 77 per cent of households possessing less than half an acre; correspondingly, as many as 4.5 per cent of households with tiny, less than half-acre, holdings and about 7 per cent of those with holdings between a half and one acre are grouped, with per capita expenditures of over Rs 21, in the same category as about 24 per cent of those with over 100 acres. This shows that agricultural labour households consisting, for example, of a woman and a man, both working and

Table 7: Percentage Distribution of Households in Each Landholding Class by Levels of Per Capita Expenditure—Rural India, 1955-56

Land Possessed (Acres)	Per Capita Expenditure Per Month (Rs)		
	0–12	13–20	21+
0	33.33	23.34	43.33
0–0.5	77.35	18.20	4.45
0.5–1.0	74.26	18.55	7.19
1.0–1.5	74.85	20.91	4.24
1.5–2.5	67.62	27.74	4.64
2.5–3.5	63.40	31.46	5.14
3.5–5.0	57.76	34.84	7.39
5.0–7.5	60.22	30.32	9.45
7.5–10	56.93	33.91	8.66
10–15	54.32	34.23	11.43
15–20	54.74	31.47	13.79
20–30	48.67	35.90	15.44
30–50	38.39	45.59	16.02
50–100	31.58	33.41	35.01
100 +	15.61	60.12	24.27
All classes	62.26	29.51	8.23

Source: National Sample Survey, Report No 140.

earning incomes, can rub shoulders with big landowning families of big size in the NSS per capita expenditure classifications.

What is equally obvious but cannot, again, be substantiated on the basis of published information of the sort being analysed here, is the implication of the differentials between the earnings of man and woman. In labour as well as cultivator families with small landholdings women generally work in contrast to those with large holdings; and these earning differentials imply a distinct disadvantage to families with more women than men, so that, other things remaining the same, families with higher proportions of females earn lower incomes per capita. The same reasoning applies to children. Children in labour and small peasant families work and add marginally to the household income but their contribution tends to be far less in per capita terms than that of the adults. For this reason, a large proportion of children, just as a high female ratio, is an economic disadvantage to the family. It can be clearly seen then, that families with high female-male ratios and high proportions of children get classified in surveys into the relatively lower per capita expenditure groups within each landholding class. This is one reason why high female proportions and high child-adult ratios and large families are systematically observed at the lower end of the per capita consumption scale.[14]

Thus the data based on classifications according to the per capita expenditure of families are less informative about the determinants of the sex ratio than those based on landholding data. However, they demonstrate a different aspect of 'discrimination', that of unequal earnings, too well known and documented to be pursued any further here.

According to the landholding data as well as those from the rural labour enquiries, labour and land-poor families tend to be small in size. The determinants of family size in relation to agrarian structure have been examined in detail in other studies.[15] The association between small families and high female proportions deserves further attention, however.

It has been shown by Visaria and Visaria [1985] that among cultivators with small landholdings the incidence of females as heads of household tends to be higher than in other rural families (Table 8). Moreover, they note that households with female heads tend to be smaller in size and to have higher female proportions. There is some evidence to show that female headship and high

Table 8: Percentage of Households with Female Heads among Cultivators according to Size of Landholding, 1961

Area	Size of Landholding (Acres)								
	Below 1	1.0–2.4	2.5–4.9	5.0–7.4	7.5–9.9	10.0–14.9	15.0–49.9	50+	All
India	14.5	9.8	6.4	5.1	4.4	4.2	3.7	3.4	7.2
Andhra Pradesh	14.5	10.8	7.9	7.1	6.5	6.3	5.9	5.7	8.8
Assam	8.0	5.0	2.7	2.0	1.6	1.5	1.3	5.5	3.5
Bihar	16.1	10.0	6.0	4.3	3.5	3.4	3.1	4.5	8.6
Gujarat	14.9	8.3	5.8	4.3	3.8	3.4	2.6	2.0	4.9
Himachal Pradesh	15.7	10.6	7.9	5.2	4.4	3.2	4.3	5.5	9.5
Jammu and Kashmir	10.9	7.3	6.0	7.4	6.9	6.4	7.5	—	7.3
Kerala	15.1	10.0	7.6	7.8	7.6	6.2	6.1	12.0	12.0
Madhya Pradesh	12.5	9.2	6.2	4.9	4.0	3.9	3.7	3.9	5.5
Maharashtra	27.1	16.4	10.9	8.4	6.9	6.1	4.5	3.3	9.5
Manipur	20.2	10.1	5.6	3.2	3.2	4.3	5.0	7.3	7.9
Meghalaya	29.2	24.8	16.1	18.0	17.8	17.1	22.1	32.8	20.4
Karnataka	20.1	14.4	11.0	9.1	8.9	7.8	6.1	4.8	10.0
Orissa	11.5	7.6	4.7	3.7	3.2	3.2	3.2	3.5	5.8
Punjab	20.6	11.4	6.3	3.2	2.1	1.7	1.5	1.5	3.9
Rajasthan	10.9	7.1	4.7	4.0	3.4	3.2	2.8	2.1	4.1
Sikkim	4.9	8.6	6.5	4.7	5.3	4.8	3.7	6.7	6.1
Tamil Nadu	14.7	11.7	8.9	7.5	6.5	6.2	5.4	6.5	10.1
Uttar Pradesh	14.3	9.3	5.6	4.0	3.4	3.0	2.9	3.3	6.9
West Bengal	8.5	5.8	3.1	2.4	2.1	2.2	2.8	5.0	4.6

Source: Census of India, 1961, Part II C (i), 'Social and Cultural Tables', table C-1, published in state volumes; cited in Visaria and Visaria [1985].

sex ratios constitute a disadvantage to families in terms of per capita consumption. In a speculative vein the Visarias say: "Also females form a higher proportion of households with smaller land-holdings perhaps because they are gradually forced to sell a part of their landholdings or get a smaller share relative to the brothers of the deceased spouse. Partly as a result, the female-headed households might include a high proportion of rural labour households . . . ."

It is possible to indulge in further speculation. The Visarias find that female heads are mainly widows (or divorced or separated persons). Now there is no reason why the incidence of widowhood should be very significantly higher among those with small plots of land; it can be so, however, if male mortalities in the relevant age groups are higher than female ones by margins relatively wider than in the bigger land size classes. This clearly points to the lack of a one-to-one correspondence between widowhood and female headship. To the extent that female head-ship results from male out-migration, this is obvious. What is not obvious is that, whatever the spirit of law and custom, women fail in general to obtain rights to ownership of (or control over) land. Thus when landholdings are substantial, even if women acquire legal titles, male relations may step in quietly or other-wise, to 'manage' the property, depriving women not only of headship in a formal sense but of much else.

This is speculative but important nonetheless, for it highlights the role of the mechanisms of property transfer and control in the determination of the relationships between sex ratio and land-holding characteristics.

At any rate, the smallness in family size among the land-poor arises in part from a greater incidence of widows heading the families constituted by them and their child dependents. The sex composition of such households has a priori to be in favour of females because of the absence of the male spouse. They are likely to be concentrated among the poor (howsoever defined) as a consequence of the female disadvantage in earning incomes and acquiring property.

Factors such as male out-migration and the bunching of families headed by widows contribute to the distinctly better-balanced sex ratios among the agricultural labour and small cultivator households, but they cannot decisively explain why these ratios— female to male—often tend to be over 1,000 in contrast to an average of 950 for the whole rural population, and even lower values among households with big landholdings uniformly all over India. The conclusion must be that although mortality rates in general can be expected to be high—higher than in the rest of the population—in such poor households, the differential between the sexes may be relatively narrower in some age groups. The consistency with which pronounced deficits of females are observed in households with large landholdings— for example in the south where generally the sex ratios are more evenly balanced—lends weight to this conclusion. This indirect inference drawn from the data on sex ratio balances discussed in this note no doubt requires more direct empirical support; also, there is scope for further analysis at the regional level of even this kind of secondary information.

However, it will be hasty to conclude that there is less discrimination against females among the poor, for mortality differentials cannot be wholly attributed to 'discrimination'. For instance the higher male death rates observed in some regions among some age groups do not imply discrimination against males. But the discrimination against females in India is real and its different dimensions are well known, whatever statistics reveal or do not. It is possible that discriminatory practices, especially in relation to nutrition and health care, are more effective among the land owning classes than in poor families, given the very low standard of living of the latter; the bias may be universal but it seems to be stronger among some caste groups and in some regions. Theorising about this is not easy, however.

No doubt, the economic value of a woman, calculated (by economists who do not distinguish human beings from commodities) on a long-run basis, may turn out to be higher for a labouring or small cultivator family than for a big farmer, given the cropping patterns and the possibility of women earning incomes. But as an explanation for the observed sex ratio variation with a better balance among the labouring poor this calculation is suspect because it is difficult to believe that it is actually made in some fashion or ingrained in culture through economic consciousness and underlies sex bias or the lack of it. For the poor, work is directly related to survival from day to day and long-run calculations may not be relevant. It is necessary therefore, to look beyond a simple economic calculus for mapping and understanding sex ratio variations.

NOTES

1 The number of females for every 1,000 males in India as a whole has declined, although not steadily, from 972 in 1901 to 935 in 1981 [Padmanabha 1981].

2 Visaria considers other factors such as spatial mobility, under-enumeration of females and sex ratios at birth, before arriving at the importance of mortality differentials for explaining the deficit of females. During the pre-independence period, the census authorities thought that the deficits of females arose mainly from the under-counting (resulting from underreporting) of females in certain age groups. Even while recognising female infanticide, the 'neglect of female life', and 'bad treatment' of women, they refer to the 'concealment' of women belonging to certain age groups among some agricultural and other high caste communities as an important factor underlying low female proportions [Natarajan 1972].

3 Some recent data show that up to the age of 35 years mortality tends to be higher among females [Padmanabha 1982]. Female mortalities are lower after the age of 35 years but life expectation at birth is lower for females than for males.

4 Visaria [1961], p 66. He suggests in conclusion that the discrimination "denies to many women the benefits of the normal biological superiority of their sex...". The superiority is presumably inferred from higher male mortalities generally observed in the western countries.

5 Apart from the difficulty of observing and assessing amounts consumed by individual members at a single meal, it has been suggested repeatedly that there is also the possibility of a bias introduced by the presence of an observer.

6 For a comprehensive discussion, see, Agarwal, op cit.

7 The 1911 Census says: In the Benares division Moore personally made most minute investigations into the facts in three hundred and eight villages; in sixty-two of these villages he found that there were no female children under the age of six years. In another part of the division, Moore found a community of Hara Rajputs regarding whom he said, "Not only are there no girls to be found in their houses now, but there never have been any, nor has such an event as the marriage of a daughter taken place for more than two hundred years...." "...the extraordinarily low female ratio of the Shekawant branch of the Kachwaha clan of Rajputs in Jaipur state, 530 females per 1,000 males, is indubitably suggestive of deliberate interference with the natural ratio, when considered with the Rajpur tradition" [quoted in Natarajan op cit, p 4]. These may be extreme cases but they illustrate the point.

8 Extracts from the different early censuses in this respect are given in Natarajan op cit.

9 For a discussion of Miller's work and some extrapolations, see, Bardhan [1982].

10 Agarwal [1986] discusses this expectation in some detail and refers to some micro evidence showing the contrary: higher levels of discrimination among the landless poor households. However, such higher levels may co-exist with

216   *Pauperising Agriculture*

better female proportions (aggregated over all age groups) for reasons to
be clarified later in this note.

11 "During baseline years female mortality consistently exceeded male mortality in all age groups except infant deaths. The age-specific sex differentials were more pronounced in children of 1-4 and 5-9 years and in the
childbearing years. Disaster tended to accentuate these sex differentials
among children. In 1971-72 (a year of food crisis) mortality of female
children of 1-4 years was 57 per cent higher than mortality of males in comparison to a differential of 40 per cent in the preceding five baseline years"
[Chowdhury and Chen 1977, p 53].

12 See Greenhough [1982], p 311.

13 Referring to fewer deaths among men than women in the 1908 famine,
the 1911 United Provinces Census Report says: "This is attributable chief-
ly to the absence of wandering. This absence of wandering was... due to
the fact that the people by 1908 had learnt by experience that government
was anxious and willing to assist them. In 1897... they had not yet obtained such confidence in government and took to... wandering in search of
work... It is these wanderers who feel the worst effects of famine, it is chief-
ly they who starve. And it is amongst them that man would most severely
feel his disadvantages and women would reap the fullest benefit of her advantage" [quoted in Natarajan 1972].

14 For further discussion of such correlations, see, Krishnaji [1984 and 1989].

15 Ibid.

REFERENCES

Agarwal, Bina [1986], 'Women, Poverty and Agricultural Growth in India',
Journal of Peasant Studies, 13, pp 165-220.

Bardhan, Pranab [1982], 'Little Girls and Death in India', *Economic and Political
Weekly*, September 4, pp 1448-50.

Chen, Lincoln C, Emadul Huq and Stan D'Souze [1981], 'Sex Bias in the Family Allocation of Food and Health Care in Rural Bangladesh', *Population and
Development Review*, 7, pp 55-70.

Chowdhury, Allauddin A K M and Lincoln C Chen [1977], 'The Interaction
of Nutrition, Infection and Mortality during the Recent Food Crisis in
Bangladesh', *Food Research Institute Studies*, XVI, pp 47-61.

Greenhough, Paul R [1982], *Prosperity and Misery in Modern Bengal: The Famine
of 1943-44*, Oxford, New York.

Krishnaji, N [1984], 'Family Size, Levels of Living and Differential Mortality
in Rural India: Some Paradoxes', *Economic and Political Weekly*, February 11,
pp 248-58.

— [1989], 'Size and Structure of Agricultural Labour Households in India'
in G Rodgers (ed), *Population Growth and Rural Poverty in South Asia*, New Delhi,
Sage, pp 121-50.

Mehrotra, G K [1974], *Birth Place Migration in India*, Census of India 1971,
Special Monograph No 1.

Natarajan, D [1972], *Changes in Sex Ratio*, Census of India, 1971, Census
Centenary Monograph No 6.

Oberai, A S and H K Manmohan Singh [1983], *Census and Consequences of Internal Migration*, Oxford, Delhi.

Padmanabha, P [1981], *'Provisional Population Totals, Series-I, India, Paper I*, Census of India, 1981.

—[1982], 'Trends in Mortality', *Economic and Political Weekly*, August 7, pp 1285-90.

Saxena, D P [1977], *Rururban Migration in India*, Popular Prakashan, Bombay.

Visaria, Pravin M [1961], *The Sex Ratio of the Population of India*, Census of India 1961, Monograph No 10.

Visaria, Pravin M and Leela Visaria [1985], 'Indian Households with Female Heads: Incidence Characteristics and Level of Living' in Jain D and Nirmala Banerjee (eds), *Women in Poverty : The Tyranny of the Household*, Vikas, 1985.

June 6, 1987.

11
Land and Labour in India
The Demographic Factor

DURING the nineteen-sixties, Daniel Thorner travelled widely over the country and wrote extensively about the changes then taking place in Indian agriculture. We still read those writings of his for analytical insights into what was then described as the new agricultural strategy, now matured into the so-called green revolution. The observations he made watching that first scene have provided the seed material for two decades of scholarly effort by social scientists here and abroad. Likewise, his earlier studies of India on land reforms, and the agrarian structure in general, have a quality of timelessness and generality that only a combination of scholarship and intuition can produce.

I refer to these works of Daniel Thorner because my own efforts during the last two and a half decades to understand the Indian agrarian economy have roots in Thorner's writings. A tribute to Thorner must necessarily refer to themes close to his heart.

Among Thorner's foremost concerns was the distribution of land among landlords, cultivating owners, and tenants. He was equally interested in the relative magnitudes of those who work on their own land and those who work for others as labourers. He attempted to assess the long-term trends in these distributions and compositions, paying attention not only to what published statistics actually mean but also to their theoretical and analytical significance. In this context, it is not clear to me from his work how much importance he gave to demographic factors. We know he had used Chayanovian ideas in formulating what he called the 'peasant economy' as a category in economic history and went on to summarise Chayanov's work as a post-Marxian theory presumably of some relevance to India. On reflection, I think, however, that it will be wrong to infer that Thorner accepted the validity for countries such as India of the so-called demographic differentiation arising from Chayanov's stylised description of the natural history of the family. Thorner has in-

deed noted in his introduction to Chayanov that the latter's theory
may work well for thinly populated countries but would need
serious modification for land-scarce economies. More directly,
he analysed the impact of land reforms as well as other forces
that shape the changes in land ownership on the processes of differentiation and the growth of agricultural labour in India.

It is not far-fetched, therefore, to infer that Thorner's interest
in Chayanov arose from and centred on the manner in which
small peasants cope with an increasing family size, or how the
small peasant economy has a tendency to persist in the face of
capitalist penetration—slowing down the polarisation process and
giving it a specific character, with semi-proletarians, rather than
those wholly divorced from the means of production, constituting
a large section of the labour force. Among other factors, it is
this kind of interpretation of Thorner that has promoted my
interest in demographic questions posed in the context of a changing agrarian structure. In what follows, I want to make some
observations on the deteriorating land-man ratio in India and
the manner in which demographic factors induce changes in the
distribution of land and thereby in the ratio of agricultural
labourers to cultivators. In doing so I will focus on inter-regional
variations both in population growth and agricultural development. I will also refer in brief to the decisive role the state has
played in promoting technological change and exacerbating
regional disparities in the productivity of land which, along with
the distribution of land, contributes significantly to the relationship between land and labour. I will indulge in some speculation about the shape of things to come during the next two or
three decades.

I

The structural change in the Indian agricultural economy, as
in other economies, has different facets: ranging from the growth
of wage labour and the development of commodity, land, and
credit markets, to the links between agriculture and industry,
and further on to the manner in which agrarian classes influence
political and economic change.

A good deal of scholarly analysis of these changes has been
set out in terms of how the capitalist mode penetrates into the
agricultural sector. Unfettered capitalist development, based upon

superior techniques of production and economies of scale, quickly puts the small farmer at a distinct disadvantage. Not merely because of economies of scale, but also because of the way the different markets—the land, labour and credit markets—tend to be inter-linked to reinforce the differential advantage. The underlying processes are too well known to be explicated here. It needs to be emphasised, however, that the processes of relative impoverishment of small peasants and the swelling of the ranks of agricultural labour are complementary to the process of capitalist and large-scale production. We may say there is only one process.

However, in retrospect, at least for the Indian case, we can recognise that the process has not been and is not an unfettered one. Indeed, why capitalist development in Indian agriculture is a slow process has been the subject of much discussion. I will not review this discussion. Instead, let me refer in brief to the role of the state.

The state has played a major role in the agrarian transformation in India in two distinct phases in the post-independence period. The first of these covers the implementation of land reforms with varying degrees of success in the different regions of India. In this context, the elimination of zamindari and other similar types of tenurial relations is undoubtedly an important landmark in Indian agrarian history, but it has not led to the realisation in full measure of the principle: 'land to the tiller'. The structure that has emerged has left intact an extreme concentration in land ownership with a small proportion of households claiming clear ownership rights to the major part of land in all the regions of India. Such a concentration meant that the large landholdings had either to be cultivated by wage labour or let out on lease on terms that changed with the times to the advantage of the owners. And since the reforms concerning tenancy that followed had more to do with the regulation of the terms of tenure than with the total abolition of tenancy, land-leasing arrangements have continued to persist, although on a declining scale, with cultivation through wage labour becoming the predominant form in the large landholdings.

Associated with the historical emergence of a large concentration in land is the steady growth of labour households in the rural population. For the late seventies and early eighties it is estimated that about 37 per cent of Indian rural households earn the major part of their subsistence from wage work. This pool of labour is drawn from the landless population and other families who have only small bits of land. However, the proportion of landless households has decreased quite substantially from about 23 per cent of all rural households during the early fifties to less than 10 per cent in recent years. This type of change suggests that increasing numbers of small peasants are seeking wage work to supplement their meagre income from land.

Along with the labourers at the bottom end of the land owner-ship scale, small peasants owning less than 2.5 acres of land have continued since the early fifties to constitute over 60 per cent of all rural households. By the early eighties this proportion has increased to about two-thirds of the rural population. There is, of course, much regional variation behind this average: in states such as Kerala, Tamil Nadu and West Bengal, where the land-man ratios are very low, the proportion of such small holdings (in terms of ownership) is over 80 per cent. There is also the variation in productivity of land so that small is not small everywhere. But even with fine adjustments, the fact that the majority is constituted by the landless and by those who do not own enough land for subsistence cannot be denied.

We know that the land ceiling laws exist merely on the statute books, and that because of their poor implementation, not much land has been redistributed. Therefore, it is likely that land reforms have made a contribution to the pattern of change in ownership described by published statistics only to the extent that it is no longer possible to establish in the case of the big owners a clear identity between families and their holdings. However, family holdings hidden from view to evade the ceiling laws will probably be in the middle ranges and may not have contributed to the observed relative swelling of small holdings. Statistics, however, cannot reveal secrets.

In any case, we need to understand the persistence and growth of the small-scale farming economy, even during the phase of rapid technological changes and the emergence of relatively higher profit-making possibilities in the large-scale sector. To some extent, the second of the two phases of state intervention that I have referred to earlier, becomes relevant in this context. From about the mid-sixties, the state has promoted a massive technological transformation: not only through direct public in-vestment in irrigation and infrastructure in general, but also

through the provision of cheap credit and inputs and by but-
tressing agricultural prices through support operations. It is true
that the benefits have accrued disproportionately to the surplus
regions and to the large surplus producers everywhere. Nevertheless, support to agriculture in general—and this is a commitment that pervades Indian politics irrespective of political
colour—must surely have provided some measure of protection
to the small farming sector against the land-accumulating propensities of the rural rich.

It is difficult to provide a conclusive interpretation of the
observed changes in land ownership, especially because, given
the large regional variation, the answers could be different in
different parts of India. Whether it is the growth of labour or
the ability of the small peasant to survive by entering into wage
work or other activities, or the adoption of enriching technological
change by the big owners, the underlying processes are complex
and have strong regional-historical roots. I have no competence
to make generalisations about these processes.

I want to restrict myself to demographic factors for two reasons.
First, it is obvious that a deteriorating land-man ratio leads to
ever-increasing proportions of smaller holdings and, in the
absence of compensating increases in the productivity of land
in such holdings, induces wage-dependence among the small
peasants. Second, despite regional variations, demographic factors act uniformly, at least to a certain extent, and the outcomes
are certainly more predictable in the short run than the manner
in which structural change takes place in agriculture.

II

Let me now consider some dimensions of population growth.
In world history there are two conjunctures identified by un-
precedented population increases in different parts of the globe.
The first of these is Europe in the 18th and the first half of 19th
centuries, and the second is the contemporary third world. These
two conjunctures have in common certain features: for example, a continuous rise—albeit at varying rates—in incomes and
living standards, especially among the middle and upper classes,
a falling death rate and a high and fairly stable birth rate. But
because the death rates in the poor countries have fallen
dramatically in recent decades, population growth rates have been

ranging above 2 per cent per annum in most countries in Asia, Africa and Latin America. In contrast, the growth rates in Europe in the 18th and 19th centuries were only of the order of 1 to 1½ per cent per annum. The reasons are well known. The control and elimination of big killers such as malaria, cholera and smallpox, as well as the development of modern and effective methods of disease prevention and cure are features more of the 20th century—especially of its second half—than of the 19th century. The importance of declining mortality as a major determinant of a likely high population growth in the future lies in the fact that mortality rates would quite predictably decline further in the coming few decades in the poor countries, and, within them, especially in the poor regions and among the poorer classes characterised by relatively higher death rates even now.

Population growth in Europe and the west in general had begun to decline from high levels from about the middle of the 19th century. This decline had been brought about by a fairly continuous decrease in fertility (barring a brief period—the so-called baby boom period after the second world war). Without going into the very complex underlying causes, we may note that the prospects of a rapid fertility decline for the next two or three decades are not very bright for most countries in the third world, especially the big ones such as India and Bangladesh. The underlying difficulties are most sharply illustrated by the Chinese case. The promotion of the one-child family norm and the coercive methods used for its implementation—reminiscent of the Sanjay Gandhi times in India—have led to impressive declines in fertility and population growth rates in China during the seventies. But with the introduction of agrarian reforms in the most recent post-Mao phase, coupled with population momentum factors, birth rates have begun to increase once again, even while death rates have tended to stabilise at the very low levels comparable to those in the rich countries. Some scholars suggest speculatively that the reasons could be purely economic: given the nature of the family production responsibility system, extra hands in the family may be economically advantageous. This is somewhat far-fetched because those who are born now will become helping hands only after a decade and a half. Others refer in this context to cultural factors—such as the preference for sons—that are surfacing once again. Whatever the reasons, it is now clear that the process of fertility transition can neither be hastened nor forced—beyond a point; it should not be forgotten that it has taken Europe and the west close to a century to achieve this type of transition and that too during a period of rapid industrialisation and all-round economic development leading in particular to both increasing living standards for workers and the provision of 'social security' (however understood).

One last point on the contrast with European history: the growing populations of Europe in the developmental phase were absorbed to a good extent by countries such as the US, Canada, Australia and New Zealand. However, nation states have become stronger since those times and national boundaries are now virtually closed. Such scope as exists for international migration—whether for semi-skilled labour (as in west Asia) or for highly-skilled technical and professional manpower (as in countries like the US or West Germany)—is wholly dictated by labour shortages of given types in the receiving countries. Regulated by strict quotas, the flows can hardly redress the international imbalances between resources and population.

Uneven regional development is of course at the heart of the matter in both the phases. The brute force of colonialism of the earlier phase has given way to economic power that underlies the present times. Only the rules of the game have changed.

III

To assess the consequences of a high rate of population growth—likely to remain so during the next two or three decades in India—on the agrarian economy, it is necessary to look at the variations in the components of growth not only across the subregions of the country but also among the different agrarian classes.

Let me consider first the differentials between the poor and the rich. It is commonly believed that the poor are more prolific and that, as the Victorian epigram has it, while the rich get richer the poor get children. Despite its strong moorings within the western intellectual tradition—carried over to the educated middle and upper classes in the third world—the belief is based more on plain prejudice than on hard facts. Careful studies show that, under conditions of uncontrolled fertility—i e, in the absence of artificial means to prevent births—fertility levels tend to be somewhat lower among the poorer classes. This is generally true for the countries in the third world but is modified to the extent that the practice of birth control is slowly spreading. Reviews suggest that both an inferior nutritional status and a longer duration of breast-feeding (among other factors) contribute to such a differentially lower fertility among the poor.

The prejudice has probably spread because of what has happened during the phase of demographic transition—the passage from high to low levels of fertility—in Europe (from about 1850). It was the educated and well-to-do classes who first began to practise birth control which then gradually spread to the poorer folk. It is only during this transitional phase that fertility levels among the poor were higher.

Nevertheless, the mistaken belief has led to much theorising about the supposedly higher reproductive capacity and its realisation among the poor. A Marxist version of such a theory reads:

When people are divorced from the means of production, they are left with only their labour to sell. To increase their income, the poor must produce more labourers per household. Thus while the rich can reinvest in capital and get richer, the poor can only 'get children'. High birth rates are therefore not the cause of continued poverty, they are a consequence of it (Karen L Michaelson (ed), *The Poor Get Children*, Monthly Review Press, 1981).

Standing Malthus on his head in this manner is of course radical rhetoric at its best, but the argument shares with Malthus some mistaken notions about poor families. The formulation may at best be valid for the transitional phase, but it does promote prejudice against the poor.

For example, in India, agricultural labour families are small on average, ranging below five in size, while for the rural population as a whole the average ranges above 5.5. Not only a somewhat lower fertility—by how much it is difficult to say—but also a higher mortality is responsible for this type of difference in the family size.

One of the important reasons why agricultural labour and small peasant households tend to be smaller on average is that they are always—in all regions of India—among the poorest. And, because poverty and under-nutrition are associated with higher levels of morbidity and mortality, the proportion of children who survive beyond the age of five years in poor families tends to be smaller than in other groups of the rural population

The implications of such demographic variation are obvious. As a consequence of narrow fertility differentials in the absence of deliberate control, and of higher death rates among the rural poor, agricultural labour and poor peasant populations are expected to grow at a somewhat lower rate than the rest of the population. However, they are not closed populations. Their numbers are affected by migration to some extent, but more importantly by the additions to the ranks of the poor through the pauperisation process. Before we discuss these factors let me turn to a brief discussion on inter-regional variations in the demographic rates.

There is a considerable variation in these rates, especially in the rural parts of the country with which I am exclusively concerned here. Data relating to the late 1980s show, for example, that the crude death rate ranged from about six per thousand in Kerala to 16 per thousand in Uttar Pradesh. Among the states with high death rates are Bihar, Orissa, Madhya Pradesh and Rajasthan. The states of Maharashtra, Punjab and Haryana have relatively low death rates, although not as low as in Kerala. In general the poorer regions of the country experience higher death rates for understandable reasons. This is even more sharply illustrated by the range in the infant mortality rate: it is about 25 per thousand live births in rural Kerala, as against an all-India rural average of slightly over 100 per thousand live births. Among the states with very high infant mortality rates are Uttar Pradesh (135), Orissa (130) and Madhya Pradesh (127) (roughly five to six times the Kerala rate).

Correspondingly, there is some variation in rural birth rates as well, but it is narrower. It must be noted in this context that there has been a marginal decline in the birth rate during the last two decades, the rural crude birth rate at the all-India level having fallen from about 38 to 34 per thousand. But the decline is unevenly spread and there is still much regional variation in fertility levels. The birth rates in rural Kerala and rural Tamil Nadu have come down sharply to 22.2 and 24.4 per thousand respectively, whereas they continue to be at high levels of over 37 in Bihar, Madhya Pradesh, Rajasthan and Uttar Pradesh. Although the correlations are not perfect, generally high birth rates and high death rates go together and characterise the demographic picture of the poorer regions of rural India.

I have discussed these inter-class and inter-regional differences in fertility and mortality in some detail because they have clear-cut and quite predictable consequences for the land-to-labour ratios.

Consider mortality first. Kerala (including rural Kerala) has already attained a very low death rate (of about six per thousand, a level that prevails in the western countries). A further reduction in this rate may not be possible because, even as infant mortality can be reduced further, deaths occurring among the old may increase. The decline in death rates, which will surely come about in the next few decades, is bound to be more prominent in regions such as Madhya Pradesh, Bihar, Orissa and parts of Uttar Pradesh and in general in the poorer sub-regions everywhere in rural India. And, within such regions, the decline would be sharper among the rural poor: agricultural labour and poor peasant families.

There is no undue optimism behind this prediction. It is based on a projection of our understanding of the history of demographic transition and also on the Indian experience during the post-independence period. The provision of clean drinking water, the spread of immunisation practices, the control of infections, and other measures of public health and those for improving access to private medical care will continue on their upward course and bring down morbidity and mortality rates. To give only two examples, gastro-enteric diseases which take a heavy toll among children below the age of five are easily controllable at relatively low costs as by oral rehydration therapy that is spreading in popularity. Deaths occurring among mothers and infants at child birth will decline with the spread of hygienic delivery practices and the gradual replacement of the traditional 'dais' by medical and para-medical personnel. I mention these two examples because, for example, infant and child deaths account for about a quarter of all deaths and child survival beyond the age of five years is an important determinant of longevity. So, given the scope for a reduction in infant mortality and the likely course of public intervention in this sphere, there is no doubt that the death rates will decrease among the poorer classes all over rural India.

Turning now to birth rates, the decline in them has begun only recently in the rural areas, and it is likely that the process of demographic transition will take the usual historical course. Given the large differentials that exist between Kerala at one extreme

228 Pauperising Agriculture

and Madhya Pradesh, Bihar and Uttar Pradesh at the other, and given that fertility will decline further in Kerala, the transitional phase is likely to last several decades. But if history repeats itself, the practice of birth control will be led by the better educated and well-to-do classes even in the countryside and will spread to the poorer families only much later.

All this means that the rural poor in the poorer regions of the country would be caught during the coming few decades in the same trap as the poor countries had been caught during the post-colonial period. This trap—I call it a trap deliberately because in the public domain we have to continue with measures for controlling morbidity and mortality—is the second phase of the demographic transition in which death rates continue to decrease while birth rates remain stable at their pre-transitional levels. This second phase will be experienced by the rural poor, even as the rural and urban rich go through the third phase characterised by a low mortality rate and a declining birth rate. We must note in this context that in Kerala the conditions for decline in mortality and fertility have been created for all sections of the population more or less simultaneously, and that is probably why the Kerala case is such a dramatic incident in the history of demographic transition.

The implications are obvious enough. Even if processes that convert peasants into paupers are held in check so that net additions to the ranks of the rural poor do not take place from outside, the poorer sections will grow at a relatively faster rate. In saying this I am not making a simple-minded projection of the past into the future. For, I have modified the transition model, taking into account inter-class differentials in demographic rates. Besides, we know that among the important correlates of both low mortality and low fertility are: a high rate of survival of infants and children, the spread of literacy and education, especially among females, a satisfactory living standard associated with expanding employment opportunities for men and women and some provisions for social security for the old-aged. In the case of the rural poor these conditions are not satisfied. Therefore, while it is safe to predict that the demographic transition will encompass the poor as well ultimately, it can only be in the far-distant future—perhaps in the second half of the next century, if not later.

In the interim, populations of the poor countries, and of the poorer sections within them, will continue to grow. An idea about the magnitude of this growth can be had from the experience of Kerala, where demographic change has been the most remarkable in India. With birth rates still above 20 per thousand and death rates plunging to a very low level—six per thousand— Kerala's population will continue to grow at between 1 and 1½ per cent. Since conditions for a further decline in fertility exist and are being promoted assiduously and therefore will be strengthened, no doubt, the rates of population growth in Kerala will come down even further and Kerala will be the first among Indian regions to achieve that demographic state of bliss: zero population growth, i e, a constant population that does not exert any pressure on the available resources. But even with the most unbridled optimism one cannot foresee this happening in the next couple of decades; it will take longer.

The poorer parts of India cannot, however, replicate easily the Kerala experience. Historical experience can perhaps be unwound fast by economists and historians to point to lessons to be learnt, but history itself cannot be speeded up. Kerala has had a long history—going back into the 19th century—of social involvement and state intervention in the fields of education and public health. And, after independence, the mobilisation of the rural and the urban poor by the communists has led not only to the effective implementation of land reforms on a scale bigger than anywhere else in India, but also to a number of other measures that provide the so-called 'social-security', recognised as a necessary condition for the transition to low fertility.

The conditions that promote a fertility decline will emerge only slowly in the rest of the country. The prospects in this respect—in the next few decades—are certainly not very bright for the poor in India in general. So, even as the population growth rates come down, mainly through the reduction in fertility among the middle and upper classes, higher growth rates are likely to prevail among the poor.

Population growth rates in any given region of course depend not only on the difference between the birth and death rates but also on net migration. However, the nature and magnitude of migratory flows within India are such that they hardly have a mitigating influence on the decreasing land-man ratio in rural areas at the state level. By far the most important of these flows is the rural-to-urban type of migration that does reduce the pressure on land. However, although such flows contribute to rapid increases in urban populations, they constitute only a small fraction of the rural population so that the rural population in the total has declined only marginally from 83 per cent in 1951 to 76 per cent in 1981. Two further points on rural-urban flows:

(1) They tend to be both localised and episodic as far as labour migration to industrial and mining centres are concerned and therefore their impact on the reduction in labour-to-land ratios can be more marked at the village or block level.

(2) The rural-to-urban flows are of course limited not only by the development of urban work opportunities but also by the fact that migration is not cost-free and finding work is uncertain. It is no wonder that within the rural-to-urban type of migration, crossing of state boundaries is a quantitatively insignificant phenomenon.

In contrast, rural-to-rural migratory flows are more prominent but they relate mostly to movements within the state boundaries. Indeed, by far the largest component of internal migration is that which takes place from one village to a neighbouring one in the same district. Moreover, labour migration accounts for only a small part of the flows, a good part of migration—that of women—arising from marriage and rules of residence.

I mention all this only to emphasise the importance of uneven regional development in agriculture (which I will discuss a little later). Inter-regional inequalities have grown and may continue to grow, but the redistribution of populations through migration does not—and probably cannot—take place on a scale big enough to bring even a marginal reduction in inter-state disparities. To give an example in this context: rural Punjab which has prospered most in the country in recent times has received during the decade of the 1970s less than half a million migrants from other states of the country. Likewise, the out-migration from rural Bihar, which has done very badly in agriculture during the last two and a half decades, is an equally insignificant flow in relation to its total population.

The situation is somewhat similar to the international imbalances between resources and population that cannot be reduced through migratory flows. While sub-nationalism within India is not yet strong enough to seal borders, there are both economic and cultural factors behind the relative immobility of the rural populations. The tenacity with which a peasant clings to his native patch is, of course, an economic phenomenon, given that even a bit of land provides a secure, if insufficient, income, but it is hard to imagine a land-hungry Bengali or Malayalee peasant migrating to Rajasthan in search of land that may be available there.

IV

During the period 1961 to 1981—on which I want to concentrate—land-man ratios have declined in all the major states in India. To assess this trend, if we look at the size of ownership holding per rural household, the decline in India as a whole is from about 4.4 acres to about 3.2 acres per household—a decrease of about 28 per cent. On the other hand, if we rely on gross crop-ped area available per person in rural areas as an appropriate measure, the decline is from 1.03 acres to 0.79 acre per person—a decrease of about 23 per cent. I shall rely on this measure, i e, gross cropped area per person, as well as the value of produc-tion per person in the ensuing discussion. The latter measure is relevant not only because it takes into account the differen-tials in cropping patterns and productivities of land, but also because it is a measure of per capita income from land—the most important determinant of welfare in the rural areas.

There is some variation in the decline in gross cropped area per person as between the different states. As I have remarked earlier, the rates of rural population growth have varied to some extent; and so have the rates at which cropped areas have ex-panded. But there are no systematic correlations between area expansion and initial levels of the land-man ratio and similarly between rates of population growth on the one hand and initial levels of per capita production, rates of growth in productivity and per capita income on the other. This is only to be expected because any mutual adjustment that takes place between popula-tion levels and resource availability—through, for example, greater expansion of areas induced by fast deteriorating land-man ratios or through lower rates of population growth in areas experiencing stagnant or declining resource and income levels—can only take place in the long run. More importantly, both population growth and area expansion have been governed by exogenous factors. In the case of population growth, the decline in mortality was the main regulating factor. And in their spatial variation, death rates, and the decreases in them, do not bear a significant relationship with the availability of land. On the other hand, in this period, the expansion of gross cropped area has come about mainly through the development of irrigation, which had nothing to do with demographic factors or demographic change.

Irrigation expansion and the improvement in cropping intensities are two important components of the green revolution and we know that the most impressive increases in this respect have been largely in the north-west. It is true that private investment in irrigation has played a big part, but this would not have been possible without the intervention of the state through its diverse activities for promoting the green revolution.

The decline in land-man ratios at moderately varying rates in all the major states contributes directly to predictable changes in the distribution of land. Other things remaining the same, these declining ratios produce a proliferation of small holdings and a reduction in the average size of holdings.

The question of size of holdings is of obvious relevance to the determination of which households have to seek wage work within agriculture outside their own farms or in non-agricultural activities. What matters most is of course not the size of holding but whether it can generate subsistence for the peasant. The issue of increases in productivity, that could compensate for a declining size in holding, is thus crucial to the pauperisation process.

Before I discuss the variations in productivity change, let me digress a bit and turn to other factors that shape the changes in the distribution of land ownership. Earlier I referred to the failure of land ceiling laws in leading to a significant redistribution of land. One must add, in this context, that some land has passed into the hands of the landless but it is too minuscule to have radically altered the distribution; moreover, much of such land is hutment land. In any case the crucial issue concerns the passage of land from the poor to the rich—a phenomenon that lies at the heart of the processes of proletarianisation and pauperisation. It is difficult to get an idea about the extent to which it has taken place (from the landholdings data which, generally, show a marginal decline in the concentration ratio perhaps because the largest holdings are not visible to the statistical eye; or perhaps a concentration in terms of surface area is not actually emerging). What is certainly true is that because the gains to the big farmers have in general been disproportionately larger, the disparities in incomes from land between the small and the big farmers are growing.

I have looked at some data (referring to 1971-72) on sale transactions in land to gain some insight into the land alienation process. Sale transactions appear to be generally minimal. At the all-India level only about one-half of 1 per cent of land has been transacted during one year. This means that if this annual rate is normal, about 5 per cent of the land changes hands every decade. More importantly, the data suggest that most of the transactions take place between and within the classes of the middle and big owners. There is no evidence of a large-scale land transfer from the poor to the middle and upper strata. In any case, the poor, although constituting about a half of the rural population, have such a small proportion of the total land that the alienation of the land they own—at the observed rates— will not radically alter the overall distribution among other owners, although the ranks of the landless will swell in proportion. So, to the extent that the perceptible decrease in 'landlessness' among the rural households is not merely statistical but real, the data would suggest that small peasants have been able to cling to their tiny plots, but are entering into wage work.

In saying this, I am not denying or even minimising the historical importance of land alienation as a describing and governing factor behind the processes of proletarianisation and pauperisation. Indeed, apart from eviction of tenants by the so-called 'resumption' of cultivation by owners (on which Daniel Thorner has written much, referring to the fifties and sixties) alienation of land from peasants to landlords, moneylenders and traders—leading to the pauperisation of the peasantry—is the very essence of Indian agrarian history. So also, the alienation of land from tribal populations is an important contemporary issue.

What I am suggesting, as a generalisation of sorts, is that the models derived from our pre-independence historical experience cannot be carried over to the present, and that we must recognise the fact that small peasants have been able to hold on to their landholdings during the last two or three decades.

The staying power—the ability of the small peasants to survive—is no doubt derived in part from the support the agricultural sector receives through various measures, including those specifically meant to benefit the small farmer. But it is also derived from their increasing participation in markets as sellers of produce. The early debates on the relatively higher productivity of land in the small farm sector have clearly shown both higher labour intensities and higher-valued crop combinations as two of the most important features of small farm agriculture. However, whether it is the extent of family labour use or the crop combination, the choices at the household level are dictated by a largely unchanging resource base and constraints upon its use, and not—in Chayanovian fashion—by the calculations on the drudgery of labour within the family as an economic unit. But when families grow in size, as they surely do, and the resource base does not expand, wage work is the only option left.

All this is admittedly a stylised description of structural change in Indian agriculture but it gives us some clues about the manner in which the components: the growth of labour, the pauperisation process, the growth of commercialisation and a slow process of polarisation, are all linked to each other through demographic factors.

The question of productivity change—to which I now wish to turn—is more complicated. The most striking aspect of this is the widening of inter-regional disparities in agricultural productivity. This story has been told and retold several times, but mostly in terms of the productivity of land and its improvement during the sixties and the seventies, and not in terms of the growth of population. It is only in north-western India (Punjab, Haryana, west Uttar Pradesh and Jammu and Kashmir) that impressive increases in per capita production have taken place during the sixties and seventies; in Andhra Pradesh and Gujarat the increase has been marginal. Maharashtra, Karnataka and Rajasthan present a somewhat stagnant picture. The rest of the country, covering the eastern region, Tamil Nadu and Kerala in the south, and Madhya Pradesh, has experienced a fall in per capita production—production not having kept pace with population.

The differences in population growth are not wide enough for demographic change to be cited as an underlying reason. On the other hand, we do know that an uneven regional development of irrigation and other resources has largely contributed to the region-specific nature of the spread of the new technology.

The importance of uneven regional development, as I have already suggested, lies in the absence of matching population flows that can redress imbalances. Of course, it is true that regional self-sufficiency was never a clear-cut policy objective. In the agricultural sector, especially in the foodgrain economy, the guiding principle has been national, and not regional, self-sufficiency and the selected engine of growth is the well-endowed farmer. Referring to foodgrain production once again, we note that the widening regional disparities are sought to be mitigated through a public distribution system, so that one can read a measure of justice in the growth strategy. But the uneven potentialities for earning income from land that remain (despite the redistribution of food) generate a corresponding unevenness in the pauperisation process. I would like to repeat, in this context, that the poorer and hitherto neglected regions are likely to experience higher rates of population growth in the next few decades.

V

I have focused on demographic factors in this note not to raise the Malthusian demons but to assess and describe the course of population growth and its consequences in a historical setting and within an analytical framework that are altogether different from Malthus's.

Indeed, the demon of population adjustment through an increasing death rate has been exorcised by history. The most striking demonstration of this is the continuous fall in death rates all over India, despite much variation in the production and availability of food, with some parts such as the eastern region experiencing declining levels in foodgrain production per capita. The trends in the production of food and in population will take their future course largely independent of each other.

But the second Malthusian demon, of population pressure on land leading to an ever-widening pool of labour and a decline in real wage rates and the living conditions of the poor, is not so easily vanquished. These prospects cannot, however, be understood in terms of purely demographic factors working in combination, as in Malthus, with the law of diminishing marginal returns to land. They have to be understood in terms of the historical evolution of a high concentration of land and the manner in which it acts as a barrier to genuine land reform on the one hand and influences the nature of technological change on the other.

May 5-12, 1990

Population and Agricultural Growth

A Study in Inter-Regional Variations

WHILE analysing the interrelationships between the components of population growth—fertility, mortality and migration—on the one hand, and the characteristics of agrarian change such as improvements in the productivity of land and the intensification of labour, on the other, we must remember two facts. First, adjustments in both directions—population levels adjusting to what the land can produce, agrarian prosperity or decay leading to higher or lower population levels; and population pressure leading to land or labour intensification and technological change—take place over long periods. Second, such adjustments tend to be spatially specific and restricted so that they can be seen clearly only in small regions.

However, the Indian experience of the two decades, 1961-81, offers some scope for analysis in this respect. A dramatic improvement has taken place during this period in technology and productivity in some parts of the country even as other regions have demonstrably stagnated. The specific questions that arise in this context are the following: Did the prosperous regions experience higher rates of population growth, either through higher rates of natural increase or through immigration, than did other regions? What are the demographic pictures of areas of stagnation and decline: are they marked by high rates of mortality and out-migration? These questions are about the extent to which population has redistributed itself over space in response to the regionally-concentrated nature of agricultural growth during this period. One can ask similar questions about the extent to which population pressure has led to land or labour intensification in areas experiencing drastic declines in the land-man ratios.

This paper is concerned with such questions. The analysis is based on data at the district and state levels relating to population, areas cropped and those under irrigation, value of production, etc. The agricultural data are borrowed from G S Bhalla and D S Tyagi, *Patterns in Agricultural Development* (1989) and refer to annual averages of three triennia: 1962-65, 1970-73, and 1980-83. The population figure for the first period refers to 1963 and is the interpolated value from the 1961 and 1971 censuses; those for the second and third periods refer respectively to the 1971 and 1981 census counts.

The analysis can provide some suggestive insights only; it cannot yield conclusive answers to the questions being raised here. One reason is that the components of population growth, births, deaths, and net migratory flows, cannot be easily estimated at the district level. A second is that even if some adjustment takes place over such a short period the lags in adjustment that must be present cannot be easily identified.

We do know that increases in productivity and production during this period were unevenly spread over space. Thus a good starting point is the magnitude of inter-regional disparities; the changing pattern of disparities over time may then be expected to be of some analytical value. Section I looks at inter-state inequalities in per capita production, productivity per hectare, and land-man ratio; it goes on to discuss what can be described as the Malthusian type of adjustment: the question asked here is whether high rates of growth in production or productivity have induced high rates of population growth at the state level. The next part of this section is devoted to the evidence on the Boserupian kind of responses, e g, land and/or labour intensification taking place in states experiencing severe population pressure or stagnation in productivity. Section II covers the same ground as Section I with districts as regional units and, naturally, is more informative about the adjustment process. The final section has some concluding remarks.

I

INTER-STATE DISPARITIES

Writing V, A, P, and W respectively for value of production, gross cropped area, rural population, and workers in agriculture (cultivators plus labourers, male and female—all in specified units) at a point of time we set out the following identities:

$$V/P = (V/A) \cdot (A/P) \qquad \qquad \dots(1)$$

i e, per capita output is the product of output per unit of land and land-man ratio; and

$$V/P = (V/W). (W/P) \quad\quad ....(2)$$

that gives an alternative decomposition of V/P as the product of value per worker and work participation rate. Similarly,

$$V/A = (V/W). (W/A) \quad\quad ....(3)$$
$$\text{and } A/P = (A/W). (W/P) \quad\quad ....(4)$$

These identities enable us to decompose the total variance across regions of a given variable into those of its components: for example, from (1) it follows that

$$Var(\ln V/P) = Var(\ln V/A) + Var(\ln A/P)$$
$$+ 2Cov(\ln V/A, \ln A/P) \quad\quad ...(5)$$

Let us begin by looking at the variations at the state level. We do know that agricultural growth was unevenly spread during this period. To assess its net impact, the trends in inter-state variation in respect of the six ratios introduced above are presented in Table 1.

Of the six ratios we are considering, in respect of three—per capita value of output (V/P), value per worker (V/W) and labour intensity (W/A)—a sharp increase has taken place in the disparities between the states during the two decades (1962-83); the widening of disparities was more marked in V/P than in V/W. It can be seen from Table 1 that the inter-state variations in the three other ratios, viz, yield per hectare (V/A), land-man ratio (A/P), and work participation rate (W/P) have remained fairly stable.

The widening in disparities is illustrated simply by the contrast between the performance of Bihar and that of Punjab. In

Table 1: Inter-State Variations—Standard Deviations of Natural Logarithms of Variables

Variable	1962-65	1970-73	1980-83
Value of output per capita (V/P)	0.2566	0.3379	0.4278
Value of output per hectare (V/A)	0.4187	0.4438	0.4201
Land-man ratio (A/P)	0.4525	0.4329	0.4632
Value per worker (V/W)	0.4101	0.4496	0.5089
Work participation rate (W/P)	0.2718	0.2023	0.2610
Labour intensity (W/A)	0.3680	0.3825	0.4105

Note: For basic data and sources see Appendix. The value figures (V) are in constant 1969-70 prices.

constant (1969-70) prices, the per capita output in these two states during 1962-65 was Rs 192 and Rs 487 respectively; by 1980-83 this range has widened: from Rs 153 in Bihar to Rs 1,134 in Punjab. Likewise, while the value per worker has stagnated at about Rs 585 in Bihar, it increased in Punjab from Rs 2,200 in 1962-65 to Rs 5,063 in 1980-83.

To understand these trends we use the two types of decomposition of V/P given in equations (1) and (2). The results are set out in Tables 2 and 3.

Table 2 shows that the increase in the inter-state disparities in per capita production has been brought about almost wholly (accounting for about 91 per cent of the total) by a weakening of the inverse correlation between productivity per unit of land and the land-man ratio. This inverse correlation, a macro-variant of the much-discussed size-productivity relationship, is of a compensatory nature, with low (high) land-man ratios generally associated with high (low) productivities, so that when it weakens (as it has, from -0.82 to -0.28, practically disappearing) per capita output variations widen. We shall discuss this phenomenon in detail later, but note here that the correlation itself is the result

Table 2: Decomposition of Variation in Log (V/P)

Year	Var(v/p)	Var(v/a)	Var(a/p)	2Cov (v/a, a/p)	r(v/a, a/p)
1963	0.0658	0.1753	0.2048	-0.3148	-0.82
1971	0.1142	0.1970	0.1874	-0.2702	-0.70
1981	0.1830	0.1765	0.2146	-0.2081	-0.28
Distribution of Change (Per Cent), 1962-83					
	100.0	1.0	8.4	90.6	

Note: In lower case letters v/p, for example, stands for ln (V/P), etc.

Table 3: Alternative Decomposition of Var (ln V/P)

Year	Var(v/p)	Var(v/w)	Var(w/p)	2Cov (v/w, w/p)	r(v/w, w/p)
1963	0.0658	0.1682	0.0739	-0.1763	-0.79
1971	0.1142	0.2021	0.0409	-0.1288	-0.71
1981	0.1830	0.2590	0.0681	-0.1441	-0.37
Distribution of Change (Per Cent), 1962-83					
	100.0	77.4	-4.9	27.5	

of a long-term adjustment process through which fertile lands tend to attract high population densities.

The alternative decomposition given in Table 3 shows that both an increase in the variation in the value per worker (77 per cent) and a decline in the inverse correlation between value per worker and the work participation rate (27 per cent) have contributed significantly to the inflation in the variance of per capita production. More on this later.

Two further decompositions of variances, respectively those of productivity per hectare and of the land-man ratio, are given in Table 4. (Let us recall that these variations have remained more or less stable (Table 2).) We see from the statistics in Table 4 some interesting changes that lie behind the apparent stability in regional variations in the just-mentioned variables.

The first part of Table 4 shows that while disparities have widened in both V/W and W/A, the inverse relationship between these two variables has considerably strengthened and has contributed to the stability in productivity variations. The second half of the table shows that across the states, area per worker and work participation rate have remained uncorrelated.

These changes in inter-regional inequalities can alternatively be described in terms of differential patterns of growth over time in the variables under study. We shall, for this purpose, restrict ourselves to the decade 1971-81 for two reasons: first, significant improvements in productivity and production started taking place only towards the end of the sixties, and their impact, if any, is likely to be clearly observable only during the seventies; and second, we are better served in respect of the relevant and comparable data for this decade than for the sixties.

Let us, to begin with, look at rates of population growth, the net result of births, deaths and migration. These rates, for the rural part of different states, are directly derived from the census counts. Estimates of crude birth and death rates (CBR and CDR, respectively) are available from the data collected under the Sample Registration System (SRS); these refer to annual averages corresponding to triennia such as 1971-73, 1972-74 and so on (and are thus based on a shifting, increasing population base). We can, however, compute the average annual rate of natural increase (i e, the excess of the CBR over the CDR) from these data. The excess of the annual compound rate of the observed population growth over the estimated annual average

Table 4: Decomposition of Variance of ln V/A and ln A/P

Year	Var(v/a)	Var(v/w)	Var(w/a)	2Cov (v/w, w/a)	r(v/w, w/a)	Var(a/p)	Var(a/w)	Var(w/p)	2Cov (a/w, w/p)	r(a/w, w/p)
1963	0.1753	0.1682	0.1354	-0.1283	-0.42	0.2048	0.1354	0.0739	-0.0045	-0.02
1971	0.1970	0.2021	0.1463	-0.1514	-0.44	0.1874	0.1463	0.0409	0.0002	0.00
1981	0.1765	0.2590	0.1685	-0.2510	-0.60	0.2146	0.1685	0.0681	-0.0220	-0.10

rate of natural increase provides us with an estimate—a crude one that can perhaps be refined by better methods—of the annual average of the rate of net migration, i e, number of immigrants minus the number of out-migrants as a ratio of the population in a given year. These statistics are given in Table 5.

The rates of population growth in rural areas (during 1971-81) ranged from 1.25 in Tamil Nadu to 2.48 in Rajasthan and the average rate of natural increase ranged from 1.59 in Tamil Nadu to 2.58 in Haryana. The estimated annual average net migration rate generally tended to be negative, indicating an excess of out-migration over in-migration—arising, no doubt, from rural to urban flows being the most prominent among population transfers. The exceptions to this are in respect of Assam and Rajasthan experiencing significant net inflows into rural areas and, to a much less extent, Himachal Pradesh, Bihar and Karnataka. The net migration rates are generally low: the highest rate corresponds to Uttar Pradesh with an annual net out-migration rate of 0.87 per cent of the total population. Similar,

Table 5: *Components of Population Growth, 1971-81*

(Per cent)

State	Annual Rates			Decadal Change	
	Population	Natural Increase	Net Migration	CBR	CDR
Andhra Pradesh	1.59	1.86	−0.27	− 6.20	−28.80
Assam	2.22	1.84	0.38	− 7.90	−32.00
Bihar	1.90	1.84	0.06	18.00	− 6.20
Gujarat	2.04	2.31	−0.27	− 9.50	−24.70
Haryana	1.98	2.58	−0.60	−10.10	−28.80
HP	2.19	2.08	0.11	−10.90	−29.10
J and K	2.15	2.22	−0.07	− 2.90	−16.40
Karnataka	1.75	1.72	0.03	−10.20	−26.80
Kerala	1.46	1.97	−0.52	−13.70	−25.30
Maharashtra	1.63	1.70	−0.07	− 4.80	−27.50
MP	1.77	2.16	−0.39	− 1.80	− 6.60
Orissa	1.49	1.66	−0.17	− 5.20	−24.30
Punjab	1.62	2.08	−0.46	−12.50	−23.40
Rajasthan	2.48	2.19	0.29	− 7.80	−17.70
Tamil Nadu	1.25	1.59	−0.34	−12.00	−22.50
UP	1.30	2.17	−0.87	− 9.40	−25.30
W Bengal	1.87	2.13	−0.26	9.60	−10.00

Source: Census and Sample Registration System.

relatively high, net out-migration rates are observed in the cases of Haryana, Punjab, Kerala, Orissa and Tamil Nadu. This suggests that out-migration is induced not only by conditions of stagnation in agriculture but also by those of prosperity. (More on this, as well as on the implications of low migration rates to the changes in land-man ratio, later.)

To see whether these variations in population parameters are related to the structure and change in agriculture, simple correlations between these parameters and the levels and changes in such variables as per capita production and yield per hectare are computed (Table 6). Most of those correlations are weak but a few are significant. Let us note these:

(a) Rates of natural increase during 1971-81 are positively associated with both changes in per capita production during 1963-71 (and hence during 1963-81) and changes in productivity per hectare. This is a restatement of the fact that states such as Punjab, Haryana, Uttar Pradesh and Jammu and Kashmir

Table 6: Population Parameters and Indicators of Agrarian Change—Simple Correlation Coefficients

(Per cent)

Levels and Changes in Production Per Capita (V/P) and Per Hectare (V/A)	Average Annual Rates 1971-81			Decadal Change	
	Population Growth (Compound Rate)	Natural Increase (CBR– CDR)	Net Out-migration	Decline in CBR	Decline in CDR
V/P 63	−0.27	0.09	0.35	0.45*	0.37
V/P 71	−0.15	0.32	0.42*	0.45*	0.23
Change (per cent)					
V/P 63-81	−0.04	0.42*	0.38	0.38	0.23
V/P 63-71	0.10	0.53**	0.33	0.33	−0.01
V/P 71-81	−0.16	0.03	0.19	0.24	0.41*
V/A 63	−0.37	−0.28	0.17	0.12	0.16
V/A 71	−0.31	−0.09	0.26	0.22	0.17
Change (per cent)					
V/A 63-81	0.07	0.54**	0.37	0.35	0.22
V/A 63-71	0.28	0.61**	0.20	0.29	0.01
V/A 71-81	−0.19	0.10	0.28	0.20	0.35

Notes: (1) * indicates significance at 10 per cent level and ** at 5 per cent level.
(2) Unlike in Table 5, net migration rates, changes in CBR and CDR are set out here as net out-migration rates, declines in CBR and CDR respectively.

experienced impressive agricultural growth along with relatively higher rates of natural increase in contrast to states such as Bihar, Orissa and Tamil Nadu characterised by poor agricultural performance and low rates of natural increase.

(b) The decline in the birth rates during 1971-81 is positively associated with the levels of per capita production in both 1963 and 1971, while the decline in the death rates is positively correlated only with the increases in per capita production. It may be noted that the decline in death rates has been far lower in Bihar, Madhya Pradesh and West Bengal—states that have experienced drastic falls in per capita production.

(c) Net out-migration rates are positively correlated to the level of per capita production in 1971, a reflection of the fact that good performers in agriculture during the late sixties such as Punjab and Haryana have recorded relatively higher rates of net out-migration.

On the whole, despite the inconclusiveness of these findings, they suggest that agrarian prosperity has promoted higher rates of natural increase through more significant declines in death rates. They also suggest that prosperity-induced rural-urban migration might have been an important factor·in rural population change during 1971-81.

Let us now see to what extent changes during 1971-81 in the

Table 7: *Correlates of Changes in Land Productivity and Labour Intensity, 1971-81*

(Simple Correlation Coefficients)

	Changes during 1971-81 in	
	V/A (Land Productivity)	W/A (Labour Intensity)
Land-man ratio A/P 1963	0.38	0.14
Land-man ratio A/P 1971	0.33	0.09
Changes in A/P 1963-71	−0.33	−0.27*
Changes in A/P 1971-81	0.29	−0.66*
Per capita production V/P 1963	0.30	0.00
Per capita production V/P 1971	0.19	−0.13
Changes in V/P 1963-71	−0.08	−0.21
Changes in V/P 1971-81	0.91*	−0.25

* denotes significance at 5 per cent level.

land-man ratio (which has declined everywhere except in Punjab) or in per capita production—the two variables standing as proxies for population pressure—have induced changes in productivity of land, labour intensity and work participation rates. The correlations given in Table 7 show that

(a) changes in productivity per hectare were positively correlated with changes in per capita production but uncorrelated with levels and changes in land-man ratios; and

(b) changes in labour intensity, i e, workers per hectare, are inversely related to changes in land-man ratios (A/P) (states experiencing drastic declines in gross cropped area per person such as Bihar, Tamil Nadu, Gujarat, Karnataka, Andhra Pradesh and West Bengal have recorded impressive increases in the number of workers per hectare).

These changes suggest a weak form of Boserupian adjustment of labour intensity to a declining land-man ratio; it is weak because the results are seen in terms of improvements in productivity only to the extent that inter-regional variations have not widened as perceptibly as in the case of per capita production.

II

INTER-DISTRICT DISPARITIES

In this section we present disparities with districts as regional units. Of the districts covered by the Bhalla-Tyagi study, only 269 are retained here because we do not have data on all the variables for the remaining districts. For the same reason the coverage in terms of the states also is different from that of the last section, Assam, Jammu and Kashmir and Himachal Pradesh not being included here.

Let us first look at the magnitude and change in inter-district variations with respect to the six ratios discussed in the previous section. The relevant measures (standard deviation of natural logarithms) are given in Table 8. Comparing the statistics here with those in Table 1, we see that, as in the case of states as units, in terms of districts also, disparities have widened considerably in per capita production, value per worker, and labour intensity (note, however, that here we are considering output per male worker). Similarly, in both cases, inter-regional variations in the land-man ratio tended to be fairly stable. In respect of the remaining two ratios, the inter-state and inter-district data exhibit different patterns: while inter-state variations in productivity per hectare and the work participation rate have tended to be minimal, inter-district variations in these two variables have widened considerably. No doubt, a part of the explanation lies in the lack of perfect correspondence between the two sets of data (in terms of coverage, and the definition of workers: male and female in the state-level data but only male in the district-level data). Also, in the district-wise analysis, the state average (of, say, per capita production) is the average of district averages which differs from the average computed directly for the whole state.

But a more important reason for the differential pattern is that the course of disparities between districts depends not only on what happens at the state level but also on what happens within states. A standard decomposition of the total inter-district variance into components: between states (B) and between districts within States (W) is given in Table 9.

It will be seen that disparities between districts within states have considerably widened, in respect of all the ratios, except the land-man ratio, especially during the seventies. This happens because of the well-documented fact that within each state, with the possible exception of Punjab and Haryana, rapid and impressive growth and the attendant changes have been confined to a few well-endowed districts. For a fuller understanding of the widening inter-district inequalities, it would therefore be necessary to study variations within each state. We do not attempt this here. Instead we proceed with decompositions of the type made in the last section.

Table 10 gives two decompositions of the variance in ln (V/P).

Table 8: Inter-District Variations—Standard Deviation of Natural Logarithms

Variable	1962-65	1970-73	1980-83
Per capita output (V/P)	0.319	0.409	0.492
Output per hectare (V/A)	0.492	0.549	0.586
Land-man ratio (A/P)	0.534	0.538	0.555
Value per male worker (V/MW)	0.357	0.431	0.517
Male workers in population (MW/P)	0.201	0.175	0.279
Male labour intensity (MW/A)	0.469	0.486	0.539

Note: Note that labour intensity, etc, are measured with respect to male workers only.

Since we have already made comparisons between inter-state and inter-district variances let us look at the covariance terms. As in the case of state-level data, the inverse correlations between land-man ratio and productivity per hectare, and between value per worker and work participation rate across the districts have declined. But this attenuation can be seen to be much less severe. For example, the first of the above correlations has decreased from −0.82 to −0.79, contributing 11 per cent to the inflation in var (ln V/P) (whereas, between states, as we saw before, the corresponding contribution was as high as 91 per cent—Table 2). Likewise, the contributions of variances of v/w, w/p and the covariance between them are also radically different, across states and across districts. This kind of a differential pattern clearly suggests that while these inverse correlations have practically disappeared in terms of states as a whole, they continue to hold (at whatever level) within each state across the districts. Two further decompositions, respectively of variances in v/a and a/p are not very informative (Table 11).

Let us now see what these trends in inter-district disparities imply to the manner in which either population or land-use variables have responded to declining land-man ratios. Since land-

Table 9: Variation between (B) and within (W) States—Mean Squares

Variable	Source of Variation	1962-65	1970-73	1980-83
V/P	B	0.86	1.79	2.85
	W	0.06	0.08	0.11
V/A	B	3.25	4.17	4.80
	W	0.09	0.10	0.12
A/P	B	3.47	3.49	3.84
	W	0.12	0.13	0.13
V/MW	B	1.55	2.40	3.14
	W	0.06	0.07	0.12
MW/P	B	0.46	0.31	0.51
	W	0.02	0.02	0.06
MW/A	B	2.56	2.93	3.33
	W	0.10	0.10	0.14

Note: B = between states (13); W = within states (255).
For each variable, the inter-district variation is broken up into the between state and within state components. The degrees of freedom are 13 and 255 respectively, corresponding to a total of 269 districts in 14 states.

Table 10: Decomposition of Var (ln V/P) between Districts

Year	Var(v/p)	Var(v/a)	Var(a/p)	2Cov (v/a, a/p) r(v/a, a/p)		Var(v/p)	Var(v/w)	Var(w/p)	2Cov (v/w, w/p) r(v/w, w/p)	
1963	0.1019	0.2421	0.2857	−0.4259	−0.89	0.1019	0.1287	0.0405	−0.0673	−0.47
1971	0.1676	0.3014	0.2898	−0.4236	−0.85	0.1676	0.1859	0.0305	−0.0488	−0.32
1981	0.2419	0.3438	0.3086	−0.4105	−0.79	0.2419	0.2676	0.0772	−0.1029	−0.36
Distribution of change										
1963-81	100.0	72.6	16.4	11.0		100.0	99.2	26.2	−25.4	

Note: v/p stands for ln V/P, etc, w/p stands for ln (MW/P) where MW is the number of male workers.

Table 11: Decomposition of Var (ln V/A) and Var (ln A/P)

Year	Var(v/a)	Var(v/w)	Var(w/a)	2Cov (v/w, w/a) r(v/w, w/a)		Var(a/p)	Var(a/w)	Var(w/p)	2Cov (a/w, w/p) r(a/w, w/p)	
1963	0.2421	0.1287	0.2206	−0.1072	−0.32	0.2857	0.2206	0.0405	−0.0246	−0.13
1971	0.3014	0.1859	0.2365	−0.1210	−0.29	0.2898	0.2365	0.0305	−0.2280	−0.13
1981	0.3438	0.2676	0.2907	−0.2145	−0.38	0.3086	0.2907	0.0772	−0.0593	−0.20

man ratios are measured in terms of surface area (gross cropped area per rural person) of varying fertility, a further classification by levels of irrigation intensity (gross irrigated area as a ratio of gross cropped area) provides some means of identifying patterns in change.

First, we look at the expansion in gross cropped area and population. Table 12 gives the average rates of increase in area and population of districts classified according to changes in the land-man ratio and the irrigation ratio.

Districts experiencing minimal declines in A/P have the highest rate of expansion in area. Of course, there is a circularity in this finding. To see how the initial levels of A/P and irrigation ratio have influenced rates of expansion in area, the data according

Table 12: Growth in Area and Population—Districts Classified by Levels and Changes in Land-Man Ratio and Irrigation Ratio

Increase in Irrigation Ratio 1963-81 (Per Cent)	Decline in Land-Man Ratio (Per Cent) 1963-81		
	Above 25	10-25	Below 10
Growth in Area (Per Cent), 1963-81			
Below 10	-8.3	8.9	35.7
10—30	-9.8	13.3	28.0
Above 30	-8.1	18.9	39.7
Growth in Population (Per Cent), 1963-81			
Below 10	37.3	39.6	34.6
10—30	38.4	40.8	35.2
Above 30	51.8*	48.9	34.8**

Irrigation Ratio (Per Cent) 1963	A/P 1963 (Hectares)		
	Below 0.3	0.3-07	Above 0.7
Growth in Area (Per Cent), 1963-81			
Below 20	3.3	4.5	1.7
20—50	8.9	6.4	18.6
Above 50	13.2	34.3	37.1

Notes: (1) The entries in the table refer to averages over the districts falling into each cell.
(2) The increase in irrigation ratio is the difference between the levels of the ratios in the two periods.
(3) * covers Alleppey, North Arcot, Giridih, Dhanbad, Santal Parganas, Hyderabad and Rangareddy and Cuddapah. ** covers all districts of Punjab except Gurdaspur.

to the relevant classification are presented in the bottom third panel of Table 12. It can be seen that area expansion has been most impressive in districts with an irrigation ratio in 1963 in excess of 50 per cent, and especially those where the land-man ratios have also been relatively high in 1963. Districts with low base (1963) levels of irrigation ratio and land-man ratio have a poor record of expansion in area. Turning now to population growth, we notice, as expected, population increases being positively associated with declines in land-man ratio (causation

Table 13: Changes in Productivity Per Hectare 1963-81—District Averages

Irrigation Ratio 1963 (Per Cent)	Land-Man Ratio (A/P) 1963 (Ha)		
	Below 0.3	0.3-0.7	Above 0.7
Below 20	24.4	35.5	37.3
20—50	33.4	46.5	76.8
Above 50	36.4	88.7	115.6
Increase in Irrigation Ratio 1963-81 (Per Cent)	Decline in A/P 1963-81 (Per Cent)		
	Above 25	10-25	Below 10
Below 10	22.2	27.9	5.1
10—30	49.9	53.3	78.7
Above 30	104.0	93.0	117.2

Note: See Note 1 to Table 12.

Table 14: Number of Male Workers Per Hectare—Level in 1963 and Change (Per Cent) 1963-81, District Averages

Productivity Per Hectare (V/A) (Rs/Ha) 1963	Land-Man Ratio (A/P) 1963 (Ha)		
	Below 0.3	0.3-0.7	Above 0.7
Level of MW/A 1963			
Below 700	—	0.409	0.274
700—1400	0.971	0.567	0.297
Above 1400	0.853	0.629	0.352
Increase in V/A (Per Cent) 1963-81	Decline in A/P 1963-81 (Per Cent)		
	Above 25	10-25	Below 10
Below 13	19.0	6.8	−11.6
13—15	10.0	3.4	− 1.7
Above 15	12.6	5.1	−13.2

Note: See Note 1 to Table 12.

possibly running both ways). Despite their poor inferential value, these data are given here to show that most districts in Punjab (except Gurdaspur) appear at the bottom right hand corner of this panel (with decline in A/P less than 10 per cent and increase in irrigation ratio above 30 per cent) and on the average record a somewhat low population growth during 1963-81 of 34.8 per cent. Since the rate of natural increase in this state was relatively high (following an impressive decline in death rates), the low rate of population growth may well be the result of prosperity-induced rural-to-urban migration. This inference is of course no more than a guess.

Table 13 gives the average increase in productivity per hectare (V/A) in districts classified according to levels and changes in A/P and the irrigation ratio. We see that productivity expansion is positively associated with base (1963) levels of the two classificatory variables. The most impressive growth has taken place, moreover, in areas experiencing high rates of expansion in irrigation and low rates of decline in land-man ratio. In particular, there is no evidence of an adjustment in terms of improvements in productivity as a response to drastic falls in the land-man ratio.

Finally, in Table 14 we present changes in labour intensity (number of male workers per hectare). The first half of this table shows that, during the base period, levels of labour intensity are, as expected, positively associated with productivity and inversely with the land-man ratio. The second half of the table gives the rates of change in the labour intensity during 1971-81. These tend to be negative in areas experiencing minimal falls in the land-man ratios, which have earlier been identified as districts with impressive records of growth in productivity. On the other hand, districts experiencing severe declines in land-man ratio record a significant increase in labour intensity. This is a weak type of Boserupian response, referred to earlier.

III

CONCLUDING REMARKS

The agricultural growth strategy employed in India, of concentrating effort and investment of resources in well-endowed, irrigated regions of the country has, of course, paid rich dividends in terms of increases in agricultural production, especially of food,

Table A1: Statewise Data

	V/P			V/A			A/P		
	1962-65	1970-73	1980-83	1962-65	1970-73	1980-83	1962-65	1970-73	1980-83
Andhra Pradesh	326.40	298.32	374.82	822.67	851.99	1265.82	0.40	0.35	0.30
Assam	342.09	319.93	320.17	1430.80	1570.97	1614.45	0.24	0.20	0.20
Bihar	192.44	190.61	153.35	795.70	901.49	921.00	0.24	0.21	0.17
Gujarat	354.41	363.70	400.51	631.89	790.83	1032.02	0.56	0.46	0.39
Haryana	429.85	576.39	679.60	687.35	1037.74	1353.85	0.63	0.56	0.50
HP	211.96	240.25	217.47	713.41	878.16	943.96	0.30	0.27	0.23
J and K	175.63	226.84	258.09	693.83	1051.22	1332.97	0.25	0.22	0.19
Karnataka	329.11	345.27	357.77	610.29	798.44	925.98	0.54	0.43	0.39
Kerala	273.47	327.77	265.75	1864.55	2197.38	2148.83	0.15	0.15	0.12
Maharashtra	305.12	199.02	325.47	505.13	418.55	693.78	0.60	0.48	0.47
MP	323.94	315.50	295.50	512.96	556.11	604.08	0.63	0.57	0.49
Orissa	324.68	290.65	298.41	937.84	901.54	887.99	0.35	0.32	0.34
Punjab	487.30	788.64	1134.38	1047.58	1644.33	2268.76	0.47	0.48	0.50
Rajasthan	251.69	301.93	267.56	321.61	420.01	445.12	0.78	0.72	0.60
Tamil Nadu	343.45	383.14	317.05	1267.44	1522.99	1675.45	0.27	0.25	0.19
UP	262.92	300.40	343.79	744.35	914.56	1214.95	0.35	0.33	0.28
West Bengal	283.74	288.89	255.81	1230.58	1376.25	1452.97	0.23	0.21	0.18

Note : V/P: value of production per capita (Rs 1969-70 prices), V/A: value of production per hectare (Rs 1969-70 prices), A/P: gross cropped area per rural person (hectares).

Source: Compiled from Bhalla and Tyagi (1989) and Census of India.

Table A2: Statewise Data

	V/P			W/A			W/P		
	1962-65	1970-73	1980-83	1962-65	1970-73	1980-83	1962-65	1970-73	1980-83
Andhra Pradesh	810.92	858.00	1017.44	1014.48	993.00	1244.12	40.25	34.77	36.84
Assam	1210.75	1570.97	1711.41	1181.75	1000.00	943.34	28.25	20.36	18.71
Bihar	586.05	686.22	585.32	1357.72	1313.71	1573.50	32.84	27.78	26.20
Gujarat	1028.66	1317.30	1483.84	614.29	600.34	695.50	34.45	27.61	26.99
Haryana	1490.68	2840.86	3195.53	461.10	365.29	423.67	28.84	20.29	21.27
HP	494.92	802.52	831.56	1441.46	1094.25	1135.16	42.83	29.94	26.15
J and K	511.84	947.25	1145.42	1355.56	1109.76	1163.74	34.31	23.95	22.53
Karnataka	888.36	1190.22	1128.43	686.99	670.83	820.59	37.05	29.01	31.70
Kerala	1824.73	2035.74	2054.91	1021.82	1079.40	1045.70	14.99	16.10	12.93
Maharashtra	721.61	601.99	918.52	700.00	695.27	755.33	42.28	33.06	35.43
MP	728.62	924.44	827.48	704.01	601.57	730.02	44.46	34.13	35.71
Orissa	1002.71	1119.16	1102.43	935.30	805.56	805.49	32.38	25.97	27.07
Punjab	2200.41	3440.49	5063.08	476.09	477.94	448.10	22.15	22.92	22.40
Rajasthan	639.45	1100.77	1043.31	502.94	381.56	426.64	39.36	27.43	25.65
Tamil Nadu	988.82	1278.46	935.54	1281.77	1191.27	1790.89	34.73	29.97	33.89
UP	820.67	1095.10	1341.03	907.00	835.14	905.98	32.04	27.43	25.64
West Bengal	1241.23	1359.53	1235.46	991.42	1012.30	1176.06	22.86	21.25	20.71

Note : V/W: value per worker (Rs 1969-70 prices), W/A: number of workers per 1000 hectares, W/P: ratio of workers to population (per cent).

Source: Same as for Table A1

Table A3: Increase (Per Cent) during 1963-81 and 1971-81

		1963-81						1971-81						
	P	V/P	V/A	A/P	V/W	W/A	W/P	V/P	V/A	A/P	V/W	W/A	W/P	P
Andhra Pradesh	33.44	14.84	53.87	-25.37	25.47	22.64	-8.47	25.64	48.57	-15.43	18.58	25.29	5.95	17.09
Assam	61.82	-6.41	12.84	-17.05	41.35	-20.17	-33.79	0.08	2.77	-2.62	8.94	-5.67	-8.14	29.93
Bihar	38.46	-20.31	15.75	-31.16	-0.13	15.89	-20.21	-19.55	2.16	-21.25	-14.70	19.78	-5.68	20.71
Gujarat	45.96	13.01	63.32	-30.81	44.25	13.22	-21.66	10.12	30.50	-15.61	12.64	15.85	-2.24	22.40
Haryana	50.75	58.10	96.97	-19.73	114.37	-8.12	-26.25	17.91	30.46	-9.62	12.48	15.98	4.82	21.69
HP	43.12	2.60	32.32	-22.46	68.02	-21.25	-38.93	-9.48	7.49	-15.79	3.62	3.74	-12.64	24.21
J and K	46.88	46.95	92.12	-23.51	123.78	-14.15	-34.33	13.77	26.80	-10.28	20.92	4.86	-5.91	23.68
Karnataka	38.22	8.71	51.73	-28.35	27.03	19.45	-14.42	3.62	15.97	-10.65	-5.19	22.32	9.29	18.92
Kerala	38.00	-2.82	15.25	-15.68	12.61	2.34	-13.71	-18.92	-2.21	-17.09	0.94	-3.12	-19.68	15.64
Maharashtra	37.37	6.67	37.35	-22.34	27.29	7.90	-16.20	63.53	65.76	-1.34	52.58	8.64	7.18	17.58
MP	42.47	-8.78	17.76	-22.54	13.57	3.69	-19.68	-6.34	8.63	-13.78	-10.49	21.35	4.64	19.20
Orissa	36.26	-8.09	-5.31	-2.93	9.94	-13.88	-16.40	2.67	-1.50	4.24	-1.49	-0.01	4.23	15.92
Punjab	35.96	132.79	116.57	7.49	130.10	-5.88	1.17	43.84	37.97	4.25	47.16	-6.24	-2.26	17.48
Rajasthan	52.25	6.31	38.40	-23.19	63.16	-15.17	-34.84	-11.38	5.98	-16.38	-5.22	11.81	-6.50	27.83
Tamil Nadu	27.45	-7.69	32.19	-30.17	-5.39	39.72	-2.43	-17.25	10.01	-24.78	-26.82	50.33	13.08	13.24
UP	36.43	30.76	63.22	-19.89	63.41	-0.11	-19.98	14.45	32.85	-13.85	22.46	8.48	-6.54	19.89
West Bengal	44.24	-9.84	18.07	-23.64	-0.46	18.62	-9.42	-11.45	5.57	-16.13	-9.13	16.18	-2.56	20.42

Note: P stands for rural population in million. Definitions of other variables are in the notes to Tables A1 and A2.

at the national level. But the price that has been paid is all too obvious: inter-regional inequalities have worsened and have been leading to political tension.

The effects of growing inequalities in food production are mitigated to some extent through the public distribution system. However, the lack of improvements in productivity and of expansion in employment, in agricultural as well as in related sectors, leaves the rural poor in the neglected regions untouched by the visible national growth.

Population movements tend to be negligible in relation to the total numbers at the district and state levels. The course of population growth has been dictated above all by a continuously declining mortality rate. The consequences of the resulting, nearly universal, decline in the land-man ratio are serious for those at the bottom end of the landholding scale. Labour intensification has to be understood thus in the context of a spatially uneven growth process and of restricted possibilities for migration for work.

An interpretation of this may be possible in terms of the models of Malthus and Boserup. However, both these are 'closed' ones in spirit and, therefore, only when the roles of the state, and of population movements are brought explicitly into the analysis, would they be useful. In particular, while the processes of adjustment between population levels and resources are undoubtedly real, they can only be described in specific historical contexts.

July 29, 1991

Index